THE MYTHS
WE LIVE BY

'Lively... Cave forces his readers to interrogate cherished beliefs and see how many of the principles enshrined in public life are not only inconsistent but incoherent, even paradoxical.'

The Herald

'At its best, *The Myths We Live By* resembles a lively tutorial, with the genial Professor Cave challenging readers' prejudices... Useful and educational.'

Sydney Morning Herald

'An elegant and erudite exposé of the hypocrisies and evasions that infect the social and political thinking of our times.'

John Cottingham,
Professor Emeritus of Philosophy, Reading University

'Britain's wittiest philosopher.'

Raymond Tallis, bestselling author of
The Kingdom of Infinite Space

T0191456

PETER CAVE lectures in philosophy for New York University (London) and the Open University. He is the author of numerous articles – some academic and serious, others humorous – and several philosophy books, including the bestseller *Can a Robot Be Human?* He has scripted and presented philosophy programmes for BBC Radio 4 and often appears in the media, taking part in public debates on matters of ethics, religion and politics.

THE MYTHS WE LIVE BY

A Contrarian's Guide to Democracy, Free Speech and other Liberal Fictions

PETER CAVE

Atlantic Books
London

First published in hardback in Great Britain in 2019 by
Atlantic Books, an imprint of Atlantic Books Ltd.

This paperback edition published in 2020

3 5 7 9 10 8 6 4 2

A CIP catalogue record for this book is available
from the British Library.

Paperback ISBN: 978 1 78649 522 8
E-book ISBN: 978 1 78649 521 1

Printed in Great Britain

Atlantic Books
An imprint of Atlantic Books Ltd
Ormond House
26–27 Boswell Street
London
WC1N 3JZ

www.atlantic-books.co.uk

DEDICATED TO

those many victims of liberal and democratic myths –
including those victims who
think they are no victims at all

CONTENTS

Preface to the Paperback Edition

Most people would rather die than think – and that is what they do.

Bertrand Russell

This book is not for the fainthearted; well, it is not for those who prefer to be untroubled by thinking, whether or not that preference outweighs their preference for life. It is not for the fainthearted because it asks readers – all of us, be we left, right, centre or nowhere – to reflect on our societies' realities and ideals. It urges us all to open our minds instead of tricking ourselves with self-deceiving comforts, easy platitudes or by simply 'looking away'. The thinking mind needs more than sighs of 'never mind'.

Think of Covid-19. Suppose the virus ravaged only the poorest in the world; suppose it left untouched earnings of major corporations; suppose it caused minimal disruption to those reasonably well off and did not hamper the travels and luxury consumptions of the wealthy. Would there be so much concern for controlling it? Would there be urgent searches for vaccinations and treatments? Suppositions to one side, contrast the vast resources deployed to provide numerous luxuries for those who can afford them with the fewer resources devoted to the provision of clean water and basic health care to the world's poorest. Ideals of human dignity – and also of liberty, rights and democracy – are easily distorted by the huge discrepancies in wealth and power.

Since this book was first published, the tricking and distortions of our lived reality – and of our gleaming ideals – are all the more in evidence. Here are two arenas of trickery recently in expansion. They relate to governments in both the United States and the United Kingdom and hence relate to the political 'right'. Were governments of different persuasions in power, other troubling examples would probably be on offer.

◂|▸

First, consider democracy. In the UK, as a result of the 2019 general election, Boris Johnson's Conservative premiership was refreshed with a large majority. That electoral success occurred despite numerous well-attested examples of Johnson not speaking the truth. Those examples were, earlier on, highlighted by many Conservative politicians as demonstrating him unfit to be prime minister, yet many of those politicians subsequently provided him with unquestioning support. Memory loss has advantages – self-serving, political advantages.

In that 2019 election period, there were the usual unjust distortions caused by the UK's first-past-the-post voting system as well as those resulting from some people being unable to register to vote, some registered voters being deterred from voting, and the distribution of misinformation to various targeted groups. 'Fake news' was supplemented by the fakery of what we may now term 'no news'. As well as refusing to release an independent report on any Russian involvement in UK politics, Johnson avoided various hard-hitting interviews, preferring instead to answer robust questions such as, 'And what shampoo do you use, Prime Minister?'

The 'no news' agenda continues with government ministers declining invitations to take part in certain flagship political interviews. 'No one was available for comment from the government' has become an oft-repeated mantra. In some cases, because the government has refused to put up ministers, broadcasters, in the name of balance, have withdrawn invitations to the opposition's shadow ministers. Thus, the trumpeting of democratic governments being 'held to account' is increasingly mythical, increasingly illusory.

⁂

Secondly, consider international law and human rights. The United States' Republican President Trump, early in January 2020, ordered a drone strike to bring about the assassination of General Qassem Soleimani when visiting Iraq. The strike also killed nine people around him; their deaths, 'collateral damage', were quickly forgotten. Soleimani was head of Iran's elite Islamic Revolutionary Guard Corps' Quds Force; he was responsible for some terrorist acts, much suffering and many murders. There was, though, no evidence of his posing an *immediate threat* to the United States or its allies. The killing – most legal experts accept – contravened international law, was itself a terrorist act and maybe a war crime. It also generated an Iranian response, leading to jittery Iranian forces mistakenly shooting down a civilian airline; nearly two hundred innocent passengers were killed. Thus it is that outrages lead to outrages.

Drawing attention to that international violation by the United States is not to defend the Iranian regime. Neither within nor outside that regime does it receive any serious acclaim as a shining example of liberalism and democracy. Contrast with the United States: the US is ever keen to polish itself with liberal and democratic credentials, seeing itself as a fine respecter of international law. Few believe that Trump's keenness for the assassination had nothing to do with his running for re-election in 2020 and his need to appear strong on US security. Trump's 'killing success' may remind us of Osama bin Laden's assassination being used by the Democrat President Obama to help his 2012 re-election. Some may recall how a certain Donald Trump of 2012 objected to Obama basking in his 'killing success'; as Trump insisted, the Navy SEALs, not Obama, killed bin Laden.

In late 2018, Saudi Arabian journalist Jamal Khashoggi was murdered – a gruesome murder – while in Saudi's Istanbul consulate. The United States and European democracies expressed outrage. Later, in 2019, the United Nations Special Rapporteur concluded that Khashoggi was the victim of an extrajudicial killing for which the Saudi Arabian state was responsible; there was credible evidence that Saudi Crown Prince Mohammed bin Salman and other high-level officials were individually liable. Unsurprisingly, our liberal democracies have allowed the matter to slide into the dusty pages of last year's news reports. Memory loss, once again, is politically convenient.

There are many instances of how respect for international law by liberal democracies is somewhat mythical. In March 2020, the High Court in London found that Sheikh Mohammed bin Rashid Al Maktoum, Dubai's ruler – horse-racing friend of Queen Elizabeth II – kidnapped his two grown-up daughters, Sheikha Latifa Al Maktoum and Sheikha Shamsa Al Maktoum. Shamsa has not been seen for over a decade. At the time of Shamsa's kidnapping – she was grabbed when in Cambridge, nearly twenty years ago – the British governmental authorities apparently ensured that further police investigations did not take place. It is not an outrageously unjustified prediction that, after a while, British relations with Dubai and the Sheikh will be as close as ever, despite the High Court judgement.

⊰∥⊱

Of course, all is not well in countries that are miles away from what we in Western liberal democracies would deem liberal and democratic. Most notable examples are the ways of the Chinese authorities. Reflect on their initial response when Dr Li Wenliang of Wuhan Hospital alerted medical colleagues, in December 2019, to the dangers of Covid-19. Had Dr Li not been silenced and the authorities acted more swiftly, it is just possible that the virus would not have spread worldwide, causing considerable disruption and so many deaths, including Dr Li's. Putting matters in perspective, though, the number of deaths and predicted deaths from the virus may be very small compared with those that occur annually through poverty.

Of course – again – we could reflect on many other examples of dubieties in our liberal democracies and not just those relating to the UK and America. Other democracies, from Australia to Israel to France, have political corruptions that tarnish their democratic credentials or undermine their commitments to human rights.

Returning to the UK, not so long ago there were investigations into links between individuals suffering cuts in welfare benefits and subsequent suicides. Curiously, some of those reports were destroyed by the government, citing data protection legislation, despite data protection authorities denying that such destruction was required. In 2020, there were court hearings concerning Julian Assange's WikiLeaks, with the United States demanding Assange's extradition. During those hearings, it became increasingly apparent that Assange had been mistreated both while imprisoned and while in court. In 2019, independent United Nations human rights experts expressed concerns over his treatment, yet the UK, apparently, shrugged them off.

Political debate, in some arenas, is under greater pressure. In both the UK and the US, criticism of Israeli policies towards the Palestinians is often rewarded by accusations of 'antisemitism'.

When the criticisms are by Jewish groups, the groups tend to be disparaged as 'fringe' and dismissed. In both the UK and the US, the term 'transphobic' is rather readily showered upon people who doubt whether, for example, biological males can rightly *be* women, grounded solely in self-certification, and receiving all the rights of biological women. As well as obvious dangers of 'tyranny by the majority', liberal democracies face dangers of tyranny by certain minorities.

Political debate is increasingly devalued. When Prime Minister Johnson and President Trump make claims that are manifestly untrue, they seem to be accepted by many – including the Prime Minister and President – as par for the course and to be laughed off. 'Who cares? So what?' mark their attitudes. That does not bode well for democracy and the importance of people's participation.

⫻

The above are examples of how, in practice, respect for democracy, for human rights, free speech and liberty are under attack. Witness in the UK how the feeling is being created that the BBC, public broadcaster much praised worldwide over the decades, must be commercialized or more or less abandoned. Witness the increases in 'no-platforming' of those who would challenge certain currently preferred views on gender, race or cases of 'historical abuse'.

The arguments in this book take us much further, though – into realizing that we are not even clear over what constitutes the ideals of democracy, human rights, liberty and so forth. We know, vaguely, the rightful direction for those ideals but lack a reliable compass and lack awareness of how far to go. We need to think, question and debate, considerably more than we do – instead of carelessly shrugging our shoulders, with sighs of 'never mind' as leaders smile and bluster while deploying 'fake news' or 'no news'. That is why I opened this preface with Bertrand Russell's wry despair at how many people resist thinking – a despair that Russell was not the first to express.

Russell (1872–1970) was an eminent philosopher, logician and political activist; he argued for social reform, sexual liberation and was active in peace protests, the latter leading to his being sent to prison – three times. The first imprisonment was his reward for protesting during the First World War against conscription. With Russell's aristocratic connections – he was 3rd Earl Russell, his grandfather having been prime minister, Lord John Russell – the then Home Secretary authorized his transfer to prison hospital with the provision of pen and paper, so he could continue writing his *Introduction to Mathematical Philosophy*. He secured that privilege via advantages of class; such privileges these days are more often grounded in wealth, silver tongues of barristers – or defendants' practice in use of walking frames.

Let me use Russell's life to highlight three important lessons. First, we should not dismiss what people say because they are poor or lacking in formal education; and we should not dismiss what people say because they are aristocratic, wealthy or 'experts'. We should look at the reasoning and values expressed – whether the values are, for example, of self-interested greed or compassion for others.

Further – and here is the second lesson – Russell's public protests as president of the CND (Campaign for Nuclear Disarmament), later of the Committee of 100, should remind us that, contrary to declarations by those in power, extra-parliamentary protests – Russell and others sitting in London's Trafalgar Square, refusing to move – are not undemocratic. They are sometimes the only way in which injustices and dangers can receive recognition. In 1851, Lord Campbell proclaimed in Britain's House of Lords, 'There is an estate in the realm more powerful than either your Lordship or the other House of Parliament – and that is the country solicitors.' Global corporations, 'the market' and market manipulators – yes, assisted by embedded legal structures for property ownership – form today's most powerful estate.

Let us remember today's most powerful estate, if inclined to mockery or condemnation of organizations such as Extinction Rebellion or of leaders such as Greta Thunberg when they are engaged in protests. Of course, that does not mean that we ought always to be uncritical of such movements; the movements and their leaders may at times come over as possessed of a religious 'greener than thou' fervour, viewing mention of any values other than green as the work of sinners who need to be shown the light.

A third lesson from Russell's life is that he changed his mind. John Maynard Keynes famously said, 'When the facts change, I change my mind. What do you do, Sir?' Russell certainly changed his mind. Both Keynes and Russell, I am sure, would recognize that we may rightly change our minds, even when the facts have not changed.

Thinking, reflecting, musing, may lead us to look at matters afresh, becoming aware of previous prejudices or false assumptions. In this work's prologue, I tell of farmyard geese arguing over which sauce will go best with them once they are cooked and ready to be eaten. With no change in the facts, the geese may one day come to see how they could be discussing a far more fundamental matter – how to flee their unfortunate fate. This book, I hope, will at least encourage us to delve into the realities and ideals of our liberal democracies and possibly even help us to flee some of the many distortions, inconsistencies and deceptions by which we live.

⊪

Allow me to add an observation from Ludwig Wittgenstein to those by Russell and Keynes. When at Cambridge, all three were much involved with each other's thoughts in the 'moral sciences' that then covered moral philosophy, logic and political economy.

Wittgenstein recommended that when two philosophers meet, they should say to each other, 'Take your time.'

This book is meant for those who prefer to think than to die. It is meant for those who are prepared to change their minds. This book – a book on certain topics within the 'moral sciences' – requires that, in thinking about these matters, we 'take our time'.

PROLOGUE

On hiding what we know

Perseus wore a magic cap that the monsters he hunted
down might not see him. We draw the magic cap down
over eyes and ears as a make-believe that there are no
monsters.

Karl Marx

This is a book about political and public hypocrisy or, more gener-
ously, political and public myths. These myths are espoused by many
politicians, judges, captains of industry, commentators, religious
leaders – the great and the good – and, more generally, by much of
the population of our liberal democracies. They are myths by which
they and we live. They are myths embraced by many with an unquestioning and unbridled enthusiasm.

Picture the following farm. The geese are arguing imaginatively,
and with gravitas, over which sauce will go best with them once
they are cooked and ready to be eaten. We may easily agree that
they could be discussing a far more fundamental matter – how to
flee their unfortunate fate – but that discussion is not on the agenda
– well, not in this version of the tale. Perhaps they are so deceived
that they fail even to grasp the possibility of escape. Perhaps a myth
holds them captive, the myth that to be eaten is how things ought
to be.

The myths of our liberal societies hold us captive; they also captivate. They relate to how things are, according to some; they also relate to how well things could be, according to others. The myths apply to certain ideals as much as to what is maintained to be the reality. They are metaphorical monsters – monstrous myths that need to be openly acknowledged, confronted, exposed, if there is to be any chance of slaying. Here are a few examples.

'We are all equal before the law' is a mantra much cloaked in praise, yet we know that its mouthing is of a myth. Some are, so to speak, more equal than others – namely, those who can afford the most talented attorneys, solicitors, barristers. That, of course, ignores a further injustice: namely, how many, many people cannot afford even to gain access to the law – to the courts; to justice. In 1215 King John of England issued the first Magna Carta, the Great Charter; it and subsequent versions are admired internationally as shining examples of first steps towards citizens' rights. British politicians celebrate such rights, bask in their glory. Clauses 39 and 40 of the 1215 Charter, all those centuries ago, forbade the sale of justice and insisted upon due legal process – yet, week after week, practices of the British and American legal systems, government policies and wealth inequalities undermine the operation of such clauses, ensuring that the shining glory of rights is deeply tarnished.

Both the political left and political right extol aspiration, ambition and realizing talents; they are curiously quiet on how they rely on millions to be in employments that few deem aspirational: street cleaners, sewage workers, slaughterers in abattoirs – the list could go on. Talk of equal opportunities continues to be fashionable, yet the ideal is as mysterious as the reality is distant.

Liberty, freedom – here the terms are used interchangeably – is much lauded in liberal democracies. Singing its virtues, businesses, particularly with the political right in support, worship free markets, curiously forgetting that we need money to enter those markets. Millions of people lack the money; hence they lack the freedom. Free markets do not thereby make people free; on the contrary, they can be oppressive, luring people into wanting what they cannot have or getting what they would be better off without.

Governments promoting freedom conveniently forget the adage that freedom for the pike is death for the minnows. Freedom for the wealthy to own vast private estates has meant that millions of people have had their liberty to roam much curtailed. Unfettered freedom for property developers can fragment local communities, replacing them with towers of luxurious apartments, owned not as homes but as investments; some locals remain, their sky views blocked, their green spaces destroyed, while others are moved to distant parts, maybe trekking back daily to work. Of course, untrammelled freedom for certain minnows is not that great either because others find themselves terrorized by gangs – by small shoals – of the alienated, alienated from society through hopelessness and that mysterious nonsense of 'equal opportunities for all'.

In many instances, related to those above, principal claims by our leading politicians, corporate executives, commentators et al. are manifestations of straightforward hypocrisy. They know what the truth is, yet they would have us believe otherwise. With a wave at a certain US president elected in 2016, they are, we may say, 'trumpists'. Trumpism with regard to truth has been manifested for centuries. 'Alternative facts' are nothing new – save, maybe, for the trumpeting of them as, in some way, entertaining. It should not, though, be entertaining to hear governments' proclamations of their respect for all human life, while promoting arms fairs and approving the export of rocket launchers and other military equipment and expertise to the Middle East with devastating consequences for millions of innocent civilians.

The intentions of politicians, intellectuals and others are, in some cases, noble; they deceive people as a stimulus, in the hope of achieving a better world. In 2010, to secure support for his Affordable Care Act ('Obamacare') that would help millions of Americans, United States President Barack Obama lied, saying that, under the Act, 'If you like your health care plan, you will be able to keep your health care plan. Period.' Obama was relying on public ignorance; his aim, in this instance, was the public good. Often, though, politicians deceive voters just to secure their own power. In Britain's 2010 general election, the Conservative Party forcibly impressed on the electorate that the then Labour government was in some way responsible for the 2008 global financial crisis and for earlier 'not fixing the roof when the sun was shining'. The party neglected to mention that it had supported Labour's earlier spending plans, had furthermore called for greater financial deregulation and would no doubt also have had no option but to bail out the banks when the crisis hit.

The cases immediately mentioned are deceptions relating to particular events. The focus of this book is the set of deceptions, often self-deceptions, concerning the pervasive myths which ground our liberal democracies. Do we, for example, have any clear idea of what, ideally, a free society would be like? When our political leaders, our bishops, imams and rabbis, speak of all human life deserving respect and dignity, does that mean that we ought to forgo our numerous luxuries, diverting funds, for example, to ensure the provision of clean water in those inhabited areas where it is currently absent?

What I have written here is sometimes provocative; sometimes it is playful. Often behind the words there is a certain anger – contempt, indignation – towards many of our leaders for what they get away with, be they politically left or right, be they religious, atheist or in between, when piously mouthing their commitments to justice, equality and liberty. In challenging our liberal democracies,

I am not implying support for those many, many states that manifestly are neither liberal nor democratic.

Of course, I am far from alone in urging that we face the truth and see the myths for what they are. My numerous letters in newspapers – from, so to speak, 'Shocked of Soho' – are little stingings, balloon puncturings, in the hope of waking people up, of opening eyes. Eyes, though, remain closed; we all, much of the time, sleepwalk even in our waking lives, manifesting varying depths of slumber.

This book is a sustained attempt at making us face our deceptions regarding cherished values of liberal democracies. Its heart is philosophical reasoning. Philosophical reasoning pushes concepts to their limits, taking arguments to their conclusions, not shying away from unwelcomed outcomes. The reasoning seeks out consistencies and inconsistencies in our actions and feelings, our 'real-life' transactions and what we declare to uphold as right. With the appeal to consistency and the exposure of inconsistencies – with incongruities between what we say that we value and what our actions show – the forthcoming chapters call us to challenge the silver tongues of our political, social and business leaders. The sentiments of this book could – indeed, should – lead some politicians, captains of industry, merchants of ideas and ideals, to feel at least a little guilty at their deceits and possibly own up. The sentiments, arguments and reflections may even encourage our leaders to go a little way towards making amends.

For some readers, this book may lead to the reflection, 'Well, we knew that all along.' Even to elicit such observations, if explicitly and reflectively acknowledged, may help people to seek to change things – for the better – though that better, as already noted, also guides us into a land of make-believe if we are not careful.

'All things conspire,' wrote Hippocrates of Kos, an ancient Greek philosopher. Lovers of 'neo-liberalism' glorify individual liberty; that typically goes hand in hand with the insistence that self-interest is people's primary motivation, which leads to praise for the right to private ownership of capital – as much as people can get – and that takes us to the claim that the social order is best served through laissez-faire, through 'free' markets. Here, then, we shall see how ideas on liberty conspire with those of equality which lead into justice, then on to humanity, discriminations and solidarity, and back to liberty. Thus, diverse themes are woven throughout the chapters, appearing in one, then reappearing later in another, with new connections. The chapters and their contents may therefore have been arranged differently; there is no magic in reading from cover to cover rather than dipping within. By the way, in what follows, I use 'United Kingdom', 'Britain' and 'Great Britain' interchangeably, save where I note in Chapter 9 how the terms cover different nationalities.

Karl Marx and Friedrich Engels are famously known for *The Communist Manifesto*, but it is Marx's *Capital: A Critique of Political Economy* (1867) that provides the heading of this Prologue. In their 1846 *The German Ideology*, they criticized philosophers for ignoring how things are:

> In direct contrast to German philosophy which descends from heaven to earth, here we ascend from earth to heaven. That is to say, we do not set out from what men say, imagine, conceive, nor from men as narrated, thought of, imagined, conceived, in order to arrive at men in the flesh. We set out from real, active men...

In contrast to Marx and Engels – though in their spirit – I examine what is said, to show how distant it is from reality, and also often from sense. I seek to remove the magic cap that covers both the reality and the ideal. I shed some darkness with the aim of shedding light.

1

What's so good about democracy?

It seemed a great idea at the time. Being a democrat and liberal, I joined the *Good Ship Democracy* for a Mediterranean cruise. It possessed vast attractions for me, not least because my fellow passengers would, no doubt, be of my persuasion: all for democracy, for equal rights, for free speech.

Trouble started when the crew noticed that there were storms to the East and rocks to the West. 'Which way should we steer – or should we turn back?' they asked.

Foolish as I am, I assumed that the ship would deploy the services of a captain or pilot with expertise and knowledge of the Mediterranean seas, storms and safe harbours. The crew explained the error of my thinking. On the *Good Ship Democracy*, it transpired, we needed to vote on such matters, on all such matters.

'But I have no idea which is the best way to go, which is the best way to vote,' I complained, feeling a little irritated – and, yes, very worried. Other passengers joined in, agreeing that voting in this context was a silly and dangerous procedure. Others, though – the travelling know-it-alls – had no doubts, waving away our complaints. 'We know what it is best to do,' they insisted. It was a pity that those with such certainty disagreed with each other over what exactly that was. What exactly was the best thing to do?

The crew told us not to fret. Before we voted, we would be provided with charts, weather forecasts and instruction guides on how to assess those charts and forecasts. That struck us as making some sense: we could then evaluate the conditions and vote accordingly. That did indeed strike us as making good sense, until we realized that different sailors were providing us with conflicting data and very different readings of the data; in fact, much of the data seemed as baffling to the sailors as to us. Further, it soon became clear that some of us were pretty gullible or careless in reasoning; and some sailors were far more silver-tongued than others. The old hands wined and dined us, eager to persuade us of their expertise; others, it transpired, had personal reasons for what they advocated: some were wanting to turn back because missing the comforts of lovers left at home; others wanted to press on regardless, in expectation of adventurous romances to come.

The voyage continued in this way – or, rather zigzagging ways – as more decisions were required, more votes taken, with little consistency of approach manifested by our votes. How we envied other cruises that seemed to know exactly how to go and where to go.

Our *Good Ship Democracy* would still be meandering across the seas, save for the rocks that it struck. We abandoned ship, with some emergency helicopters coming to our rescue, manned by the military. Fortunately, we were not asked which way to fly to reach the shore.

❖

The vignette above has at heart a fundamental criticism of democracy, as expressed by Socrates in Plato's dialogue, *Republic*. The dialogue was written around 380 BC in ancient Athens, being the first substantial and enduringly influential text of political philosophy. Surely, we need experts – philosophers, indeed – to assess the best way for a society to run; Plato referred to those individuals as 'Guardians' of the ideal society, of the Republic. Even with the charts provided when on board *Good Ship Democracy*, few of us could have made sensible judgements. Even if the electorate is well-informed, there are many doubts about how competent most members are in assessing economic likelihoods, social justice and international relations – even in assessing their own best interests. In any case, if there is a right answer, why go through the ritual of voting and why take the risk of assuming that the majority vote reaches that answer?

'Ah,' it is replied to Plato, 'no doubt we need experts for the means, explaining the different means to an end; but, in contrast to deliberating about means, we surely should all have a say in what sort of society we want, what we are aiming to achieve and what we are prepared to countenance to secure those aims. There is no "the" right answer for there is a plurality of ways of living.'

It is true that most of us cannot work out economic and social implications of a variety of different policies; experts, though, can often tell us what is likely to happen as a result of certain policies, the risks involved and how society would develop for the different groups within. We can then vote on the basis of which policies overall we prefer: that is where the democratic vote of the majority justifiably comes to the fore.

Plato would disagree. Plato's approach would have not merely an expert captain, steering us clear of rocks and storms, but a captain who would also be expert in telling us what our destination should be, which destination is best for us – best, indeed, for one and all of us.

Surely, many continue to insist, Plato is wrong in his belief in the existence of an expertise in ends. It is up to us whether we should prefer to end up in Turkey, Israel or Egypt – and it is up to us what kind of society we want. Some people may prefer a society destined towards low taxation and few social-welfare benefits; others may prefer just the opposite. Some may prefer a society that promotes free thinking, alternative ways of living and religion; others may prefer conformity and tradition. Once experts have informed us of the different viable means to the various desired ends, then it should be for us to decide which to follow.

Our reply to Plato, as implied, is grounded in a 'pluralism'; there are different ways of living, different ends, different priorities regarding the means. No expert can tell us which are the best. We have some diverse values, conflicting desires and a spectrum of attitudes to risk. As already indicated, some people prefer society to be liberal, where citizens' conduct is relatively unconstrained; some prefer a more regimented society where we all 'know our place'. Some may be easy-going over the availability of abortion, voluntary euthanasia and same-sex marriages; others, perhaps for religious reasons, would impose restrictive laws pertaining to such matters. Priorities also differ: some place health services provided by the State as of higher value than speedier rail connections. In Britain there is considerable scepticism by many about the billions of pounds to be spent on the HS2 rail project – a vanity project, as it is seen – billions that could be better spent on social care and housing.

The above observations can have light cast upon them by the philosophy of David Hume, the great Enlightenment Scot of the eighteenth century. Hume was a good-humoured man who would obliterate his philosophical melancholy and scepticism by dining, conversing with friends and playing backgammon. In his *A Treatise of Human Nature* (1738) he makes the point that preferences, passions – what we ultimately value – are not determined by reason:

> 'Tis not contrary to reason to prefer the destruction of the whole world to the scratching of my finger. 'Tis not contrary to reason for me to chuse my total ruin, to prevent the least uneasiness of an *Indian* or person wholly unknown to me. 'Tis as little contrary to reason to prefer even my own acknowledge'd lesser good to my greater, and have a more ardent affection for the former than the latter...

Being human, we naturally have plenty of preferences in common – few choose their total ruin – but we do not all possess the same preferences regarding how society should run. No expertly reasoned answer is available about which ways of living are politically best justified; hence, a mechanism is needed to determine what politically should be done. That mechanism is the democratic vote.

Some individuals would no doubt prefer to follow their own agreed way of living; they can readily grasp how others also have preferences to have their own, but different, ways. Attempted resolution by physical battle would lead to chaos for all; leaving the field, becoming hermits, has few attractions. Democracy, by contrast, has a central attraction; it offers an approach where, it seems, we can all have a say in what to say, in how we are ruled. We all can vote; we can all agree to accept the outcome. It is as simple as that – except it is not simple and not as simple as that.

Most people today approve of democracies. Dictatorships seek the linguistic privilege of deeming themselves 'democracies' sometimes even in their formal names. We have, for example, the Democratic People's Republic of Korea and the People's Democratic Republic of Algeria. Such dictatorial democracies receive much mockery from the 'true democracies' of the West. To cast serious doubt on democracy in practice there is, in fact, no need to fly off to those dictatorships enmeshed in linguistic gymnastics. We could simply look at our own Western democracies, as we shall do in Chapter 2. In this chapter the attention is directed at the defects of democracy even as an ideal to be pursued – though, to expose certain defects, we shall inevitably encounter some clashes with the practice.

It is important to note: the reasoning above regarding how democracy is needed to handle conflicting preferences was not itself justified by democratic votes. Democratic voting may justify the policies governments pursue, but it cannot justify using democratic voting – for that would be circular, akin to lifting yourself, as is famously said, by your bootstraps. Democratic voting was justified above (be it well or poorly) by reasoning regarding what individuals should rationally accept as the best way to run a society. Plato would approve of the approach – that of rationality – but, as seen earlier, argues that there are faults in the reasoning in favour of democracy.

DEMOCRACY: FAILURE IN THEORY

A democracy, in essence, consists of some machinery: there is an input from 'the people', various wheels turn, levers clang, steam hisses – and the eventual outcome is a government. What the government does is meant to bear some relationship to the interests of the people whose votes were the inputs. What is the relationship? Surprisingly, there is vagueness at a most fundamental level.

When people vote – even the most reflective – they are unclear how they should be determining their votes. What does democracy theoretically require? Listen to voters. Some openly say that they are voting in what they consider to be their best interests – or their grandchildren's best interests – or what is best for the planet. Others may be doing their best to vote on what is best for the society or best for people in general or for the poor – or to be in accord with certain religious beliefs. There is a mishmash of aims.

True, the machinery could be justified as a means of delivering a result when people's interests and aims differ; and people should simply vote in their own (perceived) best interests. The machinery, though, could be justified as delivering a proper result *only if* voters vote on what they sincerely think is in the community's best interests. In neither case, though, is the outcome satisfactory.

If people are voting in what they take to be their own interests, there is no reason at all to believe that the machinery (however it works) delivers something that is in fact in the interests of the community or even in the interests of the majority of voters. If people are voting in what they take to be the community's interests, there is no reason to believe that the machinery delivers what is in fact in the community's interests. People make mistakes both about what is in their own interests and about what is in the community's. Unless we ascend to Platonic heavens, we are stuck here in the grubby real world of mistaken views, genuine bafflement and conflicting interests. After all, the interests of corporate executives do not typically coincide with the interests of those working on factory lines. True, all may, for example, have the same interest in reducing the number of murders, but democratic voting is no reliable means to achieve that desirable reduction. In Britain a majority often call for the reintroduction of capital punishment – but that majority view could be in the belief that capital punishment deters would-be murderers, a belief for which there is no convincing evidence.

Even if we accept that people should vote on policies on an ordered-preference basis – first choice is this; second choice is that; weigh accordingly – determined by their own interests, contradictions can arise, leaving it unclear how to determine the 'right' collective decision. An example is in this chapter's endnotes. As the economist and Nobel Prize winner Amartya Sen quipped, 'While purity is an uncomplicated virtue for olive oil, sea air, and heroines of folk tales, it is not so for systems of collective choice.'

It is time to wheel on stage Jean-Jacques Rousseau, an eighteenth-century philosopher, born in Geneva, a major influence on the Enlightenment and indeed the French Revolution through his ideas in The Social Contract (1762). Here we meet his notion of the 'General Will' – the Will that advances the community's interests and upholds the interests of all the citizens. Mysteriously, the General Will is constant, unalterable and pure; mysteriously, it can be discovered if people vote for what they believe is in the community's interests. Now, it is certainly plausible that in a village, club or small enterprise, members may have a strong sense of community and will vote for what they honestly believe is best for the community – and get it right. That sense of community, though, may not be very strong when we have in view a vast nation, itself made up of very diverse groupings. Despite that, Rousseau proclaims the benefits of outcomes determined by majority votes. Here is how.

In a reasonably sized community – in fact, the larger the better – majority opinion, argues Rousseau, is more likely to be right on any matter than any individual voter. This may be laughed out of court, but it has a mathematical justification given by Nicolas de Condorcet, a liberal thinker of the eighteenth century, a thinker much exercised with problems of majority voting and collective decisions; he criticized the French revolutionary authorities and ending up dying in prison. His Jury Theorem shows the advantages of following majority votes, albeit on assumptions that are highly unlikely to hold in typical national elections. The assumptions are that all voters are cooperating to find a mutually beneficial answer to the same question and each has an equal and better-than-evens chance of getting it right – or even, in some versions of the theorem, that the average is better than evens. Then, over the long run – an important qualification – the majority is more likely to be right than any individual. Of course, we have no reason to think that each voter has a better-than-evens chance of getting things right, even if they are independently and sincerely voting for what they believe is in the national interest. Further, if they do not have the better-than-evens chance, then the mathematics shows that the majority outcome is more likely to be wrong.

An obvious practical case of a majority of those who voted getting matters wrong is the outcome of the 1933 election in Germany. Under the Weimar Republic, most people were having a bad time, but after voting in Adolph Hitler, leader of the National Socialist German Workers' Party (the Nazi Party), matters became substantially and radically worse – obviously for the Jews in Germany, but also for Germans more generally and, indeed, for millions of people outside of Germany.

There remains, of course, the fundamental challenge, namely whether there is anything that is the 'getting it right', the best for the community, for society. Perhaps it is elusive. If only we could reason better or heed the ways of Plato's Guardians or even make sense of Rousseau's mysterious General Will, our eyes would be opened to the glittering prize of 'the best'. There is, though, no good reason to believe it exists. After all, why think there is only one way of ruling, of voting – of living – that is rightly understood as in the interests of the community? In addition, even if certain minimal requirements could be shown to ground what is best for the community as a whole, it does not follow that they provide what is best for each and every member of the community. The best for all is not necessarily the best for each one and all.

Without the best in view, perhaps the value of a democracy rests on the minimal fact that 'everyone' has the right to vote, to participate. There exists equality at least with regard to that right. I acquire the same rights over others as they do over me. Even if such equality is in the interests of the community and all its members, in practice in most democratic systems, the right to vote is much constrained by various registration requirements and irregularities; they are reviewed in Chapter 2.

Still, democracy is at least meant to provide us with a way of collective decision-making. Of course, collective decisions are made in various ways – sometimes by mob and frenzy. In November 1938, Kristallnacht, or the Night of Broken Glass, occurred in Germany. It was so named because Nazi mobs smashed windows and set fire to Jewish homes, shops and synagogues, murdering and terrorizing, leading eventually to the destruction of 6 million Jews, an attempted genocide. Small groups have sometimes sought to impose their will on society regarding certain heated matters. Stirred by raving ignorance, some individuals acting together have, for instance, assaulted paediatricians, thinking them paedophiles. In South Wales, in 2000, Dr Yvette Cloete, a paediatrician, fled her home after it had been attacked, with some 'paedo' wording daubed on walls. There are different ways of collective action; at least the democratic way is intended to be peaceful – well, in physical action if not in political rhetoric.

The democratic machinery, to be democratic, needs to respect some version of universal adult suffrage: that is, the right of all adults (with a few exceptions) to vote. Obviously, there is the requirement for votes, but there is also the requirement for vetoes; the majority vote would not be permitted to overturn the universal adult suffrage, though it sometimes tinkers at the edges. Those vetoes are not the result of democratic votes. They set the framework within which democratic voting operates. Liberal democracies seek to harmonize majority voting with protection of minority rights – and that protection is justified by reference to morality, by, for example, how people deserve some degree of equality with regard to respect.

DEMOCRACY'S IMMORALITY

Why do we need a democracy? There would be no problem, were we all of a like mind; but we are not. Democracy comes to the rescue – so it seems. Everyone can have a say – and the outcome rests on majority votes, one way or another. There is present, though, a resultant deep immorality.

In committing yourself to democratic outcomes, you are giving blank cheques to you know not what. In our much-beloved democracies, we usually reach decisions, or appear to, by majority votes; in one way or another, literally or metaphorically, we raise hands. Yet we sink into confusion when the majority of hands is for what is wrong. After all, the majority could vote for me to do everyone's ironing or for a minority to be enslaved or for racial segregation.

That everyone's preferences should count equally fails to guard against such injustices.

Commitment to *whatever* is the democratic outcome, without caveat, is thus highly immoral. As steps to avoid that immorality, even the most ardent lovers of democracy recognize that democracy as majority voting requires restrictions; even the most ardent lovers of democracy know that we can have too much democracy.

The democratic appeal has often been to autonomy, to self-government; the people rule themselves. Unless we engage some fancy footwork, we should judge that claim of self-rule as risible, as a deceit, an immorality, once we focus on individual voters. After all, I am scarcely governing myself if, as a result of elections – in which, yes, I participated – policies which I opposed in my voting are now ruling my life. There is, though, as already hinted, some fancy footwork in Rousseau's Social Contract: '... every person, while uniting himself with all... obeys only himself and remains as free as before'.

Thus it is that Rousseau is often praised for his recognition of people's need for freedom, to govern themselves, yet he is also often condemned as authoritarian and totalitarian. Why? Well, recall the General Will, that Will to which majority voting magically manages to give voice, and which aims at the best interests for all. Some people may reject the resultant policies of the Will; hence – and here comes the footwork – they need, argues Rousseau, to be *forced to be free*, forced to do what is truly in their own interests, even though they fail to recognize their true interests. That, paradoxically, is true freedom, true autonomy, despite people feeling that they are being coerced, that the government possesses too much authority over their lives and, if totalitarian, *totally* dominating nearly everything they do.

We may keenly join in the condemnation of Rousseau's 'forcing to be free', but, as we shall see in Chapters 4 and 15, perhaps what is more pernicious occurs when State and corporate manipulations lead people to believe that they are acting freely and acting in their own true interests, when they are not.

Bringing Rousseau's General Will down to earth, some may argue that at least there is something that is in the interests of one and all and the community as a totality; that something is living within the democratic structure. The democratic structure requires and preserves an equality of respect for all, a recognition that all (with a few caveats) have the right to participate in civic life, to take part in elections and so forth. Democracy consequently has to place some limits on what may be enacted by 'the people' to maintain the basic democratic credentials; democracy, as said, requires a non-democratic grounding. Let us note how only after significant protests, outside of voting – of extra-parliamentary action – have democracies shown genuine interest in voting rights, minorities' rights, and, now, climate change – stirred in 2019 by Swedish schoolgirl Greta Thunberg.

Western democracies, as a matter of fact, have cohabited with all manner of immoralities. The United States' Declaration of Independence was seen as compatible with slavery; George Washington owned slaves. Even today the United States democratic practice makes it difficult in some areas for African Americans to vote. Britain, that great beacon of democracy, up to the late 1960s allowed boarding houses to display signs declaring 'No Blacks; No Irish; No dogs', without embarrassment.

There needs, then, as already noted, to be a structure to a democratic community that protects minorities – and indeed majorities – which in some way provides equality of respect. The structure, in theory, is not open to democratic change, though even here we encounter political manipulation. Witness how the judges of the United States Supreme Court are appointed by the president; those political acts can set the tone for decades regarding certain rights, such as access to abortion facilities, assisted dying et al. The idea that the law, once set – even if part of the democratic structure – is free from political engagement is a myth. That, of course, raises questions of how members of the judiciary should be appointed; such questions were high on the political agenda in 2018, with the toing and froing over President Trump's eagerness for the appointment of the conservative and controversial Brett Kavanaugh to the Supreme Court.

Even with restrictions on what a democratic vote may permit, paradoxes still arise. Some voters – and politicians – may genuinely support the democratic procedures for decision-making, yet may also sincerely believe that abortion and euthanasia are deeply morally wrong, akin to murder. If the democratic machinery churns out the result that duly leads to the legalization of abortion and euthanasia, their psychological state must surely be distressed and in something of a quandary. There is blatantly a conflict between their belief that a democratic outcome should be respected and their belief that the outcome allows murder.

There is also a paradox regarding voting, when one knows that the result is not going to be close. Why then vote? That is a good question for any particular individual to address – maybe better to spend the time doing that ironing again or reading philosophy or visiting an elderly aunt – though, paradoxically of course, if everyone reasoned thus, there would be few votes.

TWO CHEERS?

E. M. Forster, the English novelist and humanist, gave democracy two cheers, one for its permitting variety and one for its permitting criticism. Those features may indeed be of considerable value, allowing some degree of self-expression to people – and that is emphasized by exercising the right to vote. Thus, voting may have value, though it is a curious value, as the outcome has little to do with how numerous individuals have voted and many people find themselves in servitude to what the democratic machinery delivers. Despite those defects, some argue in favour of the value of democratic deliberation and participation. People engage with each other, views are batted to and fro, and possibly some views are changed for the better; sensitivities can be improved regarding the plight of others. That optimistic rendering of election periods of course is rather illusory: just take a look at the popular press.

In Britain, in 2016, the *Daily Mail*'s front page sported 'Enemies of the People' over photographs of three High Court judges who ruled that Parliament's consent was required for Britain to leave the European Union. In 2017, there was *The Sun*'s headline 'Don't Chuck Britain in the Cor-Bin', as an attack on the Labour Party's leader Jeremy Corbyn. In the United States in 2016 the *New York Daily News* ran the headline 'Drop Dead, Ted' as a response to Ted Cruz challenging the social values typically found in that city, values such as support for abortion and same-sex marriage. There are numerous such cases.

Even if deliberation and participation possess some intrinsic value, they are not of much use in securing valuable democratic outcomes. In fact, democracy may have poor instrumental value in achieving good and stable government – after all, politicians, to secure election, typically appeal to voters' short-term interests. Plato saw voters as easily swayed by demagogues – that is, by leaders whose popularity results from exploiting people's ignorance and prejudices. Aristophanes, a fifth-century BC comic playwright, also of ancient Athens, wrote the *Clouds* in which the so-called Inferior Argument, consisting of lies and bribes, wins the popular vote. Voters are also fickle. The Athenians one day voted to put to death the men of Mytilene, Lesbos, ordering soldiers to set off across the sea to effect the task. The next day the same Athenians opted for leniency, ordering another ship, carrying the changed policy, to catch the first. Happily, it did so – just in time.

Although democracy in itself may fail to secure good government, it may aid some degree of stability through acquiescence; voters buy into the belief that they have engaged in the process that has led to the government – and it is true that they have engaged, but many pointlessly so. It is worth reflecting on the following line. Belief in democracy as a good means of government may be self-fulfilling to the extent that good government requires citizens' acceptance. Citizens typically do accept democracy as the least bad form of government, being in line with Churchill's quip: 'Democracy is the worst form of government, except for all the others.'

At least democracies offer some degree of risk to politicians: the risk of political death. That should offer us hope for some humility from them, though in most cases it is not a well-founded hope. Rather, it is more an incentive for them to offer whatever they think will secure their election. Democracy can sometimes humble leaders – but so can fear of revolutions. Democracy usually achieves the humbling, when it does, in less violent ways.

A MYTH BY WHICH WE LIVE

We may ask the question of why should we – 'the people' – accept that the government has the right to govern? Democracy provides an answer: we have voted for it. Curiously, we accept that, even though we know it is highly misleading. We could give a different answer to the question: the government has a right to govern because it has served us well – yet that government could be a non-democratic government, but one that is knowledgeable and well-motivated.

That latter answer may be understood as assuming that there is a single answer to the question of what is best for society overall. As we have seen, though, there is no good reason to think that is so. True, it is possible that there exist some minimal structural conditions best for all – for example, as already mentioned, some commitment to a certain equality of rights and of respect – and democracies often, as a matter of fact, are to some degree recognizing them.

Suppose the majority vote is to exterminate all Jews, imprison all homosexuals or bring back slavery. Does the democratic vote make such policies morally acceptable? Of course not. Democratic outcomes should not be trump cards that can trump any other card played. Paradoxically, what is valuable about democracies are those elements that are not open to revision by democratic votes; those elements need not be unique to democracies. And that returns us to Plato.

Plato is surely right in challenging the crude democratic assumption that majority voting should determine ends and should determine which means to take to secure those ends. There can be reflection and reason – and passions – about ends. We can assess whether beliefs are distorted, consequences misunderstood, or the majority are supporting an obvious immorality or manifesting lack of sensitivity. Those assessments are not determined by majority votes – and we may doubt whether the majority vote is typically the right way for determining policies, even if within a framework of respect for rights. Indeed, the concept of 'democracy' has been described as an 'essentially contested concept', one that generates frequent disputes about how it is best understood, best deployed and when and where. Whichever way those arguments go, and in part because there are such arguments, democracy is valuable, if valuable at all – I dare to suggest – only as a form of *fictionalism*: we live by the fiction. We may, yet, step back and wonder whether we should live by a fiction, whether we should engage in political self-deception.

If there is a single best way for society to be run, then surely we need rulers to effect that way – and paradoxically that may require people believing that their votes matter, when we know (and perhaps at some level, they know) that their votes matter not at all. If there is no single best way for society to run, then we need competent rulers able to ensure that at least the better compromises are pursued. Once again there is no reason to think majority votes would secure that pursuit, though maybe, again, we should need people to think that they do.

The ideal 'democracy' – well, the best it can get as a minimum – is a society where there is universal adult suffrage, but where certain freedoms and rights are not exposed to voters' whims for overturning. The ideal 'democracy' has a government that governs for what is at least good for the society as a whole while compatible with its running at least reasonably well for the worse off; and that requires people believing, probably falsely, that they have an input. Many current democracies in receipt of praise are ones in which many people's votes and undistorted beliefs have little direct effect on policies. The irrelevancy of the votes and people's beliefs to outcomes need not undermine being governed well; of course, it does not remotely guarantee being governed well either.

The ideal 'democracy', in the world as it is, is perhaps one where people deceive themselves into thinking that they live in a democracy where every vote counts and – where by manipulation, good luck or divine intervention – the government is one that does its best for 'its people'.

The deceptions and self-deceptions just suggested are those deployed to secure what in practice is 'a best' for society and all its members or, at least, is as reasonably good as it can be. When we encounter Happy Land in Chapter 15, we may have our eyes opened even more to how we are deeply fooled by our liberal democracies both as ideals and as realities. Just as some would doubt whether there were any Christians in Christendom, so we may doubt, with paradoxical effect, whether amongst our democrats there are any democrats. The next chapter justifies that doubt.

2

How democracy lies

Dear reader, you lie. Well, you would have to be very exceptional for that not to be true. Think of how many times you tick boxes asserting that you have read the terms and conditions of the policy in question, yet you have not; you have just ticked. The law connives in such deceit. In using social-media services and 'smart-home' devices, there is screen after screen of terms of service for data sharing, linking to third parties' terms of service to which you have consequently 'consented', yet you have little idea of the content of those consents. The service providers maintain that through your 'consents' they have secured at least some legal protection as they take ownership of, and share out, your data. The consents here are, though, mythical. The parties are engaged in deceit.

If running a business, you no doubt often pretend to would-be clients that things are going well – in the hope of making that a self-fulfilling claim for the future. If employed, you may well feign contentment in the job for fear of the sack – or, for that matter, you may be pretending disgruntlement and an eagerness to leave, your aim being to increase your remuneration.

The corporate world more generally rests on deceit. The posters scream '75% off', yet in small print say 'up to'. In more significant ways, we have seen the deceit of banks, rating agencies and investment managers – with the resultant financial crises and the long-overdue compensations for victims of 'mis-selling', though no compensation, only hardship, for the vast majority, in America, Europe and elsewhere, who suffered as a result of the crises.

True, we can draw distinctions, when discussing how communications misfire. We can distinguish, for example, between people who lie to an audience, in that they intentionally utter untruths, and those who deliberately fail to correct an audience's false beliefs – and those who stand in the way of others discovering the truth. We sometimes lack sympathy for receivers of bad deals; we make pleas of 'caveat emptor', 'buyer beware' – whereby the responsibility buck is passed. The outcomes in such cases are much the same: people have not got hold of the truth. Deceit, one way or another, is part of the game in Western liberal, free-market democracies.

Why, then, should we expect anything better of politicians? Indeed, what is wrong with lying? It may have beneficial consequences and that may be the aim, the aim being, for example, in days of yore, 'to save a lady's honour'. With the box-ticking example, we deceitfully tick to gain access to the account, the internet, the credit facilities; we see them as to our benefit. As said, the corporate providers set the conditions requiring consent as their protection from claims and to enable themselves to claim against customers. They know full well that the pages and pages of conditions, even if read – and the irritating and hurriedly spoken conditions in transactions by phone, even if properly heard – would baffle most people by far. Society's concern for truth in these transactions may be deemed an 'institutional charade'.

Context, significance, expectations and conventions are relevant with regard to how lies and deceit are morally judged. If you ask the way to the station, you do not expect to be misled – but when reading advertisements, you accept that there are likely to be some unjustified gloss and exaggeration of benefits – as also with political manifestos. These days, though, many manipulations of voters and consumers are increasingly behind the scenes, engaged with hidden algorithms for data analyses; we, mere citizens and consumers, are typically blind to the genuine sources and paymasters of, for example, increased social-media activity, numerous tweets and emails enticing us to support – or denigrate – certain political stances or individuals.

Of course, politicians sometimes ought not to tell the truth. They may need to be secretive or 'economical with the truth', though such secrecy, when under questioning, can lead to the lying. When planning a devaluation or radical change in economic policy, financial secretaries may just have to lie – otherwise there would be adverse market reactions.

The role of context and expectations in assessing the likelihood of deceit introduces us to Ms Mandy Rice-Davies who has been much quoted because of her 'Well [giggle], he would, wouldn't he?' She was in a British court responding to Lord Astor's denial of an affair with her. They were caught up in a big 1961 scandal, when a defence minister in Harold Macmillan's government lied to Parliament. Members of Parliament lying in parliament is deemed a major parliamentary crime, yet evasions, 'inadvertent' misleadings and being economical with the truth are acceptable. The recommendation (often initially ignored) is that when in a tight corner, always tell the truth; better still is the observation (also ignored): if you always tell the truth, there is no tight corner.

Politicians' lies, even if with beneficial consequences, do not sit easily in democracies, grounded on the proclaimed necessity for an informed, not misinformed, electorate. That politicians mislead – or that they have a semi-detached relationship with the truth – seems, though, to be accepted as par for the course, as it does, these days, with regard to journalists. Many people, when asked the question 'How do you tell when politicians are lying?', nod knowingly at the responsive murmur: 'When their lips move.'

With the arrival of Donald Trump on the political scene also arrived much talk of 'post truth'. Facts, it seems, are treated by post-truth supporters as less relevant than appeals to the public's emotions and beliefs, even when the beliefs are false. There is also the casual presentation of falsehoods or, minimally, dubious claims as just 'alternative facts', thus corrupting the notion of objective facts. Such appeals and presentations are not news, political 'spin-doctoring' having been around for decades. As ever, though, there are degrees and degrees. In Britain, there was the Zinoviev letter – a fake letter published by the *Daily Mail*, just before the 1924 election, with the intention of damaging the Labour Party. During the 1945 election campaign, Winston Churchill for the Conservatives made a wireless broadcast insisting that the Labour Party's leader, Clem Attlee, if elected, would deploy the Gestapo. We could go back to Russia, 1903, with the so-called Protocols of the Elders of Zion, which received international publicity. It was a hoax, purporting to describe a Jewish plan for global domination; it was trumpeted by anti-Semites, notably by Henry Ford in the United States.

In 2002–3, there were highly misleading claims made by the United States and United Kingdom governments about Iraq's possession of 'weapons of mass destruction' ready to be deployed against the West within forty-five minutes. The deliverances of today's politicians that receive the dubious accolade of 'alternative facts' are no more outrageous. Indeed, some of today's claims are far less dangerous because they are easily shown to be false; in contrast, years of serpent windings were engaged to unravel the truth of who knew what regarding Iraq.

Let us not, by the way, fall for talk of facts as nothing but talk of interpretations and how things can always be seen differently. Sometimes they can, rightly so, but it is worth noting Clemenceau's response when asked what future historians would say about the First World War: 'They will not [or should not] say that Belgium invaded Germany.'

It can be argued that, in contrast to authoritarian rulers, democratic politicians at least are recognizing that they need to respect the people as voters when they lie to them – they have to address the electorate's worries. Mind you, they do not respect the voters sufficiently well to tell them the truth. Some politicians – without a care, it seems – speak freely of giving 'alternative facts': that is, giving claims that bear no relationship to how things are. Paradoxically that may suggest some honesty by those politicians; they are signalling that truth no longer matters to them.

With such thoughts, we may warm to W. B. Yeats, 'The Old Stone Cross' (1938),

> The Statesman is an easy man
> He tells his lies by rote.
> The Journalist makes up his lies
> And takes you by the throat.
> So stay at home & drink your beer
> And let the neighbours vote.

One lie loved by politicians of all shades, it seems, is 'the people have spoken'. How often have we been told that – and especially so in Great Britain regarding the 2016 vote to leave the European Union (EU).

THE PEOPLE

'The people' (the 'demos') are glorified in a democracy. 'Rule by the people' – that is democracy, the term deriving from the Greek *demos kratos*, meaning 'people power'. It has an aura of commendation – well, it does these days, until we meet 'populism' – in contrast with the traditional aim of the few who seek to rule *over* the people.

Consider the democracy of the United States; here is Abraham Lincoln in his Gettysburg Address (1863): '... this nation, under God, shall have a new birth of freedom – and that government of the people, by the people, for the people, shall not perish from the earth.'

At each occurrence, we may question what constitutes 'the People': the upper-case 'P' is used only when this distinctive concept of political theory is being emphasized. The simple idea is that the individuals of a State rule themselves; but, again, it is not as simple as that. The idea may be summarized as:

> the People – grant authority to
> the People – to have authority over
> the People – to secure the good of
> the People – by following what
> the People – determine.

There exists the nation's population – the people – but no democracy permits all to be involved in the democracy by way of contributing to the granting of authority, of the right to rule – and no one would think it a good idea. There are restrictions on age, on citizenship, on status, on sanity. In ancient Athens, democracy was distinguished from ochlocracy or mob rule, where the mob is led by demagogues – rabble-rousers – as Plato would see them. In nineteenth-century Britain, John Stuart Mill, the great Victorian thinker and promoter of free expression, far advanced for his day, argued to extend the franchise to include women, yet still supported a property-ownership qualification – and, controversially, thought that the educated should have more votes each than the uneducated (Mill, unsurprisingly, counted amongst the educated).

Not all those who are ruled are involved in the ruling. Democratic rulers rule the lives of those who have no chance of voting, being 'ruled out of ruling' – children, non-human animals, visiting foreigners.

Despite the above limits, the franchise, the suffrage or civil right to vote, is casually described as 'universal equal adult suffrage'. Of course, that suffrage was not determined by that franchise, but came about through protest, pressures or just good reasoning by authorities already in power. Certain limits on the franchise can clearly be justified by good reasoning. In practice, though, many limits have no good democratic justification, but derive from a variety of political self-interests.

Let us turn to how the People – those eligible to vote – determine matters. Consider a direct democracy with voting directly on certain policies. We find this in today's referendums, but a simpler model is that of ancient Athens, with a small electorate voting in the marketplace. First, note, we need a means for deciding which policies are to be proposed to be voted upon; that is usually done by those already in power. Secondly, it is understandable that only certain policies should be handled in that way, otherwise citizens would be forever voting. Imagine, today, having the electorate 'online', each week voting on the latest policies proposed – and proposed by just anyone.

The United Kingdom's 2016 referendum, whether to leave the EU, brought forth questions and doubts relating to the People and democratic decision-making. Those under age eighteen were not entitled to vote, but the outcome affects them later on when suitably aged to vote, yet having missed the vote. Indeed, they experience the consequences of the referendum for many more decades than those much older – those aged, for example, eighty-eight and entitled to vote in 2016. That, of course, holds even if living with the results of second or third or fourth referendums related to any long-term national commitment. The winners of the referendum, the 'Brexiteers' – for 'Brexit', for Britain to leave the EU – eagerly stressed their alleged belief that any request for another referendum on a related topic that could lead to remaining within the EU or immediately returning to the EU would be dishonouring the 'People's will' and would, paradoxically, be anti-democratic.

That certain decisions with significant long-term consequences should be decided on one day, on a single vote, may well strike most people, if they step back, as folly – and the outcome pretty random. It is also a strange understanding of the 'People's choice' as one whereby the People may not choose to choose again. Losers stress that point. Of course, one doubts if they would be doing so had they won. There are cases in Europe where a referendum that has not delivered the government's desired outcome has been quickly followed by a further referendum that has appropriately delivered, whether for good reasons or not. Witness the 1992–3 Danish referendums on the EU's Maastricht Treaty and the 2008 Irish referendums on the EU's Lisbon Treaty.

When things are not going the way preferred by those in power – or seem to be somewhat radical – losers sometimes complain that the results show the dangers of 'populism'. Much has been written of such dangers, if dangers they be, hitting the United States and some European countries – Britain, Hungary, Greece – but also countries of South America and beyond. What leads to radical changes in a country's political leadership is unclear. Some quote admiringly, with the rise of Donald Trump in view, the seeming foresight of Richard Rorty, an influential American philosopher, who wrote in his 1996 *Achieving Our Country*:

> … something will crack. The non-suburban electorate will decide that the system has failed and start looking around for a strongman to vote for – someone willing to assure them that, once he is elected, the smug bureaucrats, tricky lawyers, overpaid bond salesmen, and postmodernist professors will no longer be calling the shots… Once the strongman takes office, no one can predict what will happen.

Well, it took twenty years for that crack to appear. In 1945, radical change occurred in Britain; the landslide election victory of the

Labour Party with Clem Attlee becoming prime minister led to the introduction of the National Health Service (NHS), expansion of social security and industrial reorganization. As already implied, Attlee was very different from popular images of a 'strongman', one akin, for example, to Trump (as he portrays himself). Let us see, then, whether we can make much sense of populism.

POPULISM – LAZY LABELLING

'Populism' is typically deployed as a term of abuse – though ask for its definition and we meet with conflicting answers. Look at examples cited and you may wonder why the relevant electoral support counts as a populist one, whereas another does not. On the surface, populism should sit well and favourably with democracy; after all, democracy values the People having their say and populism, it seems, is a matter of the People having their say. Those comments, though, would be dismissed as naive – or populist and therefore to be disparaged.

Let us see what understanding there is of today's 'populism'. In the United States, undoubtedly Trump is deemed 'populist', yet he did not receive the largest popular vote – so, the number of people voting for a politician does not itself determine whether the politician is populist. 'Populist' has been deployed to describe the Brexit vote in Britain, but there was no overall majority for Brexit of the People entitled to vote.

Do policies determine what counts as populist? Those policies are certainly not clearly identified in terms of the political 'left' – or 'right' – for both political stances have at times been so described. In the US, Bernie Sanders, with very different policies from Trump, is also perceived as populist.

Politicians deemed populist are, we may sceptically suggest, relatively successful politicians who appeal to certain swathes of people and whose policies, personalities, even supporters, other more established politicians dislike. Certainly, those who condemned Trump, the British Brexiteers and Jeremy Corbyn's Labour Party policies as populist were inclined to disparage their supporters. In return, politicians who reap the accolade of 'populists' are critical of those in power, of establishment figures – until, presumably, they themselves secure power. Paradoxically, some populist leaders have been very much within establishment circles of the wealthy and powerful; they have been no outsiders. In Britain, Nigel Farage, a leading Brexiteer, was educated at the prestigious Dulwich College and followed his father in the City, while Boris Johnson, another leading Brexiteer, was at Eton College and Balliol College, Oxford. In the United States, as is well known, Donald Trump inherited a multimillion-dollar property empire.

'Populist' is often ascribed to those that, in some way, claim that they alone represent the People or the People's interests. Jarosław Kaczyński, a leader of the Polish Law and Justice party (PiS by its Polish acronym), asserted, '*Vox populi, vox dei*': the voice of the People is the voice of God. Without the aspect of divinity, many politicians voted in by the People – even the most partisan politicians – see themselves as acting in the interests of the People. That, then, is hardly a distinguishing feature of populists.

Populists, they are charged, endanger democracy because they see the People as a single homogeneous group in contrast to true democrats who see the people as needing to be 'free, equal and irreducibly diverse'. Well, that is how matters are seen by Jan-Werner Müller in his 2016 *What is Populism?* The charge is, though, rather odd. After all, populists recognize as well as anyone else that the policies which, for example, directly benefit the elderly are not thereby directly benefiting the young. They recognize that people have diverse employments, diverse interests – diverse heights, for that matter – but, yes, they do often insist that there is a commonality regarding how people are to flourish together in a society. Populists may emphasize solidarity being needed – of all the people pulling together – yet that is no different from the claims of run-of-the-mill politicians, though probably without the term 'solidarity' in play. In Britain under David Cameron's coalition government (2010–15), the great mantra was 'we are all in it together'.

Some see populists as making a moral claim about the nature of the People's real interests: when populist parties lose elections, that does not undermine their populist claim to be representatives of the People. Again, that is no different from the stance adopted by most politicians, though it is true that some populists emphasize how they are speaking for 'real people'; but that is political rhetoric, just as is the use of 'populist' or 'Marxist' by politicians to denigrate policies with which they disagree.

We may spot some vague policy areas that often are associated with populist stances. There is the idea that the People of a particular country have interests that conflict with the interests of foreigners seeking to enter the country; the People's interests may indeed conflict with interests of certain small groups within society, not truly part of the 'People'. On that basis, the British Conservative Party, certainly from the beginning of the twenty-first century, is populist: it is keen on radically reducing immigration; it eagerly dismisses certain groups within Britain as Marxist or Trotskyist, disparaging them as no lovers of the country in which they live.

In contrast to such populism, Zuzana Čaputová convincingly won Slovakia's 2019 presidential election as a liberal progressive, campaigning on the values of humanity, solidarity and truth. Her main opponent was Maroš Šefčovič, a veteran diplomat and EU commissioner, who opposed same-sex rights as unchristian and who was keen to deport immigrants. Paradoxically, she secured the popular vote by condemning Šefčovič's populism; paradoxically, that populism was represented by an establishment figure.

Ms Čaputová spoke in terms of a struggle between good and evil. That is another example of the murky muddle of the 'populist' label, for opponents of populists often complain that populists do not live in the real world, that they propose 'simple solutions', easy slogans – is not 'the struggle between good and evil' one? – to intractable problems and offer snake-oil remedies. Once again such charges are common between parties. During much of the 2010s, the British Conservative Party, keen on charging others as populist, sought electoral support on the simple 'solution' of austerity, in the face of many established economists who challenged that 'simple solution'.

Applications of the term 'populist' are probably as misleading as uses of 'democratic' for North Korea, Sweden and, for that matter, some periods of ancient Athens. Putting the lazy labelling of 'populist' to one side, let us return to the question of whether a democracy, in any sense, allows people to rule themselves. Do direct elections (ones not through party representatives) and direct voting on policies (through referendums) lead anywhere near to the People ruling the People?

If the idea is that the People ruling rests on the wishes expressed in voting, then unless there is complete agreement – no divergence of views – and 100 per cent voting, some people are being ruled not according to their wishes. As noted in Chapter 1, democracy is far, far from a guarantor of self-rule. There is no single 'will of the people', but individuals with individual wills. It is extremely unlikely that those individual wills all have the same goal.

Even if, on some grounds, a direct democracy is desirable in principle, it is not viable, unless we are thinking of small communities with few policy decisions. The city state of Athens, during some of the fifth century BC, operated as a reasonably successful direct democracy, with Pericles as leader, albeit the franchise excluded, for example, women and slaves – and, as seen earlier, the Athenian voters could be fickle.

Direct voting, 'direct democracies', usually give way to representative democracies (the term first coined in 1777). That is why James Madison, a Founding Father of the United States and the fourth president, refers to the United States as a 'republic' rather than a 'democracy'. Even when there is what may be seen as a direct democratic vote in the States, notably the election of president, the electoral college may prevent a majority vote from winning – thus, Hillary Clinton lost the 2016 election.

In the 2017 French election first round, Emmanuel Macron won just under 24 per cent of the votes when competing with many candidates; in the second-round 'run-off' between the two highest placed, he was standing against Marine Le Pen, perceived as extreme right-winger and populist, and he won over 66 per cent. Had Macron been running against one of the other first-round candidates who received almost as many votes as Le Pen – François Fillon or Jean-Luc Mélenchon – he may have lost. At the start of Macron's presidency in 2017 his approval rating exceeded 60 per cent; by late 2018, it was around 25 per cent. True, that was not such a swift change as the one mentioned earlier when overnight the Athenians changed their minds about putting to death the males of Mytilene. The case of Macron is, though, a fine example of both how democratic outcomes rest on various lucks and chosen procedures and how the People are misled or readily open to mind-changes.

REPRESENTATIVES

Instead of voting directly on policies, we should vote for people to represent us. Such is representative democracy; it has some good justifications of a practical nature: the representatives should have more time and resources to assess policies. They exist, though, in the grey area of representing constituents, yet not being delegated by constituents. They are meant to be representing the interests of both those who voted for them and those who did not (a seemingly impossible task). That attempts to justify their voting in Parliament, Congress or Senate in ways that their supporters may reject. In a representative democracy, rule is not so much *by* the people, but at least it is meant to be *for* the people.

A democratic conflict arises when the people disagree with a representative's assessment of what is in their best interests. That may often go unnoticed, but when a representative democracy has included a direct democracy element, as in a referendum on a highly controversial matter, there can be political havoc; Britain soon experienced that after its 2016 EU referendum. Overall, the representatives supported remaining within the EU, yet the referendum vote was to leave. Despite the millions of words written and spoken, the considerable anguish and wringing of hands, there is no 'the right answer' that all democrats should embrace regarding whether the representatives' 'will' does or does not take priority over the so-called People's 'will'. What should be obvious, though, is that one ought not to graft direct democracy procedures on to representative democracies solely for short-term political expediency.

With representative democracies, we are stepping back towards Plato – well, a little. The representatives should have, or it is hoped do have, more expertise about policies than the public. Many these days in the West are wary of such a comment because they doubt the existence of expertise – at least over sociopolitico and economic matters. That doubt is not least because millions of people have suffered hardships as a result of 'experts' running the political and financial institutions leading to the 2008 global crisis. Indeed, we should be wary of the 'expert' accolade, not because of doubts about expertise existing, but because of doubts regarding the expertise and/or motives of representatives. Representatives have to stand and use their silver tongues to be elected. Who knows their motives, beliefs and expertise? Often, they will tailor their proposals and voting patterns to those most likely to secure re-election. Because of distortions of charisma and silver tongues, there was a time in ancient Athens when officials and leaders were mainly elected by random lot. That practice – sortition – meant that all the citizens had equal chances of office; it also meant that to be elected did not rest on persuasive tactics and rhetoric.

Returning to today's world, how are our representatives selected? Democracy has no obvious means to ensure that the best would-be representatives are those 'on the ticket'. Some, it would seem, may be engaging in politics as forms of play – as games on Etonian playing fields. Some may see political engagements as competitions run every few years, competitions in persuasion. Aristophanes, in his play Knights, has the Chorus, the collective voice, commenting on the events on stage, singing: 'Demos, you have a fine sway, since all mankind fears you like a man with tyrannical power. But you're easily led astray: you enjoy being flattered and thoroughly deceived, and every speech maker has you gaping. You've a mind, but it's out to lunch.'

That is condemnation of the people who vote; it is also condemnation of politicians eager to secure public support and hence to win the electoral competition. Usually, the winnings hold for four or five years, the winnings being power and status; later on, winnings often take the form of well-paid directorships, lecture tours and celebrity-guest appearances. In Britain and the States one cannot help but notice the revolving doors between gamekeeper and poacher: ministers and civil servants as gamekeepers determine regulations, taxation policies and outsourcing to corporations; later they have become investment and tax advisers or executives of those corporations – poachers.

DEMOCRACY: ITS LYING PRACTICE

Take a look around; cast eyes on the democracies of Europe, America, India, Australia, New Zealand and elsewhere. Delve into their elections, how the franchise is determined, how candidates are selected, how political parties dominate and how governments result. By the way, Chapter 10 looks at the measures designed to ensure greater numbers of women and minority groups among representatives. Attend to the effects of wealth, of media access, of advertising, of misinformation, of how voters are persuaded to vote and how the democratic machinery counts the votes. What do we find?

Certainly, we find considerable rhetoric promoting the value of democracy, the importance of people's participation and deliberation. At election victories, we are meant to bask in proclamations of how 'the people' have spoken. Does the reality match the rhetoric? Winston Churchill commented on how a few minutes talking to voters should lead to despair about democracy as a sensible form of government – given the false beliefs and bad reasoning of many. We should add that some of those false beliefs and bad reasoning have been deliberately instilled by those seeking the electorate's votes. That may in part explain why scepticism of established leaderships, with the move to so-called populism, arises amongst many voters; they feel that they have been misled, a feeling fuelled by the global financial crisis and the adverse effects on their living standards – those adverse effects in high contrast to the flourishing of most of the apparent financial culprits.

Typically, money is a gatekeeper to power in Western democracies, especially so in the United States where, in the main, limits on political contributions by individuals and corporations have been ruled unconstitutional; to limit contributions would allegedly inhibit freedom of expression and hence offend the First Amendment. Once, when the Catholic Church dominated, some could buy their way into heaven through 'indulgences'; now, it has been noted, they can at least buy their way into political power. Wealth influences voting, be it through distortions of the media, funding of campaigns or lobbying of governments. James Harrington, a seventeenth-century political thinker – author of the utopian *The Commonwealth of Oceana* (1656) – was wise on this matter, for he recognized that any republican form of government needs an equal distribution of wealth – a 'common wealth' – otherwise the wealthy take political control. And we see today how wealth often influences which policies are proposed, which are adopted and which are quietly forgotten. It informs, yet also misinforms. It can also affect which candidates stand and, for that matter, who is elected. Obviously, being the wealthiest party at an election does not guarantee winning, but let us not fall for those siren voices whose singing would have us to believe that the amount of money spent by political parties never has an effect or has negligible effect on eventual outcome. Manifestly, money spent on campaigns is both thought likely to have an effect and does often have an effect – otherwise donors, corporations, unions and individuals would not repeatedly spend the money. It is utterly astonishing that people glorify the West's democratic elections as 'free and fair' when, in most cases, it is known that wealth, neither free nor fair, is a major factor in determining outcomes.

In Britain, for decades, a party's Members of Parliament (MPs) would select the party's leader, but gradually, over the decades, 'grass-root' members have increasingly had influence. In 2015, a rule change in the British Labour Party allowed many more people to become Labour Party members, with the right to vote in leadership elections. The outcome was that Jeremy Corbyn, a left-wing MP with mild socialist policies, was overwhelmingly elected, much to the chagrin of most Labour MPs. Putting aside the prior question of how membership of a party and its powers should be determined, many of the new active members of the Labour Party felt, not unreasonably, that they should determine who stands as Labour candidates. Most MPs see that as a threat, a process deemed 'deselection', though it could be viewed as a welcome opportunity for a fresh selection or reselection. After all, those who have been elected as MPs do not usually condemn another general election as being a process for deselecting them, though some may have an affection for Turkey's President Erdoğan's comment: 'Democracy is like a train; once you reach your destination, you get off.'

Placing referendums to one side, most democracies have representatives who represent particular constituencies; and political power typically resides with the party with most representatives elected. Consequently, the party that wins power may not have received the majority vote, for voter distribution can radically differ between constituencies. In the 1951 Great Britain general election, the Conservative Party won 321 seats, the Labour Party 295 seats, yet more people voted for Labour. Because of the United States' electoral-college buffer already noted, George W. Bush won the 2000 election, despite Al Gore, his opponent, receiving more votes. Unless proportional representation is built within the process, whereby the proportion of representatives in the legislative body tracks the proportions of the electorate's votes, such 'undemocratic' outcomes remain possible.

Democracy has been characterized as a means whereby the unwashed remind the washed of their existence, but let us remember that the washed engage in much skulduggery to mislead the unwashed. In the United States, public assistance identity papers are more likely to be used by African Americans who are more likely to vote Democrat; as a result, certain states with Republicans in local power have sought to rule those papers unacceptable as identity confirmation for casting votes. Some procedures in Britain have the effect of deterring or preventing some poor and minority groups from voting – as various independent electoral reports have shown. There are many other practical restrictions: hours of voting, the ease of reaching polling stations. For example, the articulate and well-informed can readily arrange postal votes. The burden of finding documents and queuing to vote is typically much heavier for manual workers, with long, long shifts, or those living in poverty, than for professionals and the wealthy.

For more skulduggery – in representative democracies that lack proportional representation – constituency, county and district boundaries are drawn and revised by local parties in power to their advantage. Look at certain congressional districts in the United States, look at their geographical shapes: there are clear cases of a 'party in local power' gerrymandering. That amounts to voter suppression and racial discrimination over the right to vote – in a country that proudly trumpets its democracy. Here are a couple of examples.

Some years ago, North Carolina's Republican state analysed a breakdown of turnout by racial identity and by those who lacked a driver's licence number; the Republican leadership then rearranged congressional districts accordingly. Such blatant gerrymandering has been considered in courts, with various rulings. Similar cases are Maryland's 3rd congressional district and Pennsylvania's 7th district. Gerrymandering, of course, is less likely to occur when boundaries are set by independent bodies; but when those in power have the final say – as they have in the United Kingdom, France and Greece, for example – independence is somewhat mythical. Even when there are degrees of proportional representation, governments often determine the rules to 'rule out' any representation by small parties that fail to reach a threshold of votes; that has, at times, been the case in Germany.

Certain constituencies are marginal or swing; on the basis of previous voting patterns, one can reasonably judge that only a few votes are needed to move the constituency from one party to another. Such constituencies naturally receive maximum attention by the parties, with focus groups formed so that parties may decide how to direct their advertising for best effect. Governments in power prior to elections direct resources to marginal seats to influence outcomes. Despite so-called fixed-term parliaments, in Britain governments in practice can still decide when to hold an election – as Theresa May did in 2017, after frequently denying that she would; the mind-change 'coincidentally' occurred when she was running way ahead in the polls.

Because of the structure of constituencies, districts and counties, resultant governments, as already implied, rarely have received a majority of votes – unless some proportional representation exists, as in Sweden, Denmark and many other European countries. In the United Kingdom, touches of proportionality are used for various legislative assemblies, contrasting with the 'first past the post' that curiously remains in place for the general election, the most important election, to the House of Commons. With or without proportional representation, coalition governments often result, manifesting a compromise between voters' wants, a compromise for which few wittingly voted – though the parties in coalition may, taken together, have been voted in by a majority of those who voted.

Once we have coalitions, a small government-supporting party may vote against a government policy, causing the policy to be lost, purely to 'send a message' of what it could do when a more significant policy comes to the fore: witness the antics of Northern Ireland's Democratic Unionist Party when propping up Theresa May's government in 2017–19. Witness the 'pork-barrel' politics where one or other MP or member of Congress or Senate will support legislation only if his or her constituency receives some special funding. The overall goodness or otherwise of the proposed legislation drops out of the picture. The power of small parties can sometimes far exceed what would be proportionate to their political support. In Israel's Knesset, coalition governments have at times maintained power by pursuing highly conservative policies to keep small Orthodox Judaic parties on side.

Voting is, of course, typically for a manifesto – a package – yet at the end of campaigns winning politicians pretend that the People have voted for the whole manifesto, that the government has a 'mandate from the People'. In fact, few people have read the relevant manifesto and, regarding the policies expressed, some may have voted for this policy, but not those – and many would not have voted for any of them.

Once in power, do the representatives vote according to what is perceived best for the society? Far from it: there are numerous instances of wealth, lobbying and threats of non-political preferment influencing votes in parliaments, congresses, senates. In Britain, government 'whips' have used all manner of pressures, the Dark Arts, nothing to do with the goodness of policies in question; they would often refer to the Black Book of MPs' peccadilloes and how some might 'accidentally' be made public – some even just invented – to persuade MPs to toe the party line. The level of rational persuasion is illustrated by the following: during 2016–17, a Conservative government's Chief Whip kept Cronus on his desk. Cronus was a large tarantula spider, named after the Greek god who came to power by castrating his own father before eating his own children. Not unreasonably, many MPs thought best not to argue – keen to argue neither with Cronus nor the Chief Whip.

TURNING TO MACHIAVELLI

Machiavelli, paradoxically, is not all that machiavellian, someone manipulative, prepared to do anything, solely for his own ends. Many politicians would do well to learn from the real Machiavelli – well, his good points. Let us use 'machiavellian' with lower-case 'm' when having in mind the common understanding of Machia-velli's ways.

Niccolò Machiavelli, now known as a political thinker of the Renaissance, was primarily a diplomat, committed to enhancing the power of his native city republic, Florence. He had a bad time: when the Medici family ousted the republicans, he, as republican supporter, was tortured, though eventually allowed to retire to a farm – as an internal exile. There he wrote Il Principe, The Prince, dis-tributed in 1513 – a gift he intended for the powerful Medicis, in the hope that the work would reignite his political career, as now in support of the princely dictators. He failed on that score.

Yes, Machiavelli advocated cunning, machinations and ruth-lessness – all apparently in the service of personal political success. Those are the features much admired (often off the record) by our spin-doctoring politicians, corporate sales teams, even academics ready to wield the knife for advancement. Donald Trump would seem to be machiavellian in that sense; The Prince is often read as presenting a 'Mack the Knife' stance. And yes, Machiavelli does explicitly admire the cruelty of Cesare Borgia; he advocates treach-ery, arguing that, in the real world, leaders must not be a hundred per cent committed to obeying the law and traditional morality, but need to be half beasts, possessing the fox's guile and the lion's bru-tality. Machiavelli's manly prowess – virtù – is so different from the virtues found in Plato's idea of a just society or those of Aristotle and Christianity. Machiavelli writes that a prince needs to learn 'how not to be good'.

Let us reflect a little on what is going on. We may seek morally to justify actions primarily in terms of their likely consequences, so long as we aim at desirable ends, ends worthy of desire. Cer-tainly, Machiavelli has strong consequentialist streaks. He speaks of maintaining power, of glory and posthumous fame, but they are intertwined with the Florentine State – the citizens – flourishing.

Machiavelli's Prince is not satisfied with securing illusory glory and fame; he wants the real thing, a State that flourishes for its citizens. Now, our leading politicians, many believe, lack that concern; they have motivations solely to do with the short-termism of political survival, despite frequent proclamations by them that they are acting in the 'national interest'. Witness how David Cameron's EU referendum commitment, when British prime minister, was his short-term solution regarding his political party; witness how it backfired, as many believe, for both him and the country.

As a Machiavellian prince, your aims should be noble; the immorality arises, if it does, because of the means deployed. Even here, Machiavelli shows recognizable moral concerns. He explicitly advocates maintaining traditional moral values as far as possible, using deceit and cruelty (including murder, it has to be accepted) only when necessary for the common good. In a sense, he is reminding us that moral virtue is not, as we may call it, 'episodic'. Proper kindness towards children is not to give them ice creams whenever they demand; sometimes you say no and upset them. Those episodes of seeming unkindness may in fact be continuing care for the children's interests.

Machiavelli argues similarly that seeming cruelties may be the actions of a compassionate leader, prepared not to shirk duties, acting for the greater good. True, there is an unfortunate element here: a Machiavellian leader may be genuinely concerned about the health and well-being of the city's citizens overall, but that may involve the death of particular individuals – hardly in their personal interests, unless fancying martyrdom.

When dealing with family and friends, suggests Machiavelli, sticking to traditional moral rules, or staying with virtues of honesty, compassion, courage, can be relied upon; family and friends are likely to reciprocate. In politics, adversaries cannot be relied upon. Further, Miss Fortuna – bad or good luck – throws up the unexpected; hence, princes need flexibility, a preparedness to look at things anew. Even if flexible, he notes, things often run out of a leader's control. There just is political luck – for better or worse.

Reflect on the many events outside of a leader's control. Would Margaret Thatcher have survived as British prime minister in the 1980s but for the Argentinian invasion – out of her control? Would Angela Merkel, chancellor of Germany since 2005, have had such a politically good run, but for Germany's reunification and the state of the German economy when she came to power? Had the Arab Spring, the resultant refugee crises and their effects on Europe not arose, her political decline may have been much delayed. In 1986, Olof Palme, Swedish prime minister, was assassinated; Yitzhak Rabin, Israeli prime minister, in 1995 – and, of course, most famously United States President Kennedy in 1963. Would the politics of those countries have been radically different had the assassins missed their targets or been held up by the traffic? Maybe not, but the 1914 assassination of Austria's Archduke Franz Ferdinand was undoubtedly the proximate cause of the First World War, with over 17 million people killed. Good and bad fortune can have vast outcomes as well as small; and even with the small, some large surprises may subsequently result – the so-called Butterfly Effect, not that the flappings of butterfly wings in Brazil in fact cause Texan tornadoes.

An apocryphal tale, albeit with a ring of truth, is that when asked what shaped his political strategy, the then British Prime Minister Harold Macmillan answered with something akin to 'Events, dear boy, events!' Machiavelli gives substance to that answer, saying much more than is conjured up by today's use of the term 'machiavellian'.

Machiavelli's stance – only use deceit when necessary for the common good, for example – is very different from that of many of today's politicians, where their own short-term interests seem often to be the primary motivation. Machiavelli's stance would not necessarily support governments when they chase whistle-blowers who expose actions shameful, embarrassing or morally appalling. A notable chasing, for example, has been of Chelsea (formerly Bradley) Manning and Julian Assange by the United States authorities, outraged by the 2010 WikiLeaks revelations that included some startling ones of atrocities committed by the US military against civilians in Iraq and Afghanistan. Of course, whistle-blowers break laws – of course, matters are rarely black or white – but sometimes laws need to be broken and sometimes zealous law-breakers, likeable or not, have overall done what was right.

We may hope for better things from our politicians and governments than those connected solely with self-interest. It is, though, a hope that can lead to despair – unless, as mooted in Chapter 1, behind all the political shenanigans there are leaders of Plato's ilk, leaders who know how best to steer society for a better destination, genuinely taking into account one and all.

That is, of course, a hope too far – probably far, far too far – but need it be?

3

Freedom and discrimination: burqas, bikinis and Anonymous

Allow me to quote from an anonymous journal. The writing and paper show it to be recent. I refer to the writer – I infer that it is 'he' – as 'Narrator'. Possibly Narrator is engaged in a work of fiction; possibly he is describing a real encounter. He writes:

> My troubles began when I spied the young woman, sunbathing by the sea. I could not help but find her very attractive – after all, she was reading Samuel Beckett in the original French, sipping a gin and tonic, no plastic straws in sight, and as for her smile... I realized, though, that, for me, what made her truly attractive, in contrast to others on that seashore, was her dark skin, well bronzed and gleaming brown. True, that colour was only skin-deep, but I felt sensations of desire, magnetic pulls, and wondered if I would be brave enough to say hello. I was inhibited not solely by shyness but also by guilt.
>
> I felt guilty for I was discriminating in favour of her – and discriminating against the white-skinned, against the Chinese, Japanese and many Swedes. True, they would be the lucky ones, not to have to swat my advances away – but, as member of some equality boards, I am vocal in my condemnation of discrimination by colour and, for that matter, a host of other features, even, I now remember, by sex and sexual orientation.

I managed to engage conversation with Ludmilla – yes, I discovered her name – and when I mentioned my earlier hesitation, she told me not to be so naive; attractions, at least initially, are bound to be grounded in the physical – assuming absence of telepathy. She added that she would, though, be much offended if, in the end, she was found desirable solely for her colourings of skin.

I was now on the slippery slope of discrimination. When I went to buy her some chocolates, I stormed out of the store that had veiled Muslim women serving; I chose instead to purchase from a charity shop that fought for women's freedom from the conservative Islamic dress code. Days later, when I sought to buy a cake specially iced for her birthday, I rejected suppliers that had opposed other retailers for refusing to ice cakes celebrating same-sex marriages – and we both decided against the hotel that displayed posters of President Trump in its windows, posters unadorned with added moustaches and certain historical salutes.

DISCRIMINATIONS AND RELIGIONS

Which types of discriminations are justified? That is the obvious question arising from the above vignette. In liberal democracies, how extensive should be the freedom of expression, the freedom to do what we want to do?

In this chapter, the burqa, niqab, Afghan chadri and other religious or cultural attire are the focus; they generate much controversy, especially in Europe, regarding which discriminations may or may not be permitted in the public realm. Some countries prohibit wearing in public any coverings of the face; of course, there are other countries, though hardly liberal democracies, where Muslim women must wear the burqa or similar when in public – otherwise they will suffer years in gaol. For ease, let us think of the burqa as the typical example of a religiously grounded face covering that generates considerable controversy in anti-discrimination debates, but before homing in on that matter, here are some examples where sincerely-held religious beliefs come into conflict with anti-discrimination laws.

> In the United States, the owners of Elane Photography, because of their Christian belief, declined to photograph a same-sex commitment ceremony. Elane Photography was found guilty of unlawfully discriminating on the basis of sexual orientation.

> In Britain, a Christian couple running a small private hotel was found guilty of discrimination when refusing to allow a homosexual couple, in a civil partnership, to share a bed.

> Catholic adoption agencies in Britain are no longer permitted to discriminate against potential adoptive couples in same-sex relationships; yet medical practitioners may claim exemption from involvement in abortion procedures.

As that last example illustrates, inconsistencies easily arise; well, they are inconsistencies, unless a good justification exists for certain exemptions from relevant laws. Chapter 12 notes how free expression enters here by way, paradoxically, of compelled expression: were the owners of Elane Photography being compelled to express support for same-sex commitments? Here are more seeming inconsistencies.

Couples who believe homosexual relations to be morally wrong have been barred by relevant authorities from fostering children, yet there is no bar on such couples having children or receiving IVF treatment – courtesy even of Britain's NHS. What justifies the difference? Some Muslims secure exemptions from certain Friday duties at work because of religious requirements, yet atheists with strong commitments to long weekends of debauchery receive no exemptions.

In Britain, only Sikhs are exempt from wearing helmets when riding motorcycles. 'Nature and machine' fanatics, though, may insist that experiencing wind gushing through flowing long hair – thrills of the powerful mechanical thrusting through the natural – is as important to them as the Sikh religion to Sikhs; so they too should be granted helmet exemptions. Indeed, it is more important to those 'communers with Nature', for riding motorcycles forms an essential part of their communing, whereas motorcycle riding is no essential part of Sikhism. If there are good reasons for cyclists in general to have to don protective headgear, then it is unclear why Sikhs should be exempt. True, there is, then, a cost involved in being a Sikh; the cost is that they need to travel by car, train or foot – but they would still be Sikhs.

Turn, now, to Muslim women, religiously committed to the burqa in public. Surely they, though, ought not to face the cost of being unable to enter the public realm, if face-covering bans are in force. Such bans indirectly discriminate against those Muslim women, for others may enter the public domain attired as they want. Well, that is a line that liberals commonly maintain, when rejecting, sometimes vehemently, the calls for burqa bans – liberals, unless of the French ilk and supportive of France's laïcité, a public secularism that rigidly maintains separation between the French State and religion.

⊪

Liberal democracies have a variety of laws deliberately designed to restrict certain freedoms for some, the aim being to protect freedoms of others. Liberal democracies trumpet those freedoms; they can be coy about the restrictions on others. Of course, there is little controversy over laws that forbid people physically attacking non-consenting others, though even there we encounter some uncertainties: when attacks are in defence of self and property, we have questions of the value of what is being defended and how reasonable are the means of defence.

Liberal democracies typically seek, in the main, to be secular, despite references to God in their constitutional declarations or, as in Britain, the Church of England being the established religion. A secular state, in the secularist ideal, does not discriminate at all between people on the grounds of their religion or non-religious worldviews. Yet France and others, certainly secular States, do indirectly discriminate, as just observed; France and others would also deem themselves liberal.

COMMERCE, CONSUMERS AND CONSISTENCIES

The secularism of liberal democracies, many argue for and defend, should allow for people's beliefs (not just religious ones) to be manifested in public, within any limits necessary for public order. How, then, does this work? After all, some discriminations in public are not allowed – see above – yet some are. Narrator of the vignette was in the public world, when he discriminated on grounds of skin colour with regard to possible romance – and in the public world when he discriminated on the grounds of religion and politics regarding which shops and hotel to use.

Liberal democracies have no problem with people, in the public world of market squares, streets and beaches, displaying discriminatory preferences regarding romantic partners; and no one yet argues that consumers should not be free to choose where to shop, however discriminatory. Where the State provides services, though, things are different; in Britain's NHS, patients in hospital cannot choose doctors on the basis of skin colour.

Contrasting with consumers' discriminatory freedoms, those who offer goods, facilities or services directly to the public are not allowed to discriminate on the basis of, for example, religion or sexual orientation. Declining to serve, or work with, people whose features or ways of life oppose your own is, though, very different from harming them by physical attacks. True, there would be adverse consequences for those declined, if no one else would serve them or work alongside; but if that is not so, what is the problem with such public discriminations? Well, those rejected may feel offended and not respected. There could be adverse consequences for society; it may fracture, with groups sporting those rejected features in growing tension with groups that do not. Of course, there may be no such consequences.

We should at least acknowledge some unease over anti-discrimination laws. To prevent shopkeepers and employers discriminating against, for example, homosexuals, Caucasians, Asians or Muslims, those shopkeepers are discriminated against; their freedom to serve whomever they want is blocked. The laws against discrimination are to protect the freedoms of those who would otherwise be discriminated against; in so doing, those laws restrict the freedoms of those who would otherwise discriminate.

The anti-discrimination laws are confined to areas of public life where all should be treated equally in certain respects; those laws do not touch areas of private life. Morality recognizes that individuals have specially attached relationships towards some and ought not always to adopt a detached perspective. The State, though, is detached, offering a public space, public services and opportunities where all, it is claimed, should receive equal rights to respect. In sum, anti-discrimination legislation is typically justified on the grounds that to deny certain people services because of their race, gender, disability, sexual orientation, religion or belief is disparaging, deeply humiliating and affronts their human dignity.

Let us highlight the fact that all those exceedingly disagreeable elements can also occur when denying people goods and services, especially basic goods and services, because they cannot afford their purchase – that is, because the people are impoverished and sufferers of deprivation. Curiously, that exceptionally substantial discrimination, one that affects so many, is easily – or maybe eagerly – overlooked.

A public/private distinction has been deployed above; but how clear is that distinction? It is not as simple as the paradigm distinction between the public square open to all and my private home, open only to those whom I invite. With regard to commercial activities, it is grounded in the relevance of what is on offer for what, rather than on physical location or personal preferences. A business, whether being conducted in people's homes or in market squares, has fish for sale – to derive an income. It would be irrational to sell only to the white-skinned or Christians; neither skin colour nor religion travels with the transaction. Contrast with Narrator and Ludmilla: Narrator's romantic yens being satisfied depend in part on the other's skin colour. It is a different question, though not an unimportant one, whether romance and, more basically, sexual relations should ever be determined in that way.

Membership of political parties, religions and other groups obviously is discriminatory; such groups seek only those with certain beliefs and commitments, not just payment of subscription fees. That discrimination is permitted, whether one signs up as a member in the public square or at a private meeting.

Susie lets a room in her house; she wants the rent – anyone able to pay is fine – but she also hopes for a romantic liaison with a man, so she rules out interviewing women. That is a public/private mixed example; some personal discrimination is a filter added to the public non-discriminatory input (save for the monetary, of course). The Elane photography example is also mixed; there is not just a monetary transaction – at that stage, open to the public – but also implicit statements about what the business owners personally find allowable. Courts, in that case, prioritized the public non-discriminatory aspect over the personal beliefs. Certain commercial transactions may be understood as making statements, saying something – saying something that suppliers would prefer not to say. That is discussed in Chapter 12 with the Ashers Bakery court cases.

Having dealt with business discriminations, more needs to be said about the public/private distinction before the burqa bans can be directly addressed.

DIOGENES AND PUBLIC OFFENCE

We flip back to the fourth century BC. We are in the Athenian marketplace – and we encounter Diogenes of Sinope masturbating in public. Diogenes was well-known; he begged for a living and apparently sometimes carried a lamp during the day: 'I am looking for an honest man.' He was one of the Cynics, those cynical of society's conventions; they sought a return to Nature.

'In public, he behaves like a dog,' objected the Athenians. They found his agora or market behaviour offensive, though arguably it harmed no one (apart from, according to some later beliefs, Diogenes himself). Diogenes engaged in activities that could be conducted in private, without loss. Hence, as the public world found them offensive, that is good reason to restrict such behaviour to the private; and liberal democracies do just that. Through custom or law, they generally maintain constraints on what may be done in public. That stance may have some difficulties for sexual exhibitionists.

Offence arises in different ways. Human beings typically feel that certain bodily functions, features and relationships should be for the private realm – as most cultures recognize in various areas and to varying degrees. In South Korea, it is considered offensive to be noisy on public transport; so, aware of that, most people keep the noise down. Would that there were similar consideration in Britain – and not merely when on public transport, but also when in restaurants; and not merely by the public, but also by those retailers who these days seem reluctant to allow customers to be undisturbed by thuds of amplified music.

The privacy requirement on activities depends, in part, on whether they are normally viewed as disgusting or intimate (or both). Neither in public, nor amongst friends, do most people these days in Western societies feel comfortable at vomiting or defecating, though some cultures – the Chinese, for example – accept spitting in public. Certain of those activities may be frowned upon because of health hazards. Thus it is astonishing, by the way, that in London there are few freely available public toilet facilities, bearing in mind the numerous rough sleepers.

Some may argue that the above public restrictions show societies yielding to the tyranny of majorities, but, if it is, it is a much diluted version of tyranny; and to reject the feelings of most against such activities being undertaken in public would be to accept the tyranny of a minority. The activities here in question are not being banned across the board, but only in the public realm.

In the public realm of liberal democracies, Narrator's flirtation with Ludmilla would raise no eyebrows, though when couples engage publicly in more intimate liaisons – well, again, the thought is: let the arousals happen in private and hence without offence. There is fluidity about this; customs change as tastes and beliefs change. Reflect on today's acceptability, in some countries, of male homosexuals kissing in public. Many people still find that offensive, yet repression of such activity in public hurts the homosexuals more, regarding respect for their freedom, it is argued, than toleration of such activity hurts the people offended by that freedom. Further, the repression would be discriminatory, if heterosexual kissing in public continued to be permitted.

That discriminatory point introduces puzzles of how to delineate 'the sameness' of activities: does the activity of two men kissing count as being the same as a man and woman kissing? The answer may be 'yes'; in both cases they are engaged in a valuable human intimacy. Many would answer 'no', claiming – some on religious grounds – that one is natural, the other not. Liberal democracies are not so liberal as to respect the feelings of those who deliver the 'no' answer. Liberal democracies, to put it paradoxically, have to discriminate.

Some have argued that within the public world there should be no discrimination between people over fundamental features that they cannot help. Let us work this through, taking a clear case. Introduced in 1948 by the ruling National Party with the Afrikaner Party, South Africa's 'apartheid' – Afrikaan for apartness – forced racial groups, grounded in skin colour and ethnicity, to live separately; they were deemed not to be part of the South African nation. Indeed, individuals with black skin and other features showing African ancestry were scarcely considered human by many 'white' Afrikaan speakers, an attitude not that unusual amongst many Europeans in the first half of the twentieth century. Apartheid regimes are now standardly and rightly condemned, but that ought not to be because people cannot help their skin colour. After all, if individuals with black skins – or some other pigmentation considered by the local majority as undesirable – could change the colour, it would be disparaging, morally wrong and bizarre to expect them to do so before entering the public world.

Of course, some people are unable to help being so and so and, as a result, they may feel uneasy at entering the world of others. That can relate to a sense of self-respect, of how many of us hide away with embarrassments, when feeling vulnerable – for example, if oppressed by a facial rash, a 'disastrous' hair treatment or a disability. It can also relate to an awareness of how others may feel. That is where respect for others – for example, the disabled, the facially scarred – entering the public world merits promotion over the distress, the affront, some may feel by such sights. Some affronts, though, liberal societies seek to sweep away, at least from the public gaze – for example, those needing to beg on the streets.

⊰∥⊱

Feelings of disgust and preferences for intimacies being expressed only in private can ground the offence caused by certain public behaviours – and those considerations, as noted, can restrict behaviour even when amongst friends. In a small village, indeed, the public realm may consist wholly of friends and acquaintances. What is distinctive about the public realms of towns and cities is that they are inhabited by strangers to us – and we are strangers to others. They are realms where, in the main, we are not seeking personal relationships with others, but to get on with our daily lives. They are neutral arenas where there is an assumed civil inattention, a 'disattendability'. Meeting a Diogenes of today would distract, whatever we may think about his activities. In Britain, we have the Naked Rambler, Stephen Peter Gough, who is repeatedly arrested, taken to court and, often standing in the dock naked, found guilty and imprisoned, for his public nudity, as a breach of the peace.

Many people tend minimally to feel irritated or uneasy if affronted when in the neutral public space – be it by those seeking charity contributions, beggars on the streets, the buskers now with amplified loudspeakers, or those flaunting supercars, revving with loud roars so they cannot be missed. We may be affronted by the unexpected – by Diogenes turning up – but also by the expected disturbances, as in the examples given. Of course, there are deliberate cases where disruption is the intention by way of political demonstrations.

One way of viewing the private/public distinction, in this context, is that between spaces to which one needs an invitation (be it express or implicit) and spaces to which no invitation is required. In both, certain assumptions are made, default positions accepted; yet with the invitation-only spaces, there are some joint projects in mind – a musical evening; friends for dinner – not so where invitations have not arisen. Through specially arranged invitations, what is normally a public space may sometimes, though, become private.

HOW TO SEE THE BURQA

Is any of the above helpful regarding the rights or wrongs of wearing the burqa in public? The typical liberal default position, to reiterate, is that people should be free to wear whatever they want to wear. The public realm is not by invitation only and so there is no special dress code, save, one must add, codes pertaining to customary decency (please see below on the bikini). There should be no problem with women wearing the burqa in public – yet there is. Some people are offended by it; some see it as an affront.

Here is some background. Countries that currently ban the burqa include France, Belgium, Austria and Denmark. There are some regional bans: for example, Quebec Canada and Lombardy Italy. Many liberals, including secularists, are outraged at such prohibitions; the prohibitions undermine liberalism's heart. People should be free to do what they want in public, so long as not harming others; offence is no harm. Societies should embrace J. S. Mill's 'experiments in living', so long as not experimenting under duress. Wearing the burqa and other face coverings should be permitted, even welcomed as experiments in living – though with some limitations when security comes into play or face-to-face contact is required. To discriminate against burqa wearing in public would be to close down the public space as being open to all. It would be akin to businesses offering services to the public that should be available to all, yet discriminating against same-sex couples by refusing to take their photographic orders.

In the realm of the private, notably relationships with friends, relatives and sexual partners – with Narrator's desire for Ludmilla – there is no question of demands that we should be open to all.

Human beings have preferences – prejudices – and what sort of human life would it be if no discriminatory preferences were permitted? Individuals are not offending anti-discriminatory law by declining to befriend those in burqas or preferring the company of the opposite sex. The State, though, as liberal, does not seek to befriend or un-befriend; the State ensures public arenas exist for all its citizens – no invitations required.

In much of today's Europe, in contrast to the United States, there is the tendency to think of 'religion' as restricted to the private personal realm, non-intrusive in political life. That is a change. Lord Melbourne, British prime minister of the early nineteenth century, held that religious belief ought not to enter the private realm, but be used solely to regulate the public. That was fitting for those days when Britain was described as a Christian country and not as reaching out to secularism.

These days, 'We don't do God' is the attitude of many European leaders. It is a phrase associated with Tony Blair's premiership in Britain during the 2000s, despite Blair's own religious beliefs. Interestingly, although British political leaders are no scholars of Islam, they mostly insist that they know that 'true' Islam, for example, does not urge death to apostates, enforcement of sharia law or support for jihad, for holy wars. That may well be an example of leaders hoping that saying something sufficiently often will make it so. For avoidance of doubt, that critical remark could also be addressed regarding other religions and ideologies; some evangelical Christians believe that 'true' Christianity cannot approve of homosexual relations, contraception and women and men having the same status in the Church.

Even if religion is best understood as private, religious beliefs seep into the public realm, into how things should be regulated in public space. The public/private boundary is porous. For some religious, it can be their duty to demonstrate against abortion clinics and same-sex marriages; they may be committed to comporting themselves in certain ways or affecting the public space by church bells ringing or mosques calling the faithful to prayer – frequently. Religion is, indeed, often very personal for some, tied to their identity. It is – maybe paradoxically – therefore likely to enter the public realm, the market squares; it comes with their person. From a very different angle, celebrities deliberately stand in the public world, seeking great acclaim, yet object when that public profile leads to intrusions into their private.

Returning directly to the burqa, those liberals who *defend* burqa attire are, in fact, in deep conflict with the wearers. The wearers think that it hugely matters what they wear; the liberal secularists think none of it matters. Centuries ago, witches would be burned – for heresy – be their activities in private or public. There was some idea that the community could be held responsible, collectively responsible, before God, if it did not clean up its act. The witches polluted the whole of society. They needed eradication.

Liberal secularists of today no more believe in such collective responsibility before God or gods than in witches; hence, they are typically content to let religious belief and dress be manifested in public. What excites liberals is protecting respect for individuals' autonomy, their freedom to choose – always, so long as not harming others. Banning the burqa from the public realm undermines that respect.

Burqa bans from that liberal perspective are akin to past worries about witches; they pollute the community's liberalism, as if that liberalism is a divinity that must not be upset. Burqa bans are judged as damaging multiculturalism. The bans unjustifiably demand that Muslims be assimilated into a national secularist identity. In contrast, supporters of the bans judge the public burqa display as a dangerous fragmentation of the national community, threatening the nation's sense of identity.

ANONYMOUS – THE BURQA, THE BIKINI AND PRIVACY

Allow me to introduce Anonymous. Anonymous objects to unwanted intrusions into her private life; she possesses a keen sense of privacy. She throws open her windows, to allow in the sun and breeze, but she now worries about spying drones. Her privacy, even when at home, with no spying drones, is increasingly endangered; she is troubled by data collecting when she surfs the net.

All the more so is Anonymous's privacy under threat when out in the public world, with CCTV, scanning devices and smartphone tracking. Anonymous has 'nothing to hide'; but, to maintain self-respect, she objects to those prying eyes. She needs, of course, to leave her home, to visit friends, to shop, and walk through parks, taking the air – but she wants to be anonymous. In a liberal society, she should surely be at liberty to maintain such anonymity.

With that in mind, Anonymous creates a garment in nonconspicuous colours – she is fond of dark green – to cover herself, head to toe, with face fully concealed save for eyes to see, ears to hear, mouth to speak – oh, and to breathe. Thus attired, she steps forth into the public space. Maybe some people stop and stare; maybe the guard refuses her entry into the bank; maybe the police demand to know why she is dressed so. Yet, in a liberal society that permits the wearing of the burqa in public, surely it should permit Anonymous to wear – let us deem it – her A-ttire.

Anonymous feels sad that she is driven to such lengths; she prefers a world where the public space is not so intruded upon – is not tracked by government and corporate bodies. As things stand, she has no choice but to wear A-ttire – and we should sympathize. Of course, Anonymous's stance could catch on. Others may adopt the A-ttire.

From the other end of the dress and privacy spectrum, some may determinedly choose to wear skimpy swimsuits when in towns and cities – not just when with beaches and lakes close by. They may do so to flaunt or, perhaps, just because the weather is hot and humid. They would offend some people, distract others – but so do those who wear burqas, as may also Anonymous. Nudists, eager to be unclad in public, meet similar objections of offence: recall the Naked Rambler.

Context is an important and obvious factor with regard to differential treatments – no bikinis and nudity in public in typical town centres, but fine on various seaside beaches. Context could justify differential burqa-clad treatments: with regard to secular societies, burqas are fine in public areas of mosques, but not elsewhere.

Let us muse further on Anonymous. Could a liberal secular society that permits the burqa in public have any good reason to object to the A-ttire or, for that matter, the bikini being worn in cities?

Answers could appeal to the special importance of religions; and that appeal is often accepted. City firms in Britain, for example, fear that they could be breaking anti-discriminatory laws if not permitting employees to wear their religious dress, but there would be no such breakage if they insisted that bikini wearers, nudists, hoodies and Anonymous should don the standard corporate uniform.

Putting to one side any distinctive corporate factors, the burqa manifests commitment to a deeply-held belief, recognized over centuries, with – so believers insist – consequences for eternity. There is no good reason, though, why secular societies should give religion that privileged position over, say, Anonymous. If they permit the burqa in public, they should permit A-ttire. If they permit the burqa, they should permit the bikini. If they ban both A-ttire and bikini, then they should ban the burqa.

The above may appear to be fallacious reasoning. Bikini wearing, in the city, would strike some as indecent. There may also be special good reasons for objecting to A-ttire; the liberal worry may be: what if it catches on? It could, though, catch on just because burqa wearing is permitted; they could – and should? – stand or fall together.

Assume A-attire catches on, not because of the burqa, but because of Anonymous-type objections to corporate and govern-mental prying. Were the society then to stop such prying, a liberal approach may insist that A-attire offends the idea of a public space and can no longer be justified – just as the burqa ban can be upheld as protecting the public space, unless we have any good grounds for making special exemptions for religions. That moves us along to the reasoning for the ban in France and elsewhere.

France's prohibition on any face-covering veil was upheld by the European Court of Human Rights (ECHR) in 2014, the justification being the need to secure public space for interaction. Similarly, the ban in Belgium was upheld (by the ECHR in 2017). The veil, it is claimed, generates isolation, preventing face-to-face communica-tion and integration; it separates people from the broader society. Indeed, we may see burqa wearing in public as a deliberate political or religious statement; it calls out for attention, thus offending the assumed preference, mentioned earlier, for civil inattention.

In France we also meet with some regional bans on the 'burkini', the burqa-like bikini, where the clothing represents, in the words of Prime Minister Manuel Valls, 'the affirmation of political Islam in the public space'. Curiously, the same feeling of offence against civil inattention being corrupted or worries over lack of integration have not led to the prohibition in public of nuns wearing habits, Muslim women being dressed in the hijab (it covers just the head and neck) and male Hasidic Jews sporting their distinctive curls and clad in their long black jackets.

There are, though, relevant differences. As a matter of fact, con-servative Muslim dress is associated with the version of Islam that discriminates against women and, indeed, calls for the death of apostates. Even if we accept that all the women wearing the burqa in the West do so freely, should a liberal democracy be seen as indirectly endorsing those anti-liberal views? That is the troubling question regarding to what extent should we tolerate the intolerable. Thus, even if liberal societies permitted the wearing of A-ttire, they may yet still have good reasons to object to the burqa.

Respect for individuals is respect for their autonomy. Some argue that burqa wearing can only result from oppression; no women in their right mind would willingly succumb to such restrictive attire, especially when the religion so clearly discriminates against women in favour of men. The women, it is claimed, are not acting freely, even though they may feel that they are; if so, then burqa bans are aids to their eventual autonomy, although, yes, in the short-term, the bans adversely restrict their movements. Even if some women do freely wear the burqa, restricting their freedom can be justified on the grounds of discouraging a way of life that restricts activities of those who have no genuine desire to be burqa-wearers.

Many liberals oppose the considerations just given; they oppose on the grounds of alleged inconsistency. They see the argument as running thus: women are forced into wearing the burqa; therefore, to prevent people being forced in that way, we force them not to wear the burqa – hence we have swapped one enforcement for another that is equally as bad.

The above inconsistency charge, though, should not persuade. By preventing Muslim women from wearing the burqa, the aim is to give them the autonomy to wear what they *want* – and no woman would truly want to spend her life covered up. Compelling women not to wear the burqa still permits a vast range of other options, including those taken on board by millions of Muslim women. Reflect: most countries prevent people from becoming slaves, enslaving themselves, even if they want to. It does not follow that forcing people to be non-slaves is as bad as enslaving them.

One way of testing the liberal secularist credentials on the burqa is the following. Suppose liberals have some excellent reasons to believe that in Britain, with burqa wearing spreading, more and more people will convert to a very conservative Islam, such that eventually that religion dominates the country and non-Muslim women increasingly feel uneasy, to say the least, sensing that they need at least to conform to highly modest dress in public, if not to go as far as converting to Islam.

On the above supposition, would liberal democrats, right now, shrug their shoulders and accept that, well, that just is how things turn out? Or would they recognize that they should pursue policies now to make that future unlikely to happen? If the answer to the latter is yes – and surely that is the right answer for a liberal to give – then what needs to be decided now is whether, as a matter of empirical fact, banning the burqa is more likely to prevent that undesirable distant outcome, or whether it could generate such a reaction that the distant outcome becomes all the more likely. To ban or not transforms into an empirical practical question about likely outcomes for liberal societies. Smug secularists may trumpet how tolerant they are until they face the intolerable.

In assessing these matters, account needs to be taken of the society's current customs and expectations – 'this is what we do here' – while acknowledging how they will, no doubt, change. Let us approach this via a controversial question summed as: yarmulke or yashmak?

There is little risk of the whole of any liberal society, outside of Israel, succumbing to the rituals of Judaism and the Judaic inequalities between men and women, by permitting Jews to wear the yarmulke (the kippah or skullcap): Judaism, if anything, seeks to keep others out, though it does carry dangers of promoting the value of isolated communities.

In contrast, some sincere Muslims (note: only *some*) understand jihad as the struggle to spread Islam worldwide. Permitting the wearing of the yashmak (burqa, niqab) therefore *could* encourage those Muslims to push for further steps along that jihadic political path; and that path can lead to disproportionate punishments, mistreatments of women and considerable repression. That danger may provide sufficient reason for prohibition of the yashmak, and similar, in schools, state institutions and the public realm, but not prohibition of the yarmulke. Such reasoning is based on one religion, Islam – but not the other, Judaism – being active in proselytizing. The Ottoman Empire tolerated different religions – 'the millet system', for each religion had, so to speak, its own millet, each under its own theocratic control; there was, though, a strict rule against conversions.

The above does not imply that liberal societies should have no worries about Judaism – for example, the treatment of women by certain Orthodox. Further, if there are good reasons to ban the yashmak (burqa, niqab), then – to avoid resentments, however unjustified – maybe all religious attire in public should be banned, from yarmulkes to Christian crosses. There are cases and cases, degrees and degrees – and no simple clear-cut liberal right answers. To believe so is to believe in a myth.

A gesture – probably more than a gesture – needs to made against speciesism here. Both Islam and Judaism, through dietary rules for halal and kosher meat, typically demand animal slaughter without any pre-stunning. There is strong evidence that animals, as a result, undergo unnecessary suffering; hence, we may wonder why, in many countries, the 'religious' factor holds sway in this non-stunning way. We should then rightly wonder why so many cruel activities in the production of meat and milk are, in any case, nodded through, with liberal societies drawing a veil, so to speak, over what happens on the way to, and in, the abattoir. Again, we encounter tensions, awkwardness and inconsistencies lurking in our liberal democracies.

Non-human animals aside, liberal societies, committed to equal rights between men and women, between those of different sexual orientations, may yet feel uneasy at permitting religions that promote such discriminations within; after all, members of those religions may be understood as having been, in some sense, 'indoctrinated' into holding such beliefs. Once we follow that line of reasoning, though, we need to wonder whether our holding liberal values – the promotion of sexual freedoms, of consumerism, of nail bars and bikinis – also results from indoctrination.

Let us end here with a nice example to do with face coverings:

> On 16 January 1793, a letter appeared in the *Gazzetta Urbana Veneta* from Signor Calofilo protesting at women wearing facial masks, thus hiding their beauty. A widow named Laura, sitting in a café, replied to say that, but for her mask, she would be unable to write; instead, she would have to contend with elaborate bows, whisperings and many other artful things men do when attracting women.

Venetian masks of today, in carnival time, continue a long tradition. The masks were once used in order to hide a person's identity. There were various reasons for this – to conceal their social status, to maintain secrecy of romantic liaisons, to act outside conventions – or, in Laura's case, to be untroubled. In a small way, Laura was in sympathy with Anonymous – and should we blame people who want to be free from prying eyes, listening ears, yet not be confined to home?

4

Should we want what we want?

Consider the fox – hereafter, Fox – from one of Aesop's many fables. Aesop was a Greek slave and storyteller thought to have lived around 600 BC. Fox sees that there are some fine juicy grapes on a branch above, but, however hard he tries, those grapes he cannot reach. Were we in that position, frustration may well take over; we may kick and scream, curse and sob, wanting all the more what we are unable to get. Fox knows better. Fox knows better for, being a wise old fox, he quickly realizes how silly he has been. He now sees that the grapes are sour; how could he ever have thought of wanting them? He has saved himself from hours of indigestion – and he has far more urgent things to do. He is, indeed, a wise old fox.

His partner fox – for ease, call her 'Vixen' – is not so impressed, not impressed at all. Vixen is well aware of Fox's ways. 'He cannot face reality,' she moans. 'Put an obstacle in his way and he'll persuade himself that he didn't really want what he wanted after all.'

Vixen knows that the grapes are fine. She knows that Fox also knows that they are fine – deep inside he knows, whatever he now thinks. True, she cannot reach the grapes, but it is not her style to comfort herself by self-deception. She accepts the frustration, the fact that she cannot get what she wants. 'It's weak and shameful to pretend otherwise,' she sighs, disparaging her Fox.

◦||◦

Fox goes for the easy life; Vixen faces reality. Should, magically, a ladder present itself beside the vine, Vixen would immediately climb, reaching the grapes for a refreshing and healthy snack. If Fox is to take advantage of that elevating help, he would need to somersault in his beliefs, reverting his thinking to how juicy and gorgeous the grapes are, no doubt, bound to be. Of course, we need not speculate so wildly on ladder-wise ways. Had only Fox thought a little more when seeking the grapes, he might have worked out other means for reaching the vine-laden goal.

The tale bears on matters concerning what are our 'true' wants and how a society should engage with them, especially a society that advocates the importance of informed voting, the freedom to wear religious attire in public spaces, and the liberty of buying and selling. Let us build up to such matters.

We can manipulate our wants for ourselves, out of frustration or laziness; we can engage in self-deception as with Fox. Often, though, others do the manipulating, sometimes for our benefit, often for their own. An underlying reflection is that we should not unquestioningly fall for the idea that society runs well when people are getting what they want or what they believe they want – always assuming here, of course, without harming others. A society may have citizens with preferences well satisfied, yet those preferences may not be authentic. Fox is satisfied that he does not want the grapes, yet that satisfaction has only taken hold through a distortion of his wanting. Further, even if people are getting their authentic desires satisfied – they are free because they sincerely identify with their desires; 'these are *mine*' – we ought not to conclude that that is best for them individually or for society overall.

There is often a knee-jerk response against people who tell us what is best for us. Here, what is best for us is being understood in terms of what is in our best interests. We are not yet engaging the debate of whether our interests must necessarily be guided by morality and the interests of others. The knee-jerk is even stronger when it is the government, society, customs, that are imposing themselves upon us, telling us how to behave: they may claim to 'know' what will make our lives go well, even if we do not.

Sometimes, we agree with what others tell us is for our best; but we often disagree, strongly disagree. Let us at least recognize that we can make mistakes about what is best, what will lead us to have flourishing lives – and that our freedom for ourselves to decide what to do ought not always to take top priority. That we are autonomous agents – self-governing, freely making our choices – is in liberal democracies often perceived as the highest value. While it merits considerable value, it should have no carte blanche, never to be challenged – never needing at least some developed nuances. Consider a simple example.

You want to eat the chocolate cake. That is fine – on the surface. Should we let you go ahead and dine? Even if we know that it has been poisoned or has been the flies' afternoon delight? Obviously, we should warn you. We have good reasons to think that typically people do not want to eat cakes dangerous to good health. That is an easy example where lack of information affects your wants as directed at a certain object. It is an easy example because we can inform you – and then you are free to choose whether to take a risky bite.

We may speak of judging what are your 'informed preferences' – those you would have, if possessed of relevant information, no misinformation, and in fine fettle for reasoning. All along, you wanted a safe cake. Your mistake was to think that the particular cake being eyed by you was safe; your mistake was to want that cake. So far, then, we have not challenged your autonomy; we are respecting you as a rational agent fit to govern your own life. We have helped by placing you in a better position for governing.

In the example, informed preferences are being treated as true preferences, ones that we should respect. The assumption is that things will go better for people if they are informed. That, of course, is not quite right for, even if informed, we may find ourselves unable to act on the information. Indeed, misinformation can sometimes get us to do what we ought to do, whereas accurate information might baffle us into inaction. There are various caveats suitable for mulling – but life is short.

WE WILL HELP YOU

There is a wide range of activities that governments – and other informed groups – believe to be dangerous to individuals under- taking those activities, dangerous with regard to their best interests and the community's. In varying ways and to varying degrees, governments intervene – from the prohibition of certain drugs to regulations for vehicles, buildings and sale of financial products, to advertising campaigns to reduce the intake of sugar, salt and alco- hol. The famous campaign of the last fifty years has been to reduce smoking. It is a simple example, yet one that can be used to bring out complexities in understanding the idea of 'getting what we want'.

Some smokers are, no doubt, ill-informed about the dangers of smoking. We inform them; and we credit them with abilities to appreciate the information. They are now well-informed. They may respond in three distinct ways; think of them as forming three groups.

Consider those smokers who now want to quit. They are eager for a cigarette and they get what they want – a cigarette – yet having that want satisfied is not at all satisfactory: they want to be non-smokers. Giving people what they want – here, the cigarettes – may not be giv- ing them what they truly want because they have wants not to have the want that is being satisfied. There can be second-order wants in opposition to the first order. These smokers have a second-order want; it is a want not to have the first-order wants, namely the wants to smoke.

Such smokers – frustrated reflectives – contrast with individuals who tend not to reflect; they form our second possible group. We are all like that on occasions (maybe, many occasions): we just act on the desire that overwhelms us at the time; we are, as has been termed, 'wantons'. Wantons as smokers, despite knowing of smoking dangers, remain untouched. In contrast, frustrated reflectives can and do reflect on their wants, leading them to their second-order wants and likely frustrations. Wantons lack such reflection; they are swayed by the immediacy of desires – and, in this case, they smoke, without worry.

With our frustrated reflectives, it is easy to grasp how their first-order preferences are not thereby their true preferences. For their autonomy to be operative, they need here to be satisfying their informed 'second-order' preferences. Some may simply have strength of will to give up smoking; some may succumb to cigarettes – their will is weak. The State, these days, often steps in to help both groups, especially the latter. The State may help by providing nicotine patches or by taxing cigarettes more highly or restricting the advertising of tobacco. The patches have no direct impact on those who are happy to continue as smokers; the higher taxes, of course, affect both the happy smokers and the unhappy ones. To help some – the reflective smokers wanting to kick the habit – governments intrude on the freedom of others, those smokers happy to smoke.

Forming the third group, the 'contented reflectives', are informed smokers who remain contented to smoke. They may regret the fact that there are risks; they may not care about the risks; they may be defiant. We should see them not as wantons, but as individuals pursuing their true preferences after suitable reflection. If individual liberty, individual autonomy, has high value, what can be wrong with letting our contented reflectives get on with their smoking?

What is wrong, some argue, is that these contented reflectives cannot be truly appreciating how bad smoking is for them; they lack good metaphorical eyesight into their futures. They are not much better than the wantons. Some argue that, even if they are truly grasping the risks, they are yet failing to appreciate properly (either through lack of understanding or through lack of concern) the effects on others, regarding both the dangers of passive smoking and the cost on health resources, resources likely to be deployed to deal with their lungs and cancers in due course. Governments should therefore intervene more determinedly, perhaps via programmes of nudges – perhaps by more restrictive legislation.

Government interventions have changed the desires of the frustrated reflectives, but those individuals are probably overall pleased to have been warned of smoking dangers. How, though, should we view the government interventions which aim to affect the behaviour of the wantons and of the contented reflectives? There are two distinct viewing windows, offering distinct landscapes.

One landscape on view is that of the government acting in the smokers' true interests, helping them to do what they 'truly' want to do; it is just that the smokers do not consciously realize what they truly want. Maybe one day they will come to realize; maybe they never will. Either way, the government is, in Rousseau's phrase, 'forcing them to be free'. The assumption in play is that typically for all human beings it is a mistake to smoke; for all human beings, there are some end values that hold fast. The value here is reducing the chances of bad health. The government is enabling the smokers to be acting in accord with their *true* desires; it is such a pity that these smokers fail to realize what are their true desires. We encountered that line in Chapter 3 by those critical of women who 'freely' wear the burqa.

The other window shows the government intruding upon the smokers' autonomy, their freedom. There is no pretence here that the government is helping them to be free, though what it is doing is, as far as possible, in their best interests and/or the community's best interests. In this understanding, as with the previous one, your best interests may be secured, even if you firmly believe that they are not – even if you strongly protest. Here, it is accepted that your best interests may require violations of your freedom. While 'best interests' may ideally include autonomy, making one's own decisions, sometimes one has to settle for something less than the best.

From whichever window we view matters, we see that governments – the State, the authorities – intrude upon what we take to be our freedom, our liberty, preventing us, to some extent, from being or seeing ourselves as self-governing, autonomous individuals. That may be to help us; but it may also be justified to protect the community. We encounter, for instance, government vaccination programmes and compulsory property purchases for the sake of the community as a whole, be it regarding health or (apparently) superior rail services.

'Behavioural economics' has nowadays come on to the scene, deploying discoveries in psychology to understand people's economic choices. It is as if only now has it struck economists that people do not behave rationally – for they are prone to confirmation bias, have preferences for the here and now, and a loss aversion that exceeds their hopes for probable gains. Those economists cannot have read John Maynard Keynes, the Cambridge economist of early twentieth-century Britain – an establishment figure, source of Keynesianism, yet also bohemian, being part of the Bloomsbury literary world – who wrote of people being moved by 'animal spirits' rather than rationality. With greater awareness of people's irrationality, governments are now quietly 'nudging' citizens into behaving in the best way for health and wealth. For example, because people find it difficult to opt into programmes to do with green energy, retirement planning and health checks, governments nudge them; default settings are changed so that, to avoid those programmes, people would need actively to opt out. Apathy, it seems, tends to rule.

Interventions by 'nudge' are still paternalistic – subtle 'nannying' – yet for libertarians, they are not so bad as imposing laws on people; people still retain some form of doing what they want to do. It has been suggested that such nudging makes the State rather avuncular – acting akin to a kind uncle – instead of being a harsh State nanny that must be obeyed. Apparently, a few words added to tax demands – 'Most people pay their taxes on time' – can nudge more people into paying on time than would otherwise happen.

Unsurprisingly, corporations have also taken this up – as 'sludging' – for their profits rather than community interests. Coffee bars sometimes display costs without the £ or $ sign, as there is evidence of higher sales as a result. The corporate world's sludging is often to combat the State's nudging: for example, the latter's attempt to deter purchase of 'high-energy' drinks. The corporations act as if oblivious to radical increases in obesity and type 2 diabetes among young people.

Further, corporate use of social media generates addictive needs for more 'likes', 'hits' or other forms of recognition, otherwise people online fear missing out or suffering the pain of being ignored. Various personalizing tools are to ensure that corporate marketing is well directed. Were governments to be engaged in such vast undercover attempts to manipulate behaviour, there would be outrage; but because the corporate moves are 'free-market' manifestations, there is but mild annoyance. When governments intrude on personal behaviour, be it by law or by nudges, it is condemned as the 'nanny state'; no one speaks of the 'nanny corporation'.

Returning to our individual smokers, smoking restrictions can be legitimately presented as aiding those individuals. It is, though, a commonplace to fear control by the State, whether it is thought of as 'nannying', nudging or straightforwardly authoritarian. The State ought not, it is often claimed, to interfere in our personal lives, so long as we are not harming others. That 'individualism' is linked to praising free markets, with as little regulation as possible; corporations should be free as much as individuals should – well, that apparently is the line. It gives rise to something of a paradox, or at least a tension, as will be shown after some scene setting.

GETTING WHAT YOU WANT IS GOOD FOR YOU

Well-being is a matter of what? Pleasure, work, whisky consumption? A common answer is getting what you want, often in terms of satisfying your preferences. Let 'preference satisfaction' be our watchword(s). Preferences may not all be reduced to pleasures. A fulfilled life is not thereby one solely of pleasures. Plato was wise on the matter. He pointed out that, were all that mattered to be pleasurable sensations, well, a great life would consist of deployed itching powder: sprinkle on back, itch, then the pleasure of scratching – and repeat.

Instead of satisfying preferences for 'the good life' – the Preferentist position – maybe with arguments about what those preferences are, others, Objectivists, propose the existence of objective values that any good life needs. We should desire only items that we consider desirable – that is, worthy of being desired, independently of whether we desire them. Once we spot them, we then know what it is rational to prefer. Of course, some people are irrational or swayed by immediate emotions; they may fail to prefer what is best for them – witness some smokers mentioned earlier.

The list of objective values can vary from philosopher to philosopher – that may itself cast some doubt on the objectivity – but, typically, objective values are taken to include life, knowledge, aesthetic appreciation, play, friendships. Controversies arise: placing 'an affinity with animals and the environment' on the list tends to be proposed by Scandinavians but not by South Asians. Many would argue that flourishing lives objectively require individuals to have control over their lives, to question, to aspire, whereas others, perhaps resulting from religious belief, would insist that objectively one should accept collective wisdom and be content in what one has. In botanical terms, some would promote the flamboyant crocosmia, others the more subdued speedwell.

Preferentists argue that those supposed objective values ought not to be imposed. No doubt, many people would see their well-being as involving such values, but that is simply because that is what they prefer. To risk a sexist expression, which wears the trousers? Are objective values the determining factor or are one's preferences? That is the way many philosophers see the argument, though it is misleading. Preferentists clearly believe there is one objective value – namely, people getting what they truly prefer.

As we saw with Fox, preferences can be deformed; hence Preferentists need to determine our authentic preferences. The smoking example raised that difficulty. The more we feel the need to cast doubt on whatever people say that they prefer – they cannot really prefer that; it must be because they are misinformed – the more we may be revealing a pre-commitment to certain objective values. Thus, Preferentist and Objectivist positions can draw close.

To secure the 'true' or 'authentic' preferences, we filter out distorted preferences, those arising because of poor information or poor reasoning – and those that arise in the 'heat of the moment' when we are, so to speak, throwing the rattle out of the pram. The idea is that once people are informed, reasoned and calmed down, they may recognize that they didn't really want what they thought they wanted. How often do we regret things we have said in a fit of anger or despair?

Suppose that the appropriate filtering has been completed: we may yet have individuals who, in various ways, remain individualistic. Once all the information, reasoning and so forth have been grasped, some still prefer opera to football, others, the other way round; some prefer the life of a Casanova, others the life as loyal family man; some prefer financial competitive success, others prefer a quiet life, tending the garden – or even reading philosophy. We may recall Hume with how it is not contrary to reason to prefer the destruction of the whole world to the scratching of one's finger.

Those different preferences are all very well, yet are we not inclined to think that some authentic preferences could yet be mistaken? If a woman has considerable talent for playing the violin, is she not making a mistake in preferring to count blades of grass? Consider more realistic, albeit rare, examples such as those of Bodily Integrity Identity Disorder (BIID), where people genuinely want some healthy limbs to be amputated. They are aware of all the resultant restrictions on their lives, yet have a preference to be free of the offending limbs. An extreme case was that of the Berlin engineer, Bernd Brandes, who, in 2001, after careful deliberation, stuck by his desire to be eaten; no further preferences, of course, could then be satisfied. The Preferentist, to be consistent, needs to accept that such cases can be authentic preferences; hence, they ought not to be opposed. The killer and eater of Brandes, Armin Meiwes, could also be deemed as possessing authentic preferences; and, as the cannibalism was by mutual consent, Meiwes ought not to be incarcerated, unless the episode suggests that he would endanger others, others without desires to be eaten.

FROM THE INDIVIDUAL TO THE CORPORATE

In a liberal society, as seen in Chapter 3, people should be free to do as they want, so long as not harming others. That is the aspiration, modified with certain prohibitions, regulations and nudges.

Neo-liberalism is committed to the position that businesses, companies and corporations should also be at liberty to go by their preferences with regard to what they market. What they market and how they market, though, may present barriers, preventing individuals from realizing their authentic preferences. Distortions by free markets of people's choices can be seen as akin to harming people. That is why governments, even free-market-loving governments, impose at least some regulations, regulations typically opposed by the companies.

For example, witness how corporate influence for years prevented governments from exposing tobacco's health risks; indeed, governments sometimes connived with the tobacco companies. Witness how today, food and drink companies object to regulations requiring reductions in sugar and salt and to the prohibition of 'energy-drink' sales to children. Witness how the gambling companies encourage gambling at sports venues and oppose regulations that aim to reduce addiction. In the United States, gun manufacturers fund certain politicians, ever ready to reject calls for greater gun control.

The individualism of people being free to choose how to live slides into two principles. The first, as mentioned, is that businesses, just as individuals, should be free to choose how to 'live', in their case what to produce and how to market. The second is that individuals should have as wide an array of options between which to choose. Both principles point to strong support for free markets (with some caveats, of course) where people (sellers) should be free to market whatever they choose, for other people (consumers) to have maximum choice over what to buy. That provides freedom for people as would-be buyers and freedom for people as would-be sellers. Freedom thus becomes both freedom to offer whatever one wants and freedom to bid for whatever one wants. One needs the other; one lives off the other.

That mutual freedom conceals how one can adversely affect – infect, indeed – the other, as already suggested. Sweet-sellers on the streets could cause sweet-abstainers to succumb. The sex worker, walking the streets, might catch the eye of the loyal family man – and he yields to temptation. Further, the sexual demands from consumers might lead some to decide, maybe reluctantly, to work in the sex trade, if little alternative employment around. Those are examples where the individuals concerned may well be aware that they are not engaging in what they want. They are acting because of weakness of will or because of desperate needs to earn money.

The above cases should remind us of what is obvious to all: what is on offer can affect what it is that we want and what we do. That is so obviously true without even mention of corporations' advertising and marketing projects that set out to pander to, or alter or create, desires and behaviour. In the world of large advertising and marketing budgets – the world of shopping channels, of 'buy one and get one free', of surveillance of our interests and enquiries when online – the intrusions upon us are vast, unacknowledged and often hidden behind benign-looking social-media interactions. In the political realm, the media and parties seek to 'shape public opinion'.

The mantras are simple. Consumers should be free to consume what they want. Businesses should be free to market what they want. For businesses, that can lead to two projects: one is to create consumer wants; another is to operate on existing wants, pandering to them. In fact, those projects are not that sharply delineated, for advertising and marketing may be stimulating latent wants or making people feel comfortable with surrendering to their conscious wants.

On the pandering, witness again the marketing of sugary drinks, deflecting from healthy drinks. Relate that way to Fox. Put obstacles in the way of less profitable grapes, while tempting Fox to highly profitable sweets and chocolates. When looting occurred in 2011 in London and other cities across Britain, what was stolen were trainers and iPhones; they were presumably seen as essential for possessing a status as fostered by the corporate world.

Those criticisms of business motivations are not condemnations of innovations and inventions that have considerably improved people's lives – be they in health, leisure or communication. It is misleading, though, to suggest that such improvements only occur through free markets. Sometimes they do; sometimes not. Businesses have often sought to stifle developments that would undermine their own profitability. State interventions and funding, discussed in Chapter 15, have often been sources of innovation.

With many corporate manipulations, we possess some faint awareness of their ways. That awareness is lacking with regard to details of data collections on us through social media, be the collections for commercial ends or political. It is true that consumers do not have to buy, but the power is typically on the side of the corporations in tempting them to buy. Corporations that provide gambling services have engaged various means to lure people into gambling more than they can afford, leading to addictions, debt and, in some cases, suicide.

Corporations often argue that they are innocently informing consumers of what is available or putting on offer what people desire. Their focus groups are used by the corporations simply to find out what is wanted. People, though, would not have dreamt up so many things that they wanted – nay, 'needed' – but for the advertising. Corporations undoubtedly create some wants as well as stimulating existing ones; they also make it difficult for others to get what they want – for example, to buy fresh fruit not in plastic wrappers or find soft drinks unfilled with unnecessary additives.

Outcomes of such free markets include both happy and unhappy people. Many are happy at getting what they want – at the time – yet later on are unhappy that they got what they wanted, as illness strikes home, obesity takes over or debt increases. Others are unhappy because they cannot afford what they want – though, later on, they may be relieved. Yet others are unhappy because they cannot find what they want, those satisfactions being squeezed out because commercially unviable.

HAPPY SLAVES?

The considerations above return us to Fox and what counts as true wants or what is in one's true interests. That is a worry that neo-liberalism with its free markets seeks to ignore. Our preferences are in part determined by what is available; and what is available may generate inauthentic choices. People adapt preferences to surroundings – what else would it be rational to do? – but preferences that are adapted to adverse surroundings may not be in the person's best interests or well-being. Let us look at some examples again to emphasize the point.

Consider the Stockholm syndrome, where employees were held hostage in a bank vault for six days, yet ended up defending the robbers, maybe because of the adverse conditions of their captivity. A cultural example is that of impoverished Indian women, unskilled, low caste, engaged in hard work, where they are discriminated against and where, instead of battling for justice, they accept their lot. Their preferences seem to be satisfied. As with other cases, though, we may argue that those preferences are not authentic; perhaps they are engaged in Fox's self-deception.

Zambian women live in a society where, amongst certain groups, wife-beating is commonplace and the social norm. Women, being women, are obliged to provide husbands with meals and sex, and it is the norm for husbands to beat wives who fail in those duties.

Regarding the wives' acceptance, perhaps there is more of Fox's self-deception.

Contrasting with Fox, the poor Indian women and African women may, though, be engaged in no self-deception at all. Settling for what they have now and not protesting is the best option, the only realistic option. They may quietly acknowledge, within, that they would leap at chances to live in societies where they possessed rights equal to men's. Even without that acknowledgement, even with Fox's self-deception, they would in fact leap, given the chances – well, so some would argue – for their lives would become so much better.

Suppose such chances arose, but lacked the subsequent leaping. That must be, those arguers would continue, because the women are without the imaginative or informational resources to see how much better their lives would be – or because they mistakenly fear excessive risks attached to embracing the changes. The underlying initial thought here, Preferentist and Objectivist, could be that no woman can be authentic in preferring such inequality or believing such inequality to be objectively valuable. The preference or belief has been adapted to circumstances and is difficult to dislodge.

The 'happy slave' is the paradigm of such adaption. Happy slaves are slaves who know of no better lives – and, if told of better lives and given the opportunity for them, will remain with the enslaved and familiar. To deny that staying enslaved manifests their authentic preferences and beliefs is to be motivated by some objective valuations: 'Surely, no one can truly prefer to be a slave.' If, though, after all the information and options have been properly placed before them and understood, they still prefer slavery, the committed Preferentist will have to accept that fact: they do just prefer things as they are. So be it: slavery is their authentic preference; therefore, slavery is what is best for them.

Objectivists 'know better': there is error in the slaves' grasp that makes them prefer slavery to freedom. Socially-minded Preferentists also know better. Embarrassed by the committed Preferentists' stance above, they may insist that the slaves still lack adequate awareness: were only they to be properly, truly, vividly aware of how things could be better outside of slavery, then that is what they would prefer. Thus it is that Objectivists and such Preferentists as the socially minded can both pursue political policies that advocate freedom from slavery, freedom to choose – liberty – even when individuals appear not to be grasping for such.

Do any of those considerations bear on our liberal societies of today – our consumer societies, where corporate freedom receives high priority? Some individuals, as we noted earlier, have preferences that go unsatisfied; they would prefer easier access to nutritious snacks, less pressure of commercialism and fewer exhortations to aspire for more. What, though, can be said about those who delight in the shopping, the designer clothes, the over-drinking through cheap alcohol in Happy Hours? Perhaps their preferences are inauthentic, their beliefs about what is valuable distorted. Why, though, should we think that?

We should think that, or should at least raise such possibilities, because the available information, the circumstances, the options – the zeitgeist – are mainly determined by powerful forces in the media and corporate world, forces acting in the interests of that corporate world, interests that do not thereby coincide with our best interests. And let us resist the zeitgeist's knee-jerk condemnation of the minority of the poor, with disorderly lives, who spend their little money on gambling, unhealthy drinks or who 'work benefit systems'. How well would we cope, if enslaved in dead-end work, no savings, no security – no time ever to feel properly at ease?

Whether, in our neo-liberalism, we are happy slaves – or unhappy slaves – well, that matter comes to the fore in Chapter 15 with Happy Land and some dancing bears.

5

Lives and luck: can Miss Fortuna be tamed?

Let us set the scene by way of two vignettes. They will blossom into an array of pressing perplexities.

Zach and Amelia sat the same exams for high-flying employment. Zach gets the job, not because he is wealthier than Amelia, but because his exam answers were better. Surely, his employment success is fair – but why were his answers better? He received a better university education, though not because of wealth, but because his school grades were better. Surely, that is fair, given his better grades – but why were his grades better? He attended a better school than Amelia. Surely that is fair – but is it? He attended a better school because of wealth; he was also brought up in better surroundings, with gardens, his own bedroom and with books and reading as common features of his home life. His parents could afford those surroundings and also his expensive private education: a school with excellent resources, more focused teaching and trips abroad, opening his eyes to aspirations. They paid for him to receive additional tuition in Paris when he was falling down on his French. Amelia had no such luck. Money, not just merit, can be and often is the route to success.

Here is the second:

> Anna and Belle, with the same talents, work just as hard as each other – digging. Anna hits oil, becomes very wealthy and is much admired throughout society. She shows, it is said, what sheer hard work can do. She gives some of her wealth to good causes and pops up on charity events, yet retains wealth in terms of millions. Belle hits only hard rock, ruins her back and ends up scraping a living, sometimes finding short-term work, often needing the State's welfare benefits. She is, at best, pitied or, worse, denigrated for not making anything of her life.

Both vignettes point to the role of good luck or good fortune – bad luck or misfortune – that invades lives. Let us refer to that role as that of Miss Fortuna; we met her role in political life earlier on.

The background is the political and social structure of a typical Western liberal democracy. It is a free-market economy, with competition for work and commercial rewards; there is some limited regulation and some welfare provision. Later chapters reflect on various features of that capitalism; here, the question is: what do we deserve? One stab at an underlying answer is: surely we at least deserve a fair society.

Zach and Amelia may have been born with exactly the same natural abilities (and what sense to make of that will be examined in due course), but the environmental impingings, under the control of neither, ensured Zach's greater success over Amelia's. Even if Amelia 'naturally' had far greater potential than Zach, it could have been unrealized, throttled by adverse impingings – perhaps poor schooling, poor housing and no family encouragement.

Our two examples, Zach/Amelia and Anna/Belle, display Miss Fortuna working in different ways.

With Zach/Amelia, Miss Fortune's operations are possible because of the social structure that permits them, even encourages them. The structure allows vast wealth inequalities, allowing them to be deployed to benefit one child over another. Further, the legal framework is such that employment decisions should discriminate solely on the applicant's then ability or potential to do the relevant work effectively. Because of those features Miss Fortune did not smile as much on Amelia as she did on Zach.

The Anna/Belle example, in contrast to Zach/Amelia, has Miss Fortune operating directly on Anna and Belle through factors that initially involved no human deliberation to benefit one or the other. It could have been sheer chance where they happened to thrust their spades. It could have been luck of the draw, for we could have presented Anna and Belle as engaged in spinning coins to determine upon which digging area they would work. In the example, neither knows which is the better, if even one is better. Miss Fortune is here working through external nature, in this case one of location.

Of course, the Anna/Belle example could be modified, pushing it closer to Zach/Amelia. It could have been known which plot of land would more likely deliver the goods. Perhaps because of family wealth, Anna could afford to make a higher bid for that plot than could Belle or could afford to take the financial risk, unlike Belle. That would return us to social structures as important factors in outcomes. We also have social factors and taxation policies working later down the line, where the good fortune of Anna is translated into wealth that she retains and for which she is admired. The basic Anna/Belle tale, though, is to remind us of 'natural luck'; the Zach/Amelia of 'social luck'.

Despite the obvious 'luck' in the examples just cited, there are strong tendencies for the successful to resist acknowledging the role of luck – of chance – in their own particular successes; or at least they tend to downplay that role. The mantra, particularly by the successful – a mantra that permeates government policies and society – is that people typically deserve what they get because what they get rests on their free choices; they are responsible for outcomes. That ignores the many glaring opportunities for Miss Fortuna to intervene.

Putting aside, for the moment, the luck of birth, think how many outcomes depend on whether people happened to see the job application that week, whether the train was delayed, whether they were in the right place at the right time. An opera singer, a soprano, falls ill; a young hopeful singer, in the audience, happens to know the role. The young hopeful leaps up, takes over and sings well. Her fame is made; but for that opportunity, she would have struggled in her singing career, perhaps ending in poverty.

Miss Fortuna also plays within the corporate world, the investment world and whom business people just happen to get along with on the golf course. Through technological luck, adverse weather or health scares, one company may flourish at the expense of others. Miss Fortuna's interventions are forever present.

Let us not, though, fall for the casual belief 'all is luck' – well, let us not fall for it just yet. It is a true comment by successful golfers: 'the more I practise, the luckier I get'. Even there, 'winning' shots may not win because of unexpected gusts of wind. The football match is lost because a key player slipped in the mud; the quiz team basked in winning glory only because a musician was amongst their members and they happened to get the music questions.

'EQUAL OPPORTUNITIES': A MERITOCRATIC MYTH?

In Western capitalist societies most politicians, captains of industry and pundits proclaim their support for meritocracy; people should succeed on merit. Meritocracy, it is accepted, requires 'equal opportunities', equal opportunities for all to realize their potentials. A background assumption is that 'success' be measured in financial terms and status. High-earning corporate directors are often much admired; people in high-status jobs, even if not high in wealth leagues, are praised for their success. Elsewhere questions arise whether flourishing should be understood in terms of wealth and status; here let us concentrate on the 'equal opportunities' – and, unless stated otherwise, let us ignore global implications.

It has taken many centuries for leaders explicitly to accept that societies have been riddled with prejudices, prejudices that undermine equal opportunities, preventing numerous people from realizing their potential. Consider the following:

> Two young men apply for employment in an accounts department; there is one vacancy. Undoubtedly Benjamin is the better qualified for the position; he is better in the interview, with better references and qualifications, but he fails to get the job – because he is black.

That is unfair. His skin colour has nothing to do with ability to perform well in the job; yet skin colour has stood in the way of access to the job opportunity. In the United Kingdom, the Equality Act (2010) deploys the concept of (nine) 'protected characteristics'; it is illegal to discriminate on the basis of age, disability, gender reassignment, marriage and civil partnership, pregnancy and maternity, race, religion or belief, sex and sexual orientation, though curiously not on grounds of poverty.

Caveats need to be entered: there are cases where skin colour – gender, sexual orientation – are relevant. Theatre producers may, reasonably enough, require only authentic black actors – or white – for a part. Women may prefer only women to conduct intimate examinations. Indeed, with increased awareness of 'gender fluidity', new controversies arise: a woman objects to examination by someone now deemed 'a woman' – 'she' sees her identity thus – despite displaying a beard and manly hands.

Historically there have been great injustices of the Benjamin ilk, injustices because outcomes have rested upon factors irrelevant for the work. Reflect on attitudes prevalent just sixty years ago. Even that 'living-memory' past may strike many of us as almost another country – a past when discriminations on grounds of skin colour, nationality and sexual orientation were accepted by many just as how things are or even meant to be. The United States has a strong history of unjustified discriminations, despite its constitutional insistence of equal rights. Many unjustified discriminations remain, particularly within states deeply grounded in religion as well as within certain religions themselves.

For most of today's liberal democracies, discriminations such as those above are unacceptable, at least in law. That is not to deny that there remain quite a few pockets, sometimes large pockets, where unjust discriminations persist socially. There are significant pay differentials between men and women, usually with women adversely affected, despite equal-pay legislation and much publicity given to those differentials. Of course, such differentials need not manifest men and women receiving different levels of pay for the same work; rather they may manifest men dominating the higher-status business roles, the domination resulting from earlier social expectations and educational discriminations – amounting to invisible 'No women' signs hanging on certain doors. Whether unequal proportions of men and women in various employments are typically unfair is examined in Chapter 10.

There are many discriminations less well known. The Sámi are indigenous to the most northern parts of Sweden, Norway and Finland – countries that trumpet their respect for people's rights. In practice, though, the Sámi, it seems, are much discriminated against; governments and business encourage tourism and extractive industries that adversely impact on the Sámi with regard to land ownership, reindeer herding and their traditional way of life.

In liberal societies, committed to 'equal opportunities', there remains one basic discrimination: qualifications. While 'only black people may apply' is discriminatory, 'only the qualified may apply' is not. That distinction receives rational approval, yet even that merits nuances: are those with the best qualifications for the job the best for the job? Further, as seen earlier, social structures are so arranged that discriminations earlier in life ensure that many people are excluded from those educational processes likely to lead to the required qualifications or experience. The history of a person, regarding opportunities, affects outcome – a vertical gaze. Supplement that gaze with a look across the population at a given time – a horizontal gaze – and that raises further questions of whether only the best for the job should be given the job. After all, some are in much greater need of paid employment than others. Fairness operates in different dimensions. It is far from clear which morally should take precedence.

A CLASH OF VALUES

Talk of 'equal opportunities', of 'advancement on merit', slips easily off people's tongues. Lovers of equal opportunities and advancement on merit do indeed talk the talk, but the reality is very different. Well-off owners of those tongues, often as parents, deliberately engage in projects to make things better for their own children's education rather than for the education of others. We saw that with Zach. Many are, of course (of course), keen to insist on fairness when it suits them. Some colleges discriminate in favour of applicants who, despite adverse conditions of poverty and under-resourced schools, have done pretty well; they show that they have potential. Parents of the privately educated tend to call that out as 'unfair', overlooking the unfairness of their offspring's privileged education at well-resourced schools.

There is a manifest clash between the value of fairness regarding equal opportunities and people's preferences for 'their own'. Those preferences show that the reality of equal opportunities, of desire for a meritocracy, is but myth. Here is a typical comment: 'I should be allowed to do what I want with money that I've worked hard in acquiring.'

It is the indignant cry of well-off parents, in defence of looking after 'one's own' over others. Another cry is: 'It's natural to want to do the best for your own children; we're a family.'

To the first cry, we may respond, courtesy of Miss Fortuna, that the acquired wealth, at least in part, derived from good luck. It is already, to a large extent, 'undeserved'. That point is taken further in Chapter 6. Additionally, why assume that such liberty, such freedom to do what we like with our money, should talk out the demand for fairness?

To the second cry, there is the obvious retort that what it is natural to do is not therefore what morally should be done. Of course, it fails to follow that what is natural is thereby morally wrong. The bonds of family for many people give meaning to their lives; there is nothing wrong, many ethicists argue, in 'being prejudiced' in favour of one's own, one's family. It should not even be deemed 'prejudice', but merits support, even if leading to the unfairness suffered by the Amelias of this world.

Some parents, when elderly, though, conveniently downplay the family as a unit, in one respect. They are suddenly keen that the State's welfare services should provide for their caring needs rather than the family. The 'family wealth' has – fortuitously? – cascaded down to the offspring; after all, in that respect, the family as unit comes to the fore, as the offspring happily agree. Taxing such cascades – gifts, inheritances – is, they argue, as unjustified as taxing money when transferred from one's left pocket to right.

Of course, properly there are limits to valuing the family as a single unit; consider how, in certain cultures, a dishonour brought by one family member is deemed, bizarrely, to justify an innocent member of that family being punished. In Nazi Germany, *Sippenhaft*

– kin liability – would sometimes be used to find guilty those individuals whose sole 'crime' was to be related by family or marriage to others who had indeed committed crimes against the State.

We undoubtedly have partialities – given our personal location in the world – but we can grasp the impartial; we can step back. The impartial perspective allows us to put ourselves in the shoes of others and also recognize that the interests of others merit consideration. We thus become aware of the clash between detached values – those of impartiality – and attached values which arise just because of our attachments. We, 'in our souls', have a grasp on both perspectives. That grasp does not tell us which of those perspectives ought to take priority and when. Maybe a little reasoning will assist.

'I'M ALL RIGHT, JACK'

Accept the importance to many people of how well things go for their children. Ask them this; would they consider a society fair in which whether their own children flourished rested on skin colour? Odd exceptions to one side, reason should tell them – tell us – that skin colour should be irrelevant; society should lack that discrimination. Now, ask whether they think a society fair where their own children failed to do well because at interviews they lacked resources to bribe interviewers or had lacked relevant educational opportunities. Reason again would lead them – lead us – to conclude that such a society is unfair. Society's structures, we may agree, should combat such unfairness.

Individuals, attached to their personal circumstances, may respond, 'Yes, unfair, but I and my children are in fact all right, Jack – for we're not black, we have the money to buy very good education – so, there's an end to it.' Contrast with the government of a liberal democracy. It is meant to represent all its citizens, its community; it lacks (or should lack) an attached view to *those* of its citizens rather than *these*. It does not have the 'I'm all right, Jack' attitude in favour of any particular individual or family within the society; of course, it embraces that partiality in favour of its own citizens over those of other societies – a 'We're all right, Jack' attitude.

Society's laws – where the law should intervene – should be impartial. The caveat of 'where the law should intervene' flags the problem of where to draw lines between the private and public; impersonal structures imposed by law restrict our pursuit of the personal, as revealed in Chapter 3. Western social structures have developed to reduce racial discrimination; from the State's impartial perspective, skin colour and race are irrelevant. From the impartial perspective, of equal opportunities for all, the effects of wealth are also unfair. If every child had the same genuine equal opportunities, not differing because of wealth, the apparently valuable bonds of family life would not be torn asunder. There is no reason to believe that, for such bonds to flourish, unfairness in educational, health and social opportunities is needed. After all, no one seriously argues that completely ridding racial discrimination in the public world will upset bonds of family life.

Democratic governments typically take some steps to move towards impartial equal opportunities: they provide some improved public education, living conditions and health services. Those provisions, of course, should also be justified on grounds other than equal opportunities; they could be justified on grounds of respect for people's dignity and the promotion of their well-being.

The impersonal perspective, imposed via laws restraining partialities in the public world, undoubtedly impinges on people's personal lives. The personal may fight back. Some employers and employees remain racist at work. Certain businesses resist employing Muslim receptionists, if veiled, because of damage to trade in their area; in other areas, preferences may be reversed. Securing equal opportunities obviously requires changes in attitudes as well as legislation, but let us not forget the personal, the attached realm;

it would be odd to insist that a black woman should romantically desire white and black partners equally. Recall Ludmilla and the Narrator of Chapter 3.

Let us see how far we may get if seeking genuine fairness as the highest priority within a community. Plato provides the inspiration by means of his presentation through the mouth of Socrates.

UTOPIANISM: GIVING UP ON THE FAMILY

Plato describes the ideal community, the Republic, in the dialogue encountered in Chapter 1, the dialogue conveniently entitled *Republic*. That city state, the Republic, is Kallipolis, a good place, the most excellent of cities, excellent in every respect. We may label it 'utopian' for Utopia is a 'no-place' (the Greek derivation being *ou-topia*), yet it can also be a 'good place' (the Greek derivation being *eu-topia*). Plato's Republic is a no-place for it cannot exist on Earth, with people as they are. Even if such a city existed, it would be mortal, collapsing through dissent into injustice. We can describe such a place in words, but we cannot produce it in deeds – though it may set us a mythical target at which to aim.

When Thomas More introduced the term 'Utopia' in his 1516 satire, it was presented by a certain Raphael Hythloday, the surname based on Greek for 'nonsense' or 'drivel'. Plato's Socrates, though, offers the utopian Republic – the Kallipolis – as desirable, as an ideal, albeit unrealizable; it is no idle nonsense, no daydreaming.

So far this chapter has been approaching matters via 'fairness', seeking to quell Miss Fortuna and her unsettling ways. Plato starts further back. What does a city need? 'Unity' is Plato's answer. It requires individuals to have concerns and interests in common; its people should be in harmony. When a person's finger is damaged, the person is in pain; the person is damaged. When things go wrong for a citizen, the whole Kallipolis suffers.

Plato, in pursuing the unity of a flourishing community, initially

entices readers – well, most men – by suggesting that sexual liberation would be needed, with women being held in common by all
men, each begetting children by any man who wishes for her. (Let
us put to one side the implied sexism.) The fantasy of 'women and
children in common' is found earlier in Aristophanes' *Ecclesiazousae*,
though once Plato works it through, it loses its appeal. Plato argues
that sexual relations should be compulsory, but extremely limited,
to be engaged only when for the common good, not for fun. There
would be secret manipulations by the authorities to ensure that only
the best breed with the best.

Seemingly respectable ideas of sexual partners being in common
have not, by the way, been confined to Plato. A nineteenth-century
'utopian' community, the Oneida community in upstate New York,
rejected the special love of marriage. Its founder, John Humphrey
Noyes, advocated 'complex marriage': that is, multiple sexual
partners, with birth control secured by halting actions just prior
to ejaculation. Noyes, apparently, saw it as his duty to initiate the
young women in those sexual ways.

Plato seeks justice and the justice of his Republic rests on fairness. Miss Fortuna is to be tamed – at least where nurturing is
involved. As already seen, fairness does not work well when there
are families and friends; they give rise to biases. Social structures
should hence be arranged to overcome those biases; and Plato's
Republic does that with a vengeance, with women and children
being held in common for the community. What we may think of
as naturally private relationships of family and home become community grounded. Plato, in fact, later became more realistic. In his
Laws, he accepts that families will persist, but sets laws to ensure
that landholdings are of the same size and unchanging; again, the
aim is to prevent injustices arising.

A little more needs to be explained about the *Republic*'s push
towards justice. Plato objects to all discriminations that result from

the way societies have developed through conventions and cultural pressures and preferences. Controversially for the times, reproduction apart, men and women must have equal rights. The guards – the Guardians, the rulers of society – are men and women, with the same training, who manifest relevant qualities for guardianship. The soul is, so to speak, sexless. As an aside, that stance apparently is in opposition to the view of many transgendered people; please see Chapter 14.

Partialities, as we have seen, tend to fragment and hence endanger society. Plato tries to ensure that we all – all citizens of the State, the Republic – honour and rejoice and grieve in the same things. That unifies the State into a genuine community, best for all its members. When citizens are equally affected, there is unity. 'Mine' and 'not mine' are applied in the same way by all. The Republic is communitarian.

Plato's communitarianism directly challenges the preferences most of us have for ourselves, our particular interests and attachments. The community attachment, via the impartial perspective, is simply to the community. It 'wants' what is best for the community. What is individually desirable is what is collectively so – and vice versa. As a citizen, I should be concerned for all citizens, not more so for family, friends and lovers. To overcome those 'partialist' concerns, Plato robs society of the relationships that generate such concerns. Those concerns in any case may be ill-founded.

They may be ill-founded because preferences for 'the family' perhaps express the mistaken idea that longevity – immortality, even – of parents occurs through their genes cascading down the generations. People sometimes find satisfaction in the thought that their great-great-great-grandchildren will exist, a satisfaction that far exceeds any satisfaction in the thought that the nation will continue to exist or simply that human life will exist. Why, though, value that genetic cascade? What may be valuable to hand down are

– well – values: principles and projects, ways of looking at the world that hold the community together. They may have an objectivity, but – and this plays badly with Plato – we do also, of course, value the personal links through generations, by way of, for example, heirlooms, photographs, diaries.

Most people find themselves objecting to Plato's approach, seeing it as far too radical in its egalitarianism; but that egalitarianism is lacking in one domain. Plato has no plans for ironing out differences in our natures, in what we today understand in terms of our genetic inheritances. Plato accepts that people naturally have different talents and aptitudes; they are fitted for different occupations. The community is a person writ large, with its own good – and that good needs people playing different parts, recognizing their individual stations and duties. Individual flourishing, within the community, requires playing the part one is naturally suited to play; and respect is due to all individuals playing their proper parts.

Some doubt the extent of Plato's respect for individuals given that he advocates the 'noble lie', a myth to be instilled in citizens as literally true, to justify how roles have been allotted so that all will acquiesce in their community positions. Respecting people, it is argued, involves not deceiving them: the noble lie is a blatant deception. Plato need not, though, be read in that way; his so-translated 'noble lie' could be better understood as a valuable fiction, presented as fiction, to stir the imagination, to show how a society could and should see itself. After all, Shakespeare's tragedies and Jane Austen's novels do not have to deceive us into believing the events really happened before they can open our eyes to aspects of human relationships.

The above defence of Plato's presentation of myth does not show that in fact his Republic would benefit all citizens. We may certainly doubt whether individuals doing well in their allotted community roles and accepting those roles – assuming even that happens –

amounts to their lives going well for them. Flora, the flautist, may excel at flute playing, yet may be very unhappy for she would prefer to play the violin, even if not all that well.

In shrinking the personal life, Plato promotes a totalitarian stance: community players are all centres of 'community', rather than possessors of their own individual attachments, their own private lives. Contrast with an orchestra: players are concerned for each other as differently-skilled contributors to a good performance, to the orchestral community; but as orchestral players, they are not (usually) concerned about each other's extra-orchestral private lives.

Plato's stance towards the ideal community, with everyone allotted a role, is in some ways opposed to 'pluralism', to the existence of many conflicting but rational views of what constitutes a 'good life' and how society should be organized. That opposition is not, though, a black-or-white matter: even pluralists typically accept that some social unity is required. That unity involves, at some level, all being treated with equal respect. That respect is manifested, in part, through equal opportunities – this chapter's topic. It is also manifested, in part, through democracy's equal rights, certainly to vote – Chapter 1's topic. A civilized understanding of a community, with all members being respected, contrasts – to say the least – with Robert Baden-Powell's stance in his 1908 work *Scouting for Boys*: 'Bees are quite a model community for they respect their Queen and kill their unemployed.'

With Plato's orientation, we eradicate all the external injustices, injustices from biased nurturing and personal preferences. We tame Miss Fortuna thus far. We yet embrace discriminations resulting from our different natures, our different natural talents and abilities. We can, though, play the 'unfairness' card to trump more than those manifestly unfair external discriminations.

'How unfair it is that I was born disabled.' 'How unfair it is that I was born untalented.' 'How unfair it is that I was born lazy – or hardworking.' In the next chapter, we see how complete fairness works out – or not. In the next chapter, we may see that the very ideal of the much-vaunted fairness is itself mythical.

6

The Land of Justice

We all speak of justice and fairness, even if only by way of lip service. Let us then learn from the ambassador for the Land of Justice where justice ultimately lands us – in, of course, the Land of Justice. Here the ambassador as the land's spokesman – 'spokesperson', he/she corrects – tells of its developments and characteristics.

'We recognized some time ago that there were huge discriminations on the basis of race, sex and religion, so we outlawed them as you have sought to do in your lands European, North American and elsewhere. We also realized that educational opportunities lacked fairness, when some individuals had access to those opportunities more easily than others; so we arranged that colleges and employers would take those factors into account, when assessing applicants. Needless to say, it was far from easy, both how to assess which compensations would ensure fairness and how to persuade the wealthy to come on board and accept the compensations as fair.

'Perhaps it was Miss Fortuna, but by good fortune – or was it bad? – our leaders opened their eyes more widely and saw before them the Jewel of Justice sparkling in the distance, as a beacon, a moral utopia, an inspiration. With that sparkle urging us on, we introduced laws – draconian laws, some complained – that prohibited family wealth from providing competitive educational advantage for some over others. Our land's "justice" was to be grounded upon fairness between one and all, though it posed problems when we prohibited wealthy parents from paying for their children to holi-day abroad: after all, that gave them advantages in linguistic skills, cultural awareness and confidence. We hoped that one day all could have such access.

'Equal access to the same quality of education, training and other learning came to be accepted as fair. True, some unease set in, when statistics highlighted (as they do in your countries) how chil-dren of the poor received poor healthcare, adversely affecting their potential compared with the wealthy. So it was that health services provided on the basis of wealth rather than need were prohibited. Fairness demanded that – and not solely to secure fairness in educa-tional opportunities, for fairness in quality of life and longevity was also a requirement. I note that those disparities are particularly vast in the United States and the United Kingdom.

'It took the passing of several generations, but our citizens in-creasingly came to be drawn to the sparkling Jewel of Justice; some were even awed by the sparkle. After all, how could it be fair that Tiny Tim suffered from pneumonia (through no fault of his own), with little medical care, because of Luxurious Lucy's whims for Botox vanity treatment? Her wealth effectively diverted medical resources from dealing with the more pressing needs of the likes of Tiny Tim.

'Inequalities of wealth brought about inequalities in housing, the environment, nutrition – all of which had unfair discriminatory effects on health, learning and realization of talents. Hence, to draw closer to the sparkling jewel we needed to correct further. To do so required considerable redistributive taxation. Initially, that did not go down well, though the wealthy gradually came to realize that their additional wealth did not achieve much, in view of the prohi-bitions on any services that gave them or their offspring competitive unfair advantages over others.

'Our work was done – or so we thought – for all children received the same education, opportunities and environmental impingings;

yet, as we slowly realized, our work was far from done. The jewel shimmered some way away. Even with external factors equalized, many people suffered unfairly. There were the obvious physical and psychological disablements from birth as well as those through accidents and disease later in life; we tried to compensate for them. There were also the genetic groundings of differences in abilities, capacities and talents. Some individuals possessed greater mathematical acumen than others; some with fine mathematical ability lacked interest in pursuing mathematics; some talented individuals were intrinsically lazy.

'Individuals obviously were not setting off equally in life. We made a few coarse attempts at correction by providing some children with intelligence injections, some motivational drugs and so forth; but that was all rather experimental with no secure evidential foundations.

'Fortunately – yes, it must have been the luck (some deemed it "unluck") of Miss Fortuna – we discovered ways to make "all foetuses equal". There were doubts about what should be done with regard to sexual differences, but so long as they led to no other differences of talents, motivations and interests, we allowed them to persist – so far. Some, though, still argue that something needs to be done to iron out those differences. That matter may start gaining some traction in your countries, not least because it is surprising that, despite all the concern for equality of the sexes, there is little discussion about compensating men for typically having shorter life expectancy than women.

'In our land, how to secure equality of foetuses generated considerable debate. Suppose, it was argued, we knew that this particular foetus would develop into a genius: we should be harming it – and society – were we lowering its potential to whatever all others could be lifted to. We surely ought not to "dumb down" in that way. Fortunately, our researchers solved the problem.

'Thus it came about that all infants were born with the same high level of talents, abilities, potential, and with the same eagerness to realize them. To be fair – and to cover the needs of society – we ensured that all offspring had talents for everything needed for the society. That could have posed problems.

'"Why?" you ask. Well, we could hardly have a society in which everyone wanted to be a flute player and mathematician, yet none a chimney sweep. Yes, we could draw lots for who did what, but some would end up lucky, some not; that would reintroduce Miss Fortuna, though at least the luck would be randomly distributed – and hence fair in that sense. None the less, some would end up with the good luck of doing what they wanted, others the bad luck of doing what they did not. If you had the skills and abilities to do anything, it could be frustrating for many just to be selling cheese every day instead of investigating secrets of the universe.

'Our solution was to ensure that everyone had the same level of desires and respect for all required jobs. Whatever people ending up doing, they were content with the doing – or at least as content as they would have been with any other doings.

'There were further advantages. No longer were job interviews needed: a lottery was introduced for determining who did what and how jobs were rotated between people. No one suffered unfairly for they all were content in whichever assignments they received. As people recognized that they were all equally talented – and all doing what they wanted to do – none expected to be paid more than others; none disparaged the work of others. And that is how things continue. There is harmony – well, almost.

'Some of our greybeards, near the end of life, still moan about how so much diversity of the past has been lost. No longer does it matter who is singing at our equivalent of London's Covent Garden or New York's Met because they all sing just as well. Romantic liaisons have lost much of their excitement, though some emotional differences persist. And the greybeards are right; there are some monotonous features. Games of chess always end in draws – well, nearly always, for sometimes distractions intrude more upon one player than the other. We should do something about that. We still cannot successfully predict the winners of races and football matches; Miss Fortuna manifests herself in sudden gusts of wind.

'Overall, yes, there has been a huge fall in diversity – that we recognize – but we also recognize that it has been a small price to pay, for our lives are now lit by the sparkling Jewel of Justice, of fairness.'

Our fantasy land is, of course, just that; but it reminds us that casual talk of 'equality of opportunity', if pushed to its logical conclusion and implemented, costs lives – well, costs diversity in lives. The Land of Justice has secured justice as fairness, but it is as if the land is populated by clones. It is as if there is but one person, at least with regard to many features – one person replicated throughout the land. It would strike virtually all of us as far, far from utopian; it is, rather, dystopian. The ideal turns out to be no ideal at all, but mythical – mythical even as an ideal.

There are gaps in the tale. Apart from the transition (or, perhaps we should say, 'implementation') stage, are the resultant individuals sufficiently sensitive to changes in their surroundings, to creative thinking, to rebellion, such that society could ever develop, ever improve, ever cope with environmental upheavals? Further, there will still be accidents in life, as the spokesman – sorry, spokesperson – touched upon, requiring compensations, unless genetic manipulations can ensure protection from earthquakes, absent-minded drivers and roaming tigers. That protection seems pretty unlikely, to say the least, unless we resort to a divine will.

Proposals for genetic manipulations often lead people to angry condemnation, with mutterings of 'eugenics' and 'Naziism' – and such proposals do need handling with caution. Had manipulators existed in Victorian days, they might have manipulated to ensure that all foetuses would develop into good Christians who believed that legs of tables should be covered and children of the poor were only suited for chimney sweeping and factory work. Our Land of Justice defender, in fact, is pretty vague, understandably so, in his talk of genetic intrusions and arrangements.

Whatever manipulations are engaged, a likely objection is that people's free will has been eroded. In the Land of Justice, people differ from each other in physical location. No doubt, a few bodily and psychological differences arise, but none that makes some lives go better than others – for that would be the intrusions of Miss Fortuna's unfairness.

Most of us would be horrified at such a community. Let us not, though, be too dewy-eyed about our current lives. If people in the Land of Justice knew of our lives, they would be appalled at the injustices that we allow, without qualms. Yes, we view people in the Land of Justice as 'robotic', all with the same talents and aspirations; but maybe that strikes us as a horror only because it results from human design. That could just have been the way that Nature worked in any case.

The way that Nature currently works, with existing diversities, can also be considered as creating robots, albeit robots of diverse types and who believe themselves non-robotic. Were people to become convinced that the Land of Justice is the way to go, then that too would be the result of 'Nature working'. That line of thinking should, of course, make us wonder what sense there can be to our responsibility for anything, just anything – a problem much wrestled by philosophers.

In the Land of Justice, diversity has been traded for fairness; but it could have gone in a different direction, whereby the manipulators ensured an appropriate diversity of talents with the individuals wanting to do the jobs for which they were talented. That would be in line with Plato's acceptance that people naturally have different talents and hence different roles to play in society, all of which merit respect.

HOW FAR TO GO

Talk of manipulation of foetuses – or the manipulation even earlier, if occurring at the stage of potential person creation prior to conception – has avoided tackling how we should deal with existing individuals in the pursuit of fairness. The call for equality of opportunity assumes that we can make good sense of how things could have been different and better for individuals, 'had only they been given a chance'; that is, we are applying counterfactuals to individuals – what would have happened, had the facts been different.

In the previous chapter's Zach/Amelia scenario, we dealt in the 'counter to fact': how things would have turned out had matters been different. There is nothing bizarre in everyday use of counterfactuals: had Lucinda come to the party, there would have been a riot; had Erskin not dropped the ball, the team would have won. Applying that counterfactual stance to our case studies from the previous chapter, we have:

> Had Amelia received an education as supportive as Zach's, then she would have done better in life.

We have Amelia, a flesh-and-blood individual before us, so to speak; and with regard to this woman, we can speak of things having been different; it would still have been Amelia, had those different things happened.

> Had Benjamin not been interviewed by a racist, he would have got the job.

The above examples are straightforward. How far, though, can such counterfactuals go before collapsing into absurdity – the absurdity of the individual being so changed, in the 'counter-to-fact' possibility, that it no longer makes sense to think of the individual as that individual. Consider:

> Had Julius Caesar been the United States president, he would have invaded North Korea, using bows and arrows.

> Had Donald Trump been Russian, he would still have wanted to make America great again.

We see how bizarre counter-to-fact speculations can be. Let us try some out on Amelia.

> Had Amelia, as a foetus, been genetically manipulated, she would not have developed as a female, would not have possessed her existing physical and psychological characteristics.

Would it have still been this Amelia now about whom we are postulating such differences? To take an even more extreme example, can I really make sense of how 'I' – or you – might have been born five hundred years ago or born with radically different desires, emotional characteristics and talents?

Those questions lead into troubling metaphysical perplexities of personal identity: to what extent does 'my identity' – what makes me *me* – rest on the nurturing and to what extent on the nature? What scope is there, if any, to make sense of my being responsible for my 'free' choices? The overall question, as usual, is how far to push things, how far to dig.

Although aware of digging further, many people resist digging far, for the consequences are so disturbing about our grasp of personal responsibility. With shallow digging only, some lucks can be distinguished; and 'luck egalitarianism' does just that. Its approach aims to insulate people from, or compensate people for, that bad luck which, even at a shallow level, manifestly is not within their control and affects outcomes. It is brute (bad) luck – such as being struck down by lightning or missing an interview because of motorway pile-ups. In contrast to brute luck, there is 'option luck', where people have chosen paths that have led to misfortunes: for example, placing big bets on the horses – and losing. Such choices between options that lead to inequalities do not, on this view, merit society's compensations, though usually some basic welfare safety net is proposed.

⫟

People come into existence with different talents, desires and motivations – and not just differences in shoe-size. The Liberal State typically goes some way towards instituting fairness by reducing a few external discrepancies that hinder some from realizing talents. Perhaps the Liberal State to be the Just State should go as far as Plato envisages in eliminating distortions of wealth, conventions and family preferences. Eradicating genetic differences delivered courtesy of Miss Fortuna – as in our Land of Justice – leaves us, though, with a society which seems both repugnant and absurd.

The danger of pushing things too far is no good excuse for pushing things no distance at all. Seeking the greatest number is absurd; but that does not show that we ought not to seek out some higher numbers. We should not resist going any distance because we cannot go the whole distance.

Many politicians have used 'equality of opportunity' as a calming mechanism: focus the public's attention on that – and objections to the vast differences of outcome may be quelled. The emphasis on opportunities may also divert attention from whether individuals are in a position to make use of those opportunities. The story is that once in receipt of the opportunities, people are responsible for what they make of them. Thus it is that the poor are often blamed for their poverty because, it is believed, it results from their lack of personal responsibility and aspiration. Thus it is that welfare systems distinguish between the deserving and the undeserving poor.

In the days of United States President Lyndon Johnson, the aim was to eradicate poverty. Today's rhetoric highlights personal responsibility and giving everyone fair chances for empowerment and control over their lives. The rhetoric conveniently forgets that even if all are well-qualified for jobs, it does not follow that they get the jobs; there are often supply and demand discrepancies.

⫟

SHH – DON'T MENTION THE...

Of course, the politicians' rhetoric of 'equal opportunities' is silent about the underlying absurdity raised here – of how fair chances are ultimately mythically grounded. Holding people personally responsible for their lives buys into the nonsense that they are responsible for pulling themselves 'up into existence by the hair, out of the swamps of nothingness', to quote Friedrich Nietzsche, the nineteenth-century so-called existentialist, famous for his cry 'God is dead.'

'Equal opportunities', 'fair chances' and 'personal responsibility' are used as a magician uses banter and handkerchiefs to distract from what is really going on. And, *shh*, we mustn't mention what we rely on...

In today's terms, we rely on 'failures', on people to work in jobs to which no one aspires. Now, politicians keep very quiet about that. As has been quipped, a new Jerusalem cannot be built without an effective sewerage system.

In view of the miserable jobs and soul-destroying work – which we live on – one minimal but important requirement is to secure egalitarianism at least with regard to *respect for* people, whatever jobs they are doing – indeed, to respect them, elevate them, for doing those jobs that many others would not deign even to consider. Another requirement is surely to make amends for those who are unlucky enough to have lousy jobs; we could, for example, recompense them more than we do those who have jobs that they love. Give praise to street-cleaners – and also give money.

Here is a reflection by John Stuart Mill, from his *Chapters on Socialism* (1879):

> If some Nero or Domitian were to require a hundred persons to run a race for their lives, on the condition that the fifty or twenty who came in hindmost should be put to death, it would not be any diminution of the injustice that the strongest or nimblest would, except through some untoward accident, be certain to escape. The misery and the crime would be that any were put to death at all.

The misery and crime in our liberal democracies is the suffering of the poor, those who lose out in the race or have no chance of even entering the race. It adds insult to their misfortune, notes Mill, to say, 'Well, it is because they are the weaker members of the community morally or physically.'

Shh – what cannot be said too loudly should remind us that even if wealth inequalities are not unfair, even if they contribute to society's overall well-being – even if they are 'twice blessed', an expression of R. H. Tawney, the twentieth-century social reformer – there may be other good reasons for protesting. The reasons are the effects on the poor – who do not see much, if any, of the blessings. We need to heed different equalities and inequalities.

Wealth equality (to cover both income and assets) and social equality are distinct. Those who are poor in wealth may reasonably expect not to be treated as poor in rights, respect, dignity, social status. Although the social and the wealth are distinct, humans being human often slip into admiring the wealthy, placing them on a socially high pedestal compared with the poor.

Let us place that so human disposition to one side. Assuming that a certain acceptable level of economic wealth and hence of living is available to the poorest, the highest priority may be that of social equality rather than monetary. Here, we may agree with Tawney who, in his 1931 *Equality*, suggested that what was offensive was not some people earning more than others – a counting-house worry – but that many people, because poor, are excluded from the heritage of a common civilization. For all to enjoy that heritage, what is required is rejection of the private ownership of swathes of that civilization as well as of fields and forests – and that, of course, means intruding upon the wealthy. The social and the financial are intertwined. The poor find their enjoyment restricted the more the commons are owned by corporations and private individuals. Acres of land, even some miles of seashore, are held in private hands; works of art are auctioned off, stored as investments or available only through private viewing. So-called 'public' museums, when operating as businesses, impose charges.

If some people are having good lives – their well-being is as they sincerely want and is valuable – then we may rightly accept that if someone elsewhere suddenly becomes much wealthier, that in itself does not give rise to an injustice, assuming no adverse effects on those some people. Of course, it may not reflect well on that individual if the sudden wealth, and a reluctance to share it, is but a manifestation of greed and selfishness. It may not reflect well if the lucky recipient of the wealth engages in fierce and threatening hissing when about to be plucked – as will be seen in the next chapter.

7

Plucking the goose:
what's so bad about taxation?

In seventeenth-century France, Jean-Baptiste Colbert, the finance minister to King Louis XIV, supposedly said: 'The art of taxation consists in so plucking the goose as to obtain the largest amount of feathers with the least possible amount of hissing.'

That may well be an art, but, before 'let plucking commence', there is a fundamental question to ask: are there good justifications for the plucking at all? The goose is constituted ultimately by the people of the country – and most of them do hiss and grumble about taxation, viewing it as legalized extortion, as stealing rewards of hard work. Many do their best to avoid paying; and the tax that they do pay, they pay reluctantly, scared of fines or imprisonment. Whatever can justify that imposition on people's lives?

Thomas Paine gave the answer indirectly through his support for the values of the French Revolution: namely, *Liberté, égalité, fraternité*.

Paine, English-born of the eighteenth century, was an American political activist and a Founding Father of the United States. His commitment to liberty, equality and fraternity meant that taxation was required; it was to provide benefits for children, education and the elderly. There have been plenty of attacks, though, on the acceptability of the State raising revenue by demanding money from its citizens.

St Thomas Aquinas, thirteenth-century Italian Dominican,

highly influential as philosopher and theologian, robustly criticized such demands, deeming them an assault, an unjustified one, on property. In Britain, in living memory, there occurred a major revolt against the Community Charge (the 'poll tax') that was to be a fixed levy on every individual in the country. The protests led to its demise and, for that matter, Margaret Thatcher's demise as prime minister.

Upon reflection, people usually accept the need for some taxation, but complain bitterly about its level, or at least – and more usually – its level as applied to them. Curiously, the complaint is rarely that the level applied to the complainers is too low, but that it is too high; the level is unfair. That proclaimed unfairness is often grounded in a comparison between their tax rates and the rates applied to others – or the amount actually paid compared with others. Some complainers may support differential tax rates, but believe that their higher rates ought not to be so much higher than the lower rates; others may argue that there ought to be one tax rate throughout. Those at lower-rate levels may object that they are far too close to the higher-rate, hitting their standard of living disproportionately.

There is often a more general stirring against taxation: the State is taking too much from people's income and wealth. Stirrers show how average earners are working for free until a certain date in a new year, say, in June; only after then are earners permitted to keep their earnings in full. Other unfairnesses are claimed. People are swayed by the thought that 'the same money' suffers taxation more than once: first, as income, for example, then as savings, and finally, with inheritance tax or death duty applied, when it passes to others. Tax is sometimes viewed as unjustified punishment.

The above objections all relate to 'fairness'. Tax objectors cite other worries: certain levels of taxation are disincentives to work; certain levels are needed only because of government inefficiencies or to fund undesirable projects – or to provide social welfare for people, thus disincentivizing them from work and undermining their personal responsibility for how their lives go. There are also distinct arguments about where tax should be applied – on earnings, unearned income, purchases, corporate profits, inheritances and so forth.

For completeness mention is needed of how some taxes are Pigouvian – named after Arthur Cecil Pigou, a British economist working in Cambridge in the early twentieth century. Pigouvian taxes are not primarily aimed at raising money, but to change certain behaviours; they are sometimes Chapter 4's nudges. There are taxes or tax reliefs to affect externalities that free markets and short-term business self-interest would otherwise ignore; examples are taxes and reliefs that cause businesses to steer some way away from activities that pollute the environment. There are also the 'sin taxes', aimed at reducing smoking or alcohol consumption; as ever, they have greater impact on freedoms of the poor than of the wealthy.

Whatever the reasons for taxation, there is the argument that taxation, at heart, is immoral, involving coercion: it takes something from me that is rightfully mine. That is the topic of this chapter.

A substantial assumption of the argument is that there is a clear notion of property that is proper to us, independently of any taxation being applied. That assumption merits substantial challenge, for taxation, society's laws, property rights and benefits are intermingled; we may therefore understand taxes as fees for providing a secure structure to society, past and future, a structure that, for example, upholds contracts of employment. To make sense of income 'pre-tax', we should need to grasp what that income is pre-'benefits of what the tax delivers'. Still, let us work with the common assumption – albeit mythical – that we have a clear idea of what we properly own by way of income and wealth, pre-taxation. Let us see how arguments develop.

THE FAIR DISTRIBUTION STATE: KIDNEYS, EYES AND CARESSES

A significant number of people are on dialysis machines; some will soon die because they are each in need of one working kidney. There are vast numbers of healthy people who have two kidneys each; their lives would run just as well with one fewer. Suppose an exceptionally easy procedure were developed whereby a healthy kidney could be removed from a healthy person and transferred to an ill person in need. The Fair Distribution State (FDS), as we may imagine, does just that. The State intervenes and ensures that, at least concerning kidneys, disadvantaged people (let us add: disadvantaged through no fault of their own) are helped out, without injuring others.

Our FDS has a similar policy with reference to eyes. Those of two eyes donate an eye each to enable the blind to see. The eye donor may not be able to have such a wide visual field and sense of depth, but that is a minor inconvenience compared with that of someone remaining blind. The FDS is wondering whether there could also be some sort of fairness in the distribution of sexual caresses; that is a project yet to reach fruition.

Let us run through clarifications of how the FDS works, to avoid the buzz of side criticisms and irrelevancies to the topic at hand, namely that of fairness in distribution.

Some may oppose FDS because there is inconvenience, maybe some small risks, to the healthy donors. We could ask whether anyone should object to a little inconvenience to save another's life or give that person sight. Let us suppose, though, that methods have been perfected, such that there is no inconvenience at all. Let us also suppose that procedures are developed so that life with one eye is as visually good as with two and that a single kidney always functions as well as two.

Some may oppose FDS because there may be unknown future risks or because sometimes things go wrong with the procedures. Let us suppose that none of those unfortunate events can happen.

Some may oppose FDS because, once some healthy individuals have donated accordingly, perhaps misfortunes could befall them later on, when they will then be in need. Let us assume that it will be just as easy for them to be recipients of a kidney or eye as for current recipients. Under FDS there will be sufficient available.

The above address practical problems; our FDS thought experiment is ruling those problems out, so that we may reach the nub of what is right – or wrong – about the proposal, about the FDS in its distributive practices. Once the ethics of FDS is established, the spotlight can swing directly to taxation and the similarity or otherwise to those FDS practices.

A substantial question – albeit still practical, but grounded in considerations of fairness – is that of how individual donors are to be chosen; after all, not everyone would need to donate a kidney or eye or, even, a caress. Let us put forward the Donation Lottery: all healthy people's names would be entered into a draw. The lottery would be fair; names would be picked each week – and the procedures undertaken at the donors' convenience. Many may wish hard not to 'win' the lottery; a few may want to be selected, revealing their sense of community and care for others – they want to do their bit.

Would there be any remaining objections to the FDS, now with its Donation Lottery in place?

You may respond with a determined 'yes'. What could justify the State – or indeed social pressure – imposing such so-called 'donations' from people? The State, it would seem, is invading what is rightly one's own – one's kidneys, one's eyes – for they are a person's property; they are proper to a person. There would be no objection to people voluntarily donating their organs, though even that raises the question whether the poor may be effectively compelled into 'donating' out of desperation. If, though, there are any basic moral facts, surely one is that I have a moral right to my body, at least while alive, and it ought to be solely up to me which parts I do or do not distribute.

The emphasis is on my right, as an adult, to autonomy, to govern myself. That is as clear as anything can be, when related to my body. Governing myself involves my deciding – not someone else deciding – what is to be done with and to my bodily parts, just as it involves what is to be done with and to my life. There are caveats: when the person is in no fit state to make autonomous decisions, others should intervene, but only to act in the interests of that person. Caveats to one side, even if it is accepted that the outcome, the redistribution of kidneys and eyes, would be a good overall, many would still be horrified, morally horrified at the State imposing the Donation Lottery.

Most of us, as a matter of fact, place greater value on retaining ownership of what is properly ours than on preventing the deaths of others. That is certainly what appears to be so. Given the reluctance, indignation indeed, at even the idea of people being forced to give up some luxuries to help the dispossessed, how much more would be the moral outrage at having to give up a kidney or an eye.

With that in mind, we now meet John Locke, the highly influential English philosopher of the late seventeenth century. His writings, by the way, are thought to have been the inspiration behind the 'life, liberty, and pursuit of happiness' phrase in the United States' Declaration of Independence.

In the *Second Treatise of Government*, Locke provided a starting point that can lead to an explanation of why people rightly fume at the imposition of taxes: '… every man has a "property" in his own "person". This nobody has any right to but himself.'

Of course, we are looking at this through eyes of a society where there is no government policy to enforce organ distributions. Suppose, if we can, that we grow up in a society where FDS is the normal position; it is just what happens. Most people find it perfectly acceptable. We, in that society and from its perspective, would probably be appalled, when hearing of other societies – or of our own liberal societies, centuries earlier, say – where 'self-ownership' (with the odd exception) was considered inviolable and, as a result, many unlucky people suffered blindness or died young from kidney failure.

The main objection to FDS is the enforced intrusion by the State, the community, the government – by others. That may cohere with objections to, and unease at, people, through financial desperation, being forced to sell some of their organs. With that objection in mind, let us see how we handle the next thought experiment.

Presumably, were Nature such that all people were born with at least one eye and at least one kidney, we should not object to that, even if there were fewer people with two kidneys and two eyes. Even if some of those born one-kidneyed or one-eyed wished that they had had two, it would be morally repugnant if they would prefer that twosome outcome for themselves through others having no working kidneys or no eyes at all.

Two intertwined thoughts are present. Although we may make sense of Nature delivering something better for human beings as a whole, we are reluctant to seek to achieve that 'better' by deliberate human intervention: for example, via the State. Further, individuals are disposed to believe that morally they are entitled at least to whatever good features already properly belong to them – 'I have a right to my bodily and psychological integrity' – and that trumps much else.

TAX AS LEGALIZED THEFT

Taxing people, it has been argued, is akin to taking from people what is properly theirs. The societies in view are those where paying taxes is compulsory and where people are, to some degree or other, opposed to paying; they pay or pay in full (unless they can get away without paying) only out of fear of the consequences of non-payment. A supplementary reflection is that even when people consent, the fact that the State would still impose the taxation, were people not to consent, is also objectionable.

We shall need to address nuances, but the vivid picture is that mentioned above: people are having effectively to work for so many months a year, during which all their earnings are 'stolen' by the State. They are akin to forced labourers, slaves – to the extent that they are working for nothing and not voluntarily so.

The strongest claim is that taxation – not property – is theft. It is akin to the enforced 'donation' of a kidney, an eye, a caress. Taxation steals our labour which is as much our property as our limbs. In our ideal FDS, the enforced donation did not harm the donors at all; yet many, from today's societies, find the FDS morally repugnant. Enforced taxation, some would argue, is even worse – for losses through tax payments do, to some extent, restrict taxpayers' lives and hence harms them. Paradoxically, the extremely wealthy are often most vocal in their opposition to taxation, where the taxation makes negligible impact on their quality of life – save that they lack control over that portion of money lost through the taxes.

The 'forced-labour' argument – 'slavery' – if it has any plausibility, applies most obviously and directly to taxation on income received through working. The argument may also apply indirectly to taxation of capital's gains, dividends and interest, in as far as the capital derived from the earnings. It more plausibly can be seen simply as theft, rather than involving slavery, when it is hitting

capital that one has justly received, for example, through inheritances. When we come to sales taxes, well, they may be perceived as
unjustified intrusions upon voluntary transactions.

Let us orientate the discussion, by first relating it more explicitly to what is proper to one, one's property, assuming sense can be
made of that, and then, secondly, review exceptions and weaknesses.

⑁⑁

As seen earlier, Locke advocated the importance of the individual
ownership of one's self, yet at least the 'earth' was in common to all.
Things, though, change. Picture the world thousands of years ago:
individuals toiled on the land and in so doing, according to Locke,
'mixed their labour' with that land. As a result, people succeeded
in growing produce, in rearing chickens for eggs, cows for milk;
some may have struck gold or oil (recall Anna in Chapter 5). That
labour-mixing, for Locke, generates the rightful individual ownership of land.

The labour-mixing defence of property ownership is readily
open to challenge. Mixing yourself with something does not usually
give you ownership of that something. It would be quite bizarre to
think that sexual intercourse would lead a man to own the woman
impregnated; it would be odd to argue that breathing out gave you
a right over the air as yours – or that the little boy who urinates in
the Nile now owns that river or even just a portion of its waters. The
'mixing' is not key.

What may be key is the fact that one has worked on something;
that generates some right of ownership. How extensive, though, is
the ownership and how intensely must be the working? You labour
on the land, succeed in growing olive trees and harvest the olives.
Perhaps the olives can be reasonably argued to be yours, maybe also
the trees, but, in addition, the land – and, if so, just as far as the
roots extend or will extend or could extend, or wider still?

We should also challenge Locke's starting assumption. Rather than treating the land as in common, but open to private ownership, we could have treated it as remaining in common, but able to be borrowed, on temporary loan. Locke ignores that possibility, simply arguing:

> Thus the grass my horse has bit; the turfs my servant has cut; and the more I have digged in any place, where I have a right to them in common with others, become my property, without the assignation or consent of any body. The labour that was mine, removing them out of that common state they were in, hath fixed my property in them.

Perhaps, contrary to Locke's line, private ownership of property acquired in that way is akin to theft. Locke recognizes that if we needed the consent of all, before we could take the apples and acorns, we should probably starve; but that has nothing to do with the requirement that the land fall into private ownership.

Mixing your labour these days, be it as toiler of the soil, worker in a factory or serving in a shop – be it trading for an investment company or teaching students – does not remotely provide you with ownership of that upon which you labour; it is already owned in nearly all cases by others. We may yet salvage Locke's approach, for you have used up some labour, expended your energy, taken up your time – and all that in exchange for wages, salaries or other remunerations. Your labour, energy, time were as much yours as your kidneys. The combination has been transformed into money – and that is, therefore, also yours.

Whether or not the above is a good argument, the State, the Revenue, the tax authorities take some of that money that is properly yours. Is not that disrespecting you, treating you solely as a means to the Revenue's ends? Here are some reasons why the right answer may be 'no'.

By remaining in the country, people are giving tacit consent to the law in general and to taxation in particular. Yes, they may be reluctant to pay their taxes; yes, they may decline to pay, were there no threats of punishment – but their engagement in this society is sufficient indication of consent, at least of sorts.

The reply is that merely remaining within the country does not manifest consent; consent depends, in part, on options available. As David Hume pointed out, in response to Locke, staying on a ship hardly counts as consent to the captain's orders when the only alternative is to jump overboard into a raging sea. If mere presence in a country manifests consent to its laws, then protestors against the laws are engaged in a contradictory activity. The riposte is that in as far as we support the democratic process (whichever one it is), if we do, then we are under obligations to obey democratically grounded laws, including taxation ones. The response to the riposte is that we should not be obliged to obey immoral laws – and enforced taxation is as immoral as theft of a kidney or eye, despite its acceptance in the FDS.

Consent or not, people receive benefits as a result of paying their taxes. That is another attempted justification for why people ought to pay taxes. Were people not to pay, there would be no benefits provided by the State – no justice system, no national defence, no social security – but that on its own does not show that I ought to pay. I could be a 'free-rider'; the benefits would still be available, unless most other people also failed to pay. That others do pay, though, suggests that it is unfair if I do not join in and pay.

The above fairness argument can rightly be rejected. Just because I enjoy various facilities provided through taxation, I am not therefore obliged to pay for them. If, unsolicited, a company sends me some champagne, the company has no right to demand payment or indeed return. And that applies whether I enjoy champagne – or not. If a young lady takes me to an oyster bar, buys oysters for me which I enjoy, surely I am under no moral obligation to take her out in return – unless there is a well-established convention in play.

There are further problems with the 'benefits-received' consideration. At best, it may show that one ought to pay those taxes related to received benefits – lighting in the streets, say – but not to those unreceived or unwanted. The State may still be viewed as running a protection racket; if you do not pay up (that is, pay the taxes due), then you or your property will be impounded. In fact, even the most 'libertarian' anti-tax individuals do not typically reject all taxation. They defend any taxation necessary to protect people's autonomy and property.

Thus it is that taxation to pay for defence, internal and external – and the justice system – is defended by many who otherwise treat enforced taxation as immorally intrusive. That may appear paradoxical; it could, though, be argued that rationally individuals would (or should) voluntarily pay for what is necessary to protect what is properly theirs. Echoes, from Chapter 3, of Rousseau with his 'forced to be free' may gently sing here. Mind you, some of the anti-tax league may feel sufficiently powerful to forgo any State protection; others may, with good reason, be so down about their lives, so dispossessed, that they no longer care. Those to one side, the vast majority of the anti-tax league support what is known as the 'Night-Watchman State'.

The Night-Watchman State is the minimal State, one that upholds justice, deters theft, fraud and violence – but that is it. It chimes with Ronald Reagan's 1981 Republican quip over proposed expansions of taxation to run government and secure its policy aims: 'Government is not the solution to our problem; it is the problem.' The Night-Watchman State can hence be deemed morally legitimate, even without the consent of all those to be governed; it is necessary for the structure of justice and defence. It is worth emphasizing the following: we have here at least one exception to the insistence that a person's property ought not to be intruded upon.

NIGHT-WATCHMAN STATE: COERCIVE OR LIBERTARIAN?

Many accept that, in practice, street lighting is a good; roads and other infrastructures are necessary. They are community benefits. Committed libertarians see the ideal as such benefits arising from people voluntarily agreeing to fund them directly, rather than through the State and coercive taxation. Do we really think, though, that individuals, working separately for their own benefit, would manage to create a well-thought-out street and services plan, from sewage systems to transportation, for a whole city? That is impractical; it is, so to speak, for the birds, mythical birds. Are libertarians, then, to accept no coherent infrastructures – with roads going so far, then stopping when the next community refuses to fund? Look at the City of London, where individual planners have been allowed, more or less, to 'do their thing', leading to a chaotic skyline. Overall, practical benefits outweigh some disruption to autonomy through taxation – as already acknowledged over defence and justice.

What particularly angers people of a libertarian persuasion is, it seems, the use of taxation to redistribute wealth, taking from the well-off to give to the poor, through social-security benefits, health services and education provision. When it is pointed out that such services cover risks that can arise for anyone, some insist that they would rather cover those risks themselves or simply take the risks. Apparently, they are prepared to live in a society where the poor are destitute, urchins scavenge for food and people die in the streets – save for any voluntary charitable interventions. Many libertarians accept the truth that *morally* we should provide for others; the objection is to the State compelling us to provide for others. That compulsion is itself immoral, it is claimed. Further, it does not make the taxpayers themselves into morally fine agents for they are being forced to help.

If libertarians sincerely recognize the morality of helping the dispossessed, they could reasonably reflect that some intrusions on individuals through enforced taxation to provide such help is justified, bearing in mind that charitable donations, solely on a voluntary basis, are likely to be insufficient and whimsical. The inviolability of individuals is broken to provide the minimal State – which they accept. Similarly, then, saving the lives of the destitute – another worthwhile aim akin to protection and justice – permits certain violations of autonomy, unless libertarians selfishly believe that violations are only permissible when to the direct benefit of the individuals violated.

Here is a further reflection. It is far from clear that voluntary charitable donating is morally superior to 'enforced donations' through taxation. Think of how donors can be emotionally manipulated to give and how they have to decide upon which charity. Think too of how unfair it is for those beggars or charities that miss out. In addition, it is demeaning for people to have to beg for 'charity' as opposed to receiving State benefits as of right. Even the provision of State benefits, indeed, needs handling with care. Many eligible for benefits do not take them up because of the need to reveal personal information; there is also the associated indignity and shame in applying. Those factors point to making certain social benefits universal, available to all, even to those who do not need them – after all, the taxation system can correct for that.

Before we seek to justify taxation further, let us see whether the basic libertarian position is morally all that it is cracked up to be.

The libertarian position emphasizes that I should be at liberty to do whatever I want with what is properly mine – my body, my possessions rightfully acquired – so long as not harming others. A much discussed argument – from the American philosopher Robert

Nozick, writing in his 1970s book *Anarchy, State and Utopia* – is given to show how even if we commenced with an egalitarian society, equal in the distribution of money, voluntary transactions would quickly lead to radical inequalities.

Consider the Three Singers. There used, in fact, to be the much praised and highly successful 'Three Tenors' – José Carreras, Plácido Domingo and Luciano Pavarotti – who performed together. Hundreds of thousands of people want to attend concerts by our three famous and splendid singers. The people voluntarily pay for tickets; the singers earn vast amounts, making them far wealthier than spectators and far wealthier than the orchestral players, support staff et al. Inequalities have arisen – through people being at liberty to do what they want with their money. What can be wrong with that?

Here are some wrongs. Through the inequalities generated, many other people have liberties curtailed. They cannot freely roam the land; after all, many areas are owned by the wealthy few, and so to roam would be to violate the owners' properties. Those lacking the wealth are priced out of certain markets; property ownership, concert tickets, rail travel effectively go to the highest bidders. Wealth inequalities lead to a disdain directed at the poor as well as to fears suffered by the wealthy who worry about their property; they end up living in gated communities or surround themselves by CCTV. Wealth inequalities can distress the poor, causing envy towards the wealthy, fuelled in part by the advertising that encourages them to aspire to wealth and spend. True, there is frequent rhetoric in favour of the 'trickle-down' effect, whereby wealth seeps down because of, for example, menial jobs becoming available for the poor to service the rich; but the evidence undermines the truth of that highly convenient rhetoric (please see Chapter 15).

In view of the outcomes just given, is it correct to argue that ticket-buyers for the Singers typically engaged in voluntary actions?

There is good reason to answer 'no'. Actions, to be voluntary, require agents to be well-informed. The ticket-buyers, though, were not at all well-informed with regard to the longer-term adverse outcomes of their buying activities – adverse because of effects of the large wealth inequalities, just cited.

The above are relevant factors why taxation, at least on such 'voluntary' commercial transactions, can be justified: namely, to help to reduce the loss of liberty for the poor. The taxation is not an intrusion upon someone's property; for the transactions are being taxed, not the individual singers – though, true, they end up with less. We do not know, though, the intentions of all ticket-buyers; some may positively support the Singers becoming vastly wealthy, while others may want some of the ticket costs to be used to foster future talent.

The libertarian argument appeals to the importance of permitting voluntary transactions. It also rests on the assumption that what is being transferred has been justly acquired. Let us now turn explicitly to that assumption.

Consider what is owned by the wealthy. Has it been justly acquired? Were we to trace how land and other property has been acquired over the centuries, has it been through voluntary transactions? If we step back sufficiently far, we see land acquired by conquest, businesses flourishing through slavery, fraud and threats to workers. There is no good reason to think that we typically know which property is rightfully owned now, if rightful ownership depends on historical transactions being just.

Even if cases exist of unsullied ownership where the whole wealth has been justly acquired directly, it has not been justly acquired in all respects, if the owners have made use of facilities resulting from unjustified taxation. That contaminates the purity – well, that should be the libertarian argument. Taxation of such owners might be deemed as causing a further wrong; but it might, instead, be seen as a compensatory, albeit crude, attempt at correcting earlier wrongs.

There remains the moral repugnancy of, apparently, disrespecting owners in taking some of their wealth or income through taxation, against their will. According to Immanuel Kant, the highly influential Enlightenment philosopher, respect involves not treating people solely as a means to an end. Redistributive taxation is, though, treating the taxed solely as means to secure the outcome of wealth redistribution; yet is that necessarily a manifestation of 'disrespect'? No – for even when taxing people, the State may yet respect them, paying heed to their circumstances. Taxation levels may be set to ensure that the wealthy's taxed lives are not seriously taxing for them and their opportunities are not significantly disrupted. Respect involves attitudes of concern; simply doing nothing to violate people's ownership of their assets does not manifest any genuine concern for those individuals. Indeed, taxing them usefully helps them to sense some degree of community with others.

RETURNING TO KIDNEYS AND EYES

Whatever the hisses against taxation, most people feel very differently about the State taxing our wealth and the State insisting that we share out eyes and kidneys. There is a significant gulf between what is proper to a person being a person – the body and mind – and what property that person possesses. Perhaps that partially explains why a rape may be far more horrendous for a woman than her bank account being raided. Consider this thought: a compassionate woman may well share her food with a starving man – and others may recognize it as their duty to share in such circumstances – yet few would see compassion or duty as demanding that they should share their bed with a man starved of sex. It is not terribly controversial that the State should ensure sufficient basic goods, such as food and shelter, for all its citizens to have reasonable lives; it would be controversial, no doubt, were the State to provide services for those people who would otherwise have sexual desires unfulfilled. That

thought leads to wider questions of what constitutes human flourishing and whether people have a right to, for example, a family life,
to be loved and not to be left lonely. Chapter 11 offers some exploration of human rights, but here ownership and the intrusions of
taxation need to be pursued further.

Let us recall, ownership of myself, of intimacies, makes sense
prior to any laws and life in society whereas ownership of my earnings and wealth is not so easily grasped as prior to law and society.
Within a society, there are of course distinctions to be made relating
to the person. People find loss of personal objects more disturbing
than loss of the impersonal; a theft of love letters typically is more
intrusive than theft of the television.

What constitutes an individual has fuzzy edges: the artificial
leg may become part of me; the blind may feel their guide dogs
as their eyes. The integrity of an individual's body and mind has a
good claim as the starting point for counting what truly belongs to
someone. The FDS left people sufficiently intact; the revised Nature
(speculated above) that ensured everyone had at least one working
kidney and eye did not undermine people's ability to lead flourishing lives. That thought experiment does not generate societies so
alien that we should be baffled how to make sense of them. That
thought experiment is far removed from the fairy stories used to
mock caricatures of utilitarianism – of securing the greatest happiness of the greatest number – with groups of healthy people being
treated as plantations, whereby organs and limbs are grown to sell
to others.

In contrast to the latter repulsive scenarios, suppose Nature or
culture had developed Western societies such that people 'naturally'
found it obvious to share far more of their possessions, welcoming
forms of redistributive taxation. In those developed societies, it
would strike people as bizarre – morally outrageous – to consider
that things would be so much better for people to become selfish,

with the resultant poverty, sometimes extreme, for many. In those developed societies, people would find it bizarre to start supporting laws and cultures of today's typical liberal democracies where competition and individualism are praised far more than cooperation and community.

Bearing in mind the perspective of how things could naturally or culturally have been, it is not so unreasonable, within our actual society, to promote the value of sharing; after all, some small communities have done so, praising solidarity, with all members contributing to the group's welfare. In the eighteenth century, some small Shaker groups – Believers in Christ's Second Appearing – were started; in the following century, they spread across New England and some Midwestern states. Other nineteenth-century communities included George Ripley's Brook Farm in Massachusetts and Robert Owen's New Harmony in Indiana. We should reflect how during the twentieth century trade unions, promoting a sense of solidarity, manifestly ushered in better working conditions and employment rights – yet both unions and the emphasis on workers' rights are now frequently viewed with scorn by neo-liberals as unnecessary hangovers from a past and irrelevant age.

Today, we may look to Marinaleda, a small social-democratic agricultural municipality in the province of Spain's Seville. For nearly forty years, it has been led by the left-wing Sánchez Gordillo with, in the main, the support of its citizens. Its land has been shared out amongst the citizens and, over those decades, Gordillo has sought to dispel myths of liberal democracies. As the town's website maintains, democracy is 'a way to deceive people into believing they are part of a project when in fact they are not needed at all'. Gordillo likens capitalism to King Midas: everything it touches turns to gold, commodity, trade and death; the capitalist system is necrophilous. The survival of socialist Marinaleda is, of course, not guaranteed; a right-wing government coming to power in the region could well impose the capitalist touch, bringing about this municipality's death.

It can be argued that what may work by way of small communities has no chance of success in large industrial societies, yet we should remember that, even in those societies, institutions can bind and bring forth solidarity. This can come about through social benefits being universal, with everyone possessing a stake in the community. In Britain – so far – the NHS is free at the point of delivery to all. There is no means testing; and the NHS, despite much underfunding, continues to receive huge public support.

Once taxation is accepted as properly justified in principle, there remain questions of detail. Who and what should be taxed? Should there be differential rates, different allowances, different reliefs depending on the income source? Should taxes be applied on the basis of consumption, wealth, capital gains realized or gifts? With so many factors, it is astonishing that people are keen to argue that, for example in Britain, the 20 per cent income tax rate is maybe fair, but the 40 per cent certainly is not. How could one tell?

In the 1960s in Britain, Prime Minister Harold Wilson's government introduced a 95 per cent supertax rate; Wilson received the mocking accolade of 'Taxman', George Harrison's 1966 Beatles' song, despite having recommended all the Beatles for the award of the MBE (Member of the British Empire). British governments have since proudly announced how much income tax rates have been reduced, yet are rather silent with regard to how Value Added Tax over the years has moved from 10 per cent to 20 per cent, a tax that impinges far more on those of low incomes compared to those on high incomes.

There is a vast range of tax rates internationally and historically. In some countries, the 'race to the bottom' is the game – that is, to the lowest tax rates in order to attract businesses. Many European countries have corporation tax around the 22 per cent level, but Ireland's is around 12.5 per cent and the United Kingdom has been heading below the 20 per cent level to 19 per cent and aiming for lower still. We could cynically wonder why the rates matter to those countries that allow creative accounting and complex corporate structures whereby profits made at home are magically transferred to 'tax havens'; the (British) Virgin Islands has zero corporation tax. Let us muse a little on that international element.

Countries lure corporations and wealthy individuals to become resident; that may well improve the country's average standard of living, its wealth and economic prosperity. The lure succeeds, in part, when some countries outbid others regarding low tax levels. Matters, though, are not remotely that simple. Mariana Mazzucato's *The Value of Everything* (2018) shows how Apple Inc., for example, benefited from technology derived from publicly funded work in California, yet over the years has formed subsidiaries in different states and countries, avoiding vast amounts of tax otherwise due. It has 'extracted value', pitting countries and states against each other.

That we have countries – distinct nations, distinct States – is probably justified by way of effective administration and citizens' local participation; but an outcome, as noted, is that States, eager to attract global corporations, compete by lowering levels of corporation tax. As a result, many people can suffer greater poverty because the tax competition reduces the nation's ability to increase tax revenues and hence make improved provision of welfare services, despite the increased economic activity. Global justice is also undermined, being at the mercy of international corporate trading policies, policies that minimize tax liabilities and hinder global redistribution. Tax havens, for example, typically have no significant economic activity and are far from transparent, yet strangely are homes to thousands of international companies, often subsidiaries

of major international banks – and, strangely, major liberal democracies have allowed them to flourish. The Latin tag may come to the
fore: *cui bono?*; who benefits? And, of course, when there are suggestions for taxing global transactions, there are cries of horror from
corporate and financial leaders.

⫘

Inheritance taxes – estate duties; death duties; gift taxes – often
receive special distaste from the public, a distaste urged on by libertarians.

One typical objection to those taxes is that they deter would-be
givers from saving; yet, curiously, that they may deter receivers from
working, and adversely affect those who do not inherit, is forgotten.
To the cry that such taxes are unfair, consider an employee whose
£25,000 annual earnings are taxed; is it fair that someone else
receives an inheritance of £25,000, yet pays no tax? If inheriting is
thought so desirable, whereby the elderly pass assets to the young,
it would be fairer to use the tax system to spread the inherited sums
across the younger generation as a whole instead of unfairly benefiting just a lucky few.

Inheritance tax is often singled out and condemned as double
taxation. That clearly is false regarding the recipient; and the taxes
on death, of course, do not then affect the deceased. Further, double
taxation is accepted in many walks of life. When I pay the plumbers,
I pay them out of taxed earnings; and they are then taxed. When I buy
the piano out of taxed earnings, I pay Value Added Tax. In any case,
the number of taxes is irrelevant; the worry should be the cumula-
tive effect. True, there are additional factors pertinent to inheritance tax. Maybe parents who save to give money to their offspring
are behaving more virtuously than those who squander money, but
maybe they are not; after all, they are helping to undermine equality
of opportunity, perhaps even encouraging sloth in their offspring.

Once again, there are degrees and degrees here, regarding the help (typically) that parents may justly give to their children.

Let us mull matters over further – and more fundamentally. Tax on inheritances is a means of limiting the intergenerational transfer of advantage. Of course, we need caveats. We may recognize, for example, that there is a big and relevant difference between on the one hand a small farm-holding that passes through the generations where all are involved in the farming and, on the other hand, large portfolios of shares inherited by children simply as a 'something for nothing'. Further, we may question beliefs that 'our' young – many better off in health, rights and technology than earlier generations – deserve also to do better financially, even if tax reliefs for them mean lower benefits for the elderly poor.

In summary, it is baffling what counts as 'fair' when we consider different taxes and rates. Curiously, in the United Kingdom, it is considered fair that winnings from lotteries and other gambles are untaxed, yet earnings typically are taxed. We encountered such bafflement about fairness in other arenas earlier in this work. We should once again be reminded that, regarding many of these societal matters, siren voices demanding definitive right answers are siren voices that leave us with no right answers; they sing to mythical ideals. We need to accept that, for many of these questions, answers need to recognize cases and cases, degrees and degrees, though we rightly should urge a sense of humanity, compassion and solidarity rather than the 'I'm all right, Jack' motif. When there are the usual corporate demands for lower levels of taxation – when international trading taxes are much rejected – it is again worth asking: when the lowering and rejections succeed, who benefits from that success? *Cui bono?*

8

'This land is our land'

The United States of America is swamped with immigrants; Great Britain is swamped with immigrants – as are Germany, Sweden, Australia, and even North Korea. All the countries of the world are populated by immigrants. Well, they are if by 'immigrants' we mean 'those who are newcomers to the land'. From the viewpoint of those who lived one hundred years ago, virtually everyone in every land now is a newcomer to the land. Of course, from the viewpoint of today, some have arrived in a country more recently than others; some are more 'newly-come-d' than others.

'What a foolish observation,' respond many: anxiety about immigrants and immigration is not a worry about our children coming into existence in this land – it is not directed at generation replacement (though that merits some discussion) – but is a worry about the numbers of people in a country who were not born in that country or are not offspring of people born in that country. It is a worry about the non-natives present in a land. The central distinction is between natives and foreigners. Within a country, history trumps geography; even if you are 'here', you may not belong here for you lack the right history.

Natives are those possessing relevant historical connections with the land – 'this land is our land' – though the depth and length of connections vary. Those who lack relevant connections may yet be living in the land or trying to gain access to that land, but their historical connections are with elsewhere.

'This historical land' is highly important for many nations or groups, but we should remember that many groupings, without distinctive territory, may be as much a nation, a culture, a community, as one possessed of continuous life in a particular territory. Witness the plight of the Jews over centuries: they have held together, through a narrative of struggles for survival, despite having no 'land of their own' for many, many centuries.

A particular patch of land need not be essential to a group's identity; France would still be France, even if located in South Asia. There is more to nationhood than its land. To use an Aristotelian comment, you can put a wall round a city, but you do not make a city with a wall. A city, a nation, typically is tied to a particular territory, but that is neither sufficient for its identity nor is it necessary.

Migrations have been and are big news. They have varied from people escaping civil wars in Syria, to those of the EU's free movement of labour, to the flight of people from Venezuela because of its economic collapse. There were the Rohingya Muslims fleeing from Myanmar to Bangladesh, understandably so, given the United Nations' evidence of Myanmar's senior military being engaged in a genocide. Mexicans, looking for work, slip illegally into the United States, much to the chagrin of President Trump and supporters.

For many European countries, the aim has been to prevent or severely limit entry by the desperate – some poor, some well-off – from North Africa. They are so desperate that they risk their lives on Mediterranean waves, crowded on fragile crafts, to secure refuge and better lives. During the first couple of decades of the twenty-first century, hundreds of thousands have landed on the Italian island of Lampedusa, the Greek island of Lesbos and other Aegean islands. They have been fleeing Libya and Tunisia, later also Eritrea and Somalia. Thousands have perished in their attempts; thousands have suffered appalling conditions. In 2014, organizations around the Mediterranean propounded the Charter of Lampedusa, grounded in the idea that as human beings we all inhabit the Earth as a shared space; thus, nations should not seek to prevent migrants from the full exercise of human rights.

Despite the Charter, European countries have argued over their responsibilities in helping Italy and Greece to deal with the influx of desperate people. Some countries showed generosity – Germany and Sweden, for example – though many made at best small gestures of help. Hungary adopted a 'keep them out' policy with the construction in 2015 of high razor-wire fencing on the Hungarian-Serbian border. Contrast with the initial response by Germany; in 2016 alone, it welcomed over a million fleeing migrants. In the generous nations, though, opposition to the generosity quickly grew. It is worth noting, by the way, that the countries receiving most of the migrants are the far more impoverished Lebanon, Jordan and Turkey.

Political debate in Britain has highlighted the need for humanitarian aid to help those outsiders eager for safety. Political debate also has highlighted the financial burdens and disruption such migrants are for receiving countries. Some popular pronouncements against accepting the migrants, even those being rescued from choppy seas or found clinging to undercarriages of trains or lorries, are that the migrants are just opting for an easy life and should be sent back. The pronouncers would do well to reflect on, seriously reflect on, Warsan Shire's poem 'Home'. It vividly expresses how no one casually endangers lives of their children and themselves, 'burning their palms under trains', 'feeding on newspapers'.

Businesses often quietly welcome immigrants as sources of cheap labour; other groups often oppose because of adverse effects on nationals regarding jobs and wage levels. There are other factors relevant to migrations more generally; qualified people leaving destitute countries are more needed at home than in the flourishing West. As ever, there are competing values and considerations. If the predictions regarding global warming come true, with many areas flooded and resources lost, radical mass migrations will occur, leading to intense conflicts, upheavals and worse.

JURISDICTION

Why think that any population of natives, of citizens – any community, any individual – has a rightful jurisdiction over a parcel of land? Justifying the territorial rights of populations that have, through the generations, lived in the same land is difficult enough; it is even more difficult when people have fought or continue to fight over that land as their historical territory. The most controversial and internationally highlighted example is the continuing struggle over the 'Holy Land' between Palestinians and Israeli Jews. There are similar sufferings of the Kurds who seek their homeland, separate from Turkey and Syria. With the 2019 presidency of Brazil's 'Tropical Trump' Jair Bolsonaro, indigenous communities fear for their territorial autonomy and foresee dangers of further commercial erosion of the Amazon rainforest.

Historically, territorial rights were violated through colonization, with the extension of the British Empire and other empires. There are many groups and injustices now largely forgotten – Tasmanian Aborigines, the Indians east of the Mississippi River – and there are current cases little noted: do the Uyghurs (in China) have a legitimate claim to self-determination? Thomas Malthus, whose 1798 work *An Essay on the Principle of Population* argued that population growth, unless controlled, would exceed food supply, questioned the morality of colonization. Colonization would be bad for the indigenous peoples; the peoples would either be assimilated

into the conquering groups or led into mass migrations – or exter-
minated. Over the last century, versions of all three have occurred,
though there have also been some relatively successful policies of
decolonization.

We could be radical. No one has a right to own the sunsets, the
air, the oceans; perhaps land should be added to that list. We could
think of land as belonging to all human beings – or, better, all creatures – and resist Locke's argument (of Chapter 7) that land worked
upon can properly pass into private, individual ownership. Some
view land as belonging to God, on loan to all creatures in common.
Once we have the idea of 'this is mine' – be it for land or other significant resources – strife is, as Rousseau emphasized, the outcome.
Maybe we ought to follow the line of Pierre-Joseph Proudhon, the
nineteenth-century French anarchist, who perceived property privately owned to be akin to theft. Karl Marx, though critical of the
'property is theft' mantra, had a similar view over land and means of
production; there is no problem, though, about the private ownership of socks, a toothbrush and, these days, smart mobile phones.

The underlying dispute can be seen thus. We are all equally citizens of the world. Political boundaries impede movement; morally
they ought not to do so. Borders should be open, or at least more
open, with restrictions imposed only when justified by overall benefits. Certainly, to open them for others fleeing disasters is not
merely some touching compassion, but a moral duty. That is a 'cosmopolitan' position – the word derives from the Greek for 'citizen
of the world' – whereby all human beings are understood as being
members of one universal community. That understanding should
be encouraged; it does not conflict with people also having certain
local obligations. In contrast, a 'nationalist' position perceives the
State, a political state, as possessing the right to control its territory
and who may reside within; after all, nationals have built infrastructures which belong to them. Permitting entry may be on grounds

of prudence, to avoid external instabilities intruding upon the nation; it may be on grounds of charity – but not those of any absolute moral duty.

That 'closed-border' attitude can manifest fears of 'the other'; but it can be understandable self-interest; immigrants increase costs for social-welfare provision – well, that is a typical complaint. Contrary to much popular belief, though, immigrants to well-developed countries usually overall contribute to economies, through business enterprise, provision of services and paying taxes, helping to provide for the native older generations.

Today's reality is the nationalist position. Today's land ownership, states and territorial controls have resulted from force, battles, coercion and deals, whereby the weaker have reluctantly submitted to the stronger. Seeking a source for what is rightfully the land of a people is a hopeless task. True, we may take little steps back into history; but how far back?

In the early eighteenth century, Britain forcibly took Gibraltar and eventually compelled Spain to cede it. Gibraltar is now British – yet justly so? In 1830, the European settlers in America had their way: their President Jackson signed the Indian Removal Act. The outcome was the forced removal of native American tribes from their homelands. The march of the Cherokee Nation led to around four thousand unnecessary deaths. Are there many significant international demands for European Americans to give back the land? Not at all. The power of the United States, the native American removals being nearly two centuries ago, together with the impotence of the natives, all contribute to the original injustice and its horrors fading away into distant memories, the tales from previous generations remaining as mere scraps in the dusty pages of history.

The most outstanding case, as already noted, of territorial conflict for 'our land' is Israel and Palestine. The conflict suffers all the more from the unhappy weavings of religion, with both sides' insistence that the Holy Land is exclusively their land. There are plenty of other instances of sufferings through territorial disputes. There has been the Russian 2014 annexation of Crimea, declaring it as rightfully Russian. We have the battles in the Middle East for an Islamic State, and, as mentioned, the determination of the Kurds for their own country. In the 1990s, the break-up of Yugoslavia led to distinct nation states and horrors of ethnic cleansing. Serbia, for example, sought to secure a Greater Serbia by cleansing some territory of Muslims. That led to massacres and war crimes, with Ratko Mladić, Bosnian Serb commander, eventually receiving a prison life sentence for genocide and other atrocities.

The above observations may encourage us to ask again what it is that morally gives natives, the nationals, 'the people', rights over 'their' land. The answer may well be 'nothing'. Let us, though, assume that natives, through long historical connections, do possess the rights. The topic here, on that basis, is to evaluate whether those rights justify refusing entry to foreigners, strangers, non-natives. The strength, the weight, the confidence in the 'my land' rights, may well be a factor in determining how open or closed borders should be. We should in any case note that there is more to morality than rights. Consider the following little tale, from Marcel Proust, recognized as one of the world's greatest novelists. The tale occurs in his *Remembrance of Things Past*. Monsieur Cottard, already in his dinner jacket, shrugs his shoulders when his wife timidly asks if he could bandage the cut vein in their cook's arm; blood is pouring. 'Of course I can't,' he groans. 'Can't you see I've got my white waistcoat on?'

Cottard has things out of perspective. Assume that I have a right to my tie: it would be irrational to insist that that right trumps someone's need for the tie to stem a blood flow, thus saving a life. Assume Cottard has a right to be attending the dinner, wearing his white waistcoat in pristine condition: should that trump manifesting the virtues of compassion and generosity by helping the cook?

WHAT IS A NATION STATE?

What, according to international law, makes Great Britain, Germany, the United States, Sweden legitimate States? Well, a land, a territory, is needed for an authority to effect its laws over a population. Statehood is taken to require the following: the authorities maintain social order over the land in question, with the population's consent. Maybe those two conditions are sufficient for the State's legitimacy, for its sovereignty, though both conditions need caveats recognizing, for example, that the requirement is that the people who consent have had some ties with that territory and 'the people' here does not imply each and every one.

Any State is coercive; to justify such coercion, the State must, at least at some level, respect its constituents, its members, nationals, citizens (using the terms loosely, as interchangeable, here). Of course, within many national territories, there are swathes of land and natural resources unused. The State, then, needs some justification for its exclusive control over those unused areas. Hugo Grotius, a seventeenth-century Dutch jurist, termed such areas as 'the lump', including lakes, forests, deserts and mountains. It was Grotius, indeed, who formulated the idea of 'freedom of the seas', with the seas as international territory. There are related questions over which principles to adopt when a nation state does control certain areas, such as tropical rainforests, rivers or those containing rare species, that affect other nations' well-being.

Even if we accept that nation states have rights over relevant territory, determined in an internationally agreed way, that does not show that it is right to have nation states rather than, say, world government or informal groupings. Nation states can, though, possess instrumental value for a manifest good; they can provide the best practical means for people to have some input into government and hence some sense of autonomy regarding the laws under which they live. True, nation states can give rise to nationalism; they also can give rise to patriotism.

There are bewildering and conflicting attempts to separate nationalism (often condemned) from patriotism (often defended). When a country consists of one cohesive nation, nationalism and patriotism are likely to amount to similar attitudes and beliefs. A feel for the distinction, though, is shown in the following. Nationalists may be seen as seeking to preserve the integrity of their nation; they do so by keeping strangers out. Patriots show loyalty to their country, pride in their country, by welcoming strangers in.

Nationalists are sometimes understood as, and criticized for, believing that their nation's values are superior to others', whereas patriotism is more a loyalty to one's country. Now, if a nation has some clear values, then sometimes that 'superiority' claim may be true; after all, a nation's values that firmly reject torture may, reasonably enough, be accepted as superior to – that is, morally desirable over – ones relaxed about torture. What may be disreputable about some nationalists is a belief that certain moral values are exclusively theirs; others are incapable of grasping them. The liberal impulse is strongly to reject that exclusivity; that liberal impulse is, though, curiously muffled when engaging with religions – religions that may speak of only Jews being the chosen people or of only a Christian way of life offering the possibility of eternal bliss.

The nation of a particular territory may be seen as possessing certain typical characteristics, be they understood in terms of the people's race, ancestry, ethnicity or culture. (For 'race', please see notes on page 324.) Assuming still that there is such a thing as the justified 'nation state' controlling a territory, possessed of laws and culture, how, morally, should the State treat would-be immigrants, strangers, foreigners who want or need to enter? Well, we should take into account the effects upon, the requirements and wants of, the receiving State's nationals – and the effects upon, the requirements and wants of the would-be immigrants, were they to be refused entry or permitted entry. There may also be some distinctive obligations to certain outsiders; they may deserve special treatment because of the receiving nation's earlier (mis)use of those countries, their people and resources. We should need to assess the effects of, for example, British, French and Dutch colonial policies.

In the case of Britain and its then empire, the Labour government's British Nationality Act of 1948 introduced the status of 'Citizen of the United Kingdom and Colonies'; it applied amazingly to all Commonwealth subjects – then a quarter of the Earth's population – and it recognized their right to work and settle in Britain and to bring their families. British borders were, thus, pretty open, though proportionately few took advantage. Over the decades, though, hostility towards immigrants arose – 1958 saw race riots in London and Nottingham – leading to the Act's entry conditions being much tightened. In 1962, the Conservative government's Commonwealth Immigrants Act introduced entry based on certain skills and prospects; the effect 'just happened' to impinge mostly on those would-be immigrants from the Caribbean, Africa and Asia. Margaret Thatcher's Conservative government made more radical changes, with the British Nationality Act of 1981; British citizenship was now defined such that only those born in Britain, or the children and grandchildren of those born in Britain, possessed the right to enter Britain. No longer was it allegiance by dominions, history, desire, but largely by ties of blood.

Immigration controls of most countries have typically been racist or nationalist. The United States 1924 Immigration Act was based on eugenics later used by the Nazis; it restricted immigration from Southern and Eastern Europe in favour of the 'superior'

Northern and Western Europeans. Jewish refugees at that time were restricted entry. In 1905 the United Kingdom's Aliens Act was aimed at reducing Jewish immigration.

Since 2010, the United Kingdom's policy has been very determinedly that the country should be a hostile environment to 'illegal immigrants'. Its hostility, though, has led to considerable suffering, detention, even deportation, for many perfectly 'legal' United Kingdom citizens who lacked relevant paperwork and who looked West Indian or African. They are people of the so-called 'Windrush generation', those African-Caribbean individuals who legally entered the country in 1948 on the HMT *Empire Windrush* – and later – often in response to Britain advertising job vacancies to them. Initially, Theresa May's government sought to shrug off such cases, until adverse political reactions overwhelmed it.

Regarding those who seek entry, they form a spectrum, from people in desperation, escaping torture, now clinging on to boats on raging oceans – refugees or asylum seekers – to those unable to find work in their own countries – economic migrants – to those who simply want to live in the receiving country, perhaps preferring a higher quality of life or joining family members already resident. We need, of course, to put to one side those who are tourists and temporary guests.

Refugees, in principle, are seeking refuge, in the hope that one day they may return to their homeland; that contrasts with those migrants who are aiming for the receiving country to become their home. How receiving nations respond to either group varies, but they are increasingly reluctant to take such groups, unless bringing talents and/or cash. The problems arise because of the different feelings we typically have regarding friends as opposed to strangers; some, though, view it as a conflict between friends and enemies.

MY HOME: CLARISSA, JUSTINA AND TESSA

Features that we possess in common help to hold us together. The natural example is the family: biology, nurturing, initial proximity – they typically glue people, attaching them to each other. There are exceptions. Those attachments are usually deemed morally valuable; they are seen as so valuable that we place them above detached values, above values that seek equality of treatment. As touched upon in earlier chapters, we give preference to our child, our mother, our lover, rather than to someone else's. Families and friendships, for most people, are highly significant constituents of flourishing lives.

We also deliberately choose to tie ourselves into associations even though they lack any immediate biologically or intimate linkage; we form clubs, colleges, orchestras, local societies. Criteria are set, determining club membership: musical preferences, talent at chess or commitments to beards. Associations' rules manifest preferences for some people over others. A political party accepts as members only people who commit to its policies; the golf club allows membership only to those who pay the fees and promise obedience to the rules.

Freedom of association, as with attachments of family life, necessarily entails a freedom to exclude – and with a nation state that extends to its territory. Let us, then, try the family home, as an attempted analogy for a nation state.

You awake one morning and find a couple of intruders: Clarissa and Tessa. Their breakfast is your smoked salmon and champagne. They broke in. Until more is said, if any more needs to be said, we should surely agree that they have no right to your property. They are trespassing. Although you would be within your rights to expel, would you be acting morally in doing so? After all, we should not assume that exercising your rights is always morally acceptable; we saw that assumption questioned via Proust's white waistcoat tale. We need reasons (ideally good reasons) for how we treat other people, in this case for expelling Clarissa and Tessa.

Clarissa is so-called because she is Champagne Lover par excellence. She has a home of her own and a good quality of life, save that she wants champagne and likes your landscaped garden. We may all reasonably feel you are under no obligation to support her champagne-guzzling ways; we are not hypothesizing that, without champagne, she would collapse into mental illness. She has no right to your champagne – or garden or home – and you are not acting badly in demanding that she desists and leaves.

Tessa is a Torture Sufferer. She is a victim. Were you to exercise your property rights, she would be back in the hands – the chains, electrodes and beatings – of her torturers. It would surely be callous, cruel, unkind – to say the very least – to insist on your rights and remove her from your property. To provide Tessa with safety does not entail that she has a 'right' to live with you, be it temporarily or permanently. You ought, though, to provide her with safety – your desire for undisturbed use of your home can be overridden by the morality: here, the virtues of kindness and generosity – but for how long depends on other factors, as do the facilities which she may reasonably request. Is she entitled to all the benefits enjoyed by your family? How disruptive will she be?

We could picture many cases along the spectrum between Clarissa and Tessa. Picture Justina. She has a Just Acceptable Life in a distant land where she lived; she would much prefer to be living in your property, where there are far greater opportunities courtesy of your library, your conversation and internet speed.

With Clarissa and Tessa – and versions of Justina along the spectrum – you have just a few particular individuals in front of you to handle. A further dimension to the discussion would be added were there large groups of Tessas intruding upon your home, squeezing into every room. There would then be problems of who, if any, of a group may be allowed to remain. First in? Most deserving? Most like you? Most desperate? Ones you take a shine to? Should it be by random selection?

⫶

Is 'home intrusion' a good analogy with which to work for understanding how a country ought to deal with immigration? The countries in our sights are, of course, liberal democracies such as the United States, Great Britain, France, Sweden. Being democracies, the governments may claim that they are representing their nationals; the nationals, through their government policies, 'speak as one'. Earlier chapters here have challenged that as mythical, but let us see how far it takes us.

Compatriots – the nationals of a particular land – have their humanity in common; but they also have humanity in common with outsiders, foreigners, would-be immigrants. That common humanity does not itself mark any distinction that could justify the differential treatment of non-nationals compared with nationals. There is, though, far more to a nation's glue than its shared humanity.

Compatriots to a greater or lesser extent – depending on migrations to date – have histories and language in common, maybe significant ancestral genealogical overlaps; they hold to certain basic values and commitments. They accept the society's laws and conventions; they engage in voting, identify with a political or social culture, even speak of a 'national identity'. A Frenchman once commented to Lord Palmerston, a nineteenth-century British statesman, twice prime minister, 'If I were not a Frenchman, I should wish to be an Englishman.' Palmerston replied, with England at the height of its imperial power, 'If I were not an Englishman, I should wish to be an Englishman.'

Pride in one's national identity may yet live with awareness of a chaotic history which gave rise to that identity and its structure of similarities and dissimilarities between the nationals. The 'True-Born Englishman', according to the author Daniel Defoe, writing in 1700, was the heir of the 'Customs, Sirnames, Languages, and Manners' of an 'Amphibious Ill-born Mob'. Incursions and invasions were the foundations of Englishness whose:

> *Relicks are so lasting and so strong,*
> *They ha' left a Shiboleth upon our Tongue;*
> *By which with easy search you may distinguish*
> *Your Roman-Saxon-Danish-Norman English.*

The English identity embraced the previous invasions; yet now, as Britain, it may prefer relatively closed borders. It is not, though, closed to linguistic changes through foreign interventions: contrast with the linguistic purity sought by the Academies of France and Italy.

Having outlined a nation state and its nationals, let us review the reasons for preventing outsiders from entering the nation's territory. We look here in this chapter at the 'Justina's or 'Clarissa's rather than the desperate 'Tessa's. Our observations need the caveat 'for the most part'. Moral demands to one side, we have reasons concerning first, how migrations affect the economic prosperity of receiving nations and, secondly, migrants' effects on legal, political, institutional and social features of those receiving nations. A third reason rests on those features to which nationals feel distinctively attached as theirs, as part of their narrative. That merits a chapter (the next chapter) of its own, for exploration – and where, later on, the 'Tessa's come to the fore.

First, regarding economic prosperity, there is a host of economic relationships within a liberal democracy, involving free markets, ways of trading, regulations and State interventions. Immigrants could obviously uphold those relationships; they may be keen to enter the country just because of its economic opportunities. Lovers of free markets for goods and services, if consistent, should promote free movement at least of labour, if not of people more generally. Thus it is that, internally, the United States has free movement between its states. Thus it is that the EU has free movement between its nation states; that is much supported by the corporate world, given the potential for attracting cheap labour from abroad. Corporate eagerness for free movement, as within corporate support for globalization, can also be to enable easy production relocation from the home country to countries with lower production costs.

Even if free trade, including free movement of people, is beneficial economically or even if it is judged possessed of intrinsic value – and both claims may be questioned (please see Chapter 15) – there may yet be good reasons that justify severe restrictions.

Depending on numbers, the entry of migrants may undermine employment prospects of some nationals in the receiving country. At least those nationals, though, could participate democratically, with resulting policies in theory prioritizing citizens' interests. Those in other countries, notably the impoverished, had little say, if any, in the policies of the receiving country; citizens of those impoverished countries may suffer adversely, losing the skills and talents of the migrants leaving for greener pastures.

Significant differences exist between the domestic and international stage; they undermine any convincing analogy between free movement within a country and free movement between countries. Within, free movement between regions may effectively be partly 'directed movement'; governments often introduce subsidies for certain industries, regeneration programmes and tax incentives.

The aim can be to spread the prosperity within the nation. On the international stage, there is no single effective authority with the aim of spreading prosperity between all nations. There is no international body that determines how best to direct 'free' movements between countries. International movements of people result from a mishmash of interests of the powerful, be they governments or global corporations – be they political, military, financial or incompetent – mixed with handling, mishandling or not handling the needs of millions of people, ranging from the desperate to those who would just like somewhere better. The mishmash is occasionally sprinkled with touches of humanity.

On economic grounds, there are no decisive overall reasons supporting heavy restrictions against migrations. That is no comfort to those nationals who do miss out on rehousing or lose jobs because of migrants arriving; that may be of comfort to some intending migrants. One additional factor relevant here, politically and rhetorically often highlighted, is 'undeserved benefits', where the moral mingles with the economic. Migrants, it is often claimed, secure benefits that exceed any contributions. That is, of course, true of some nationals. It may be true of all nationals in as far as they rely on benefits secured from abroad through histories of exploitations. It is not then distinctive of migrants. Usually, in fact, evidence points, as noted earlier, to receiving countries securing overall net economic benefits.

⁂

It is time to look at the second features mentioned: the basic legal, political and social. These are the institutions of democracy, involving an effective judiciary, police, social justice, elections, free speech and debate. The United States border authorities thus ask such penetrating questions as: 'Do you intend to overthrow by force the government of the United States?' Years ago, probably in the 1950s, a British celebrity, Gilbert Harding, wrote, 'Sole purpose of visit.' Today, that would be an unwise quip.

There are further institutions in which much of a nation's public takes pride as part of its identity. In Britain, they include the NHS, the BBC, the national galleries and certain sporting events such as Wimbledon's tennis. The BBC's world-famous *Last Night of the Proms* can manifest an interesting display of differences in identity. Some groups wave the United Kingdom's Union Flag; the event is distinctively British. Others wave the EU flag, seeing the musical event as distinctly European. Maybe some feel that they must commit to being either British or European, but not both. Would-be migrants could well grow to value – some already do value – those institutions and events. As with the economic and political considerations, they may be migrating to reach a land where such institutions hold sway.

Let us assume that the would-be immigrants do hold to the receiving country's basic political, institutional and social values. Once within the land, they may affect outcomes for the nationals, by their free speech, their votes, while still acting within the nation's accepted ways. They are taking part in what is believed to be valuable by the receiving country: it is difficult to see, then, why a country should object to others joining in.

Of course, a country may become so crowded, infrastructures so burdened, that there are good practical reasons for entry limits. Witness the plight of the 700,000 Rohingya who fled from Myanmar into Bangladesh during 2017 – and the plight of the people of Bangladesh, unable to cope. Such examples, though, fail to justify increasing restrictions on migrants to prosperous countries where overall economically and socially there is no damage. Were there to be some such damage – perhaps loss of jobs to some nationals – we could then awkwardly ask, why give preference to the people already in a country – in effect, to the 'first come'? They have had that luxury, through good fortune, compared with the would-be migrants.

We should remember, though, that the would-be migrants have the relative luxury of drawing close to entering receiving countries, in contrast to more desperate people unable even to make the journey.

So far, we have seen no good reason for a general opposition to 'open borders' for liberal democracies, save practical ones of numbers and political security. That perhaps is because we have not yet dealt with the third consideration, the consideration which makes full use of the ideas of a people's attachment to 'their nation' and of the right to self-determination. Those ideas are next for discussion, as are the Tessa cases of desperate refugees and asylum seekers. Those ideas direct us to reflect that while migrants may benefit a society economically, may be law-abiding and may value the society's political and social institutions, there can yet be justified challenges to allowing their entry. Let us see.

9

Community identity:
nationalism and cosmopolitanism

'We Greeks invented democracy' is a mantra of some Greeks. In the United Kingdom, governments are inclined to speak of upholding 'British values', apparently ignorant of how for centuries such values included 'values' of injustice, sexual inequalities and trading in slaves – and today continues with acceptance of people sleeping rough, children attending school hungry and the poor unable to pay for access to justice. The United States' Declaration of Independence which is so highly valued – especially by the National Rifle Association, keen for citizens to be free to bear arms and hence for arms to be sold – coexisted with slavery for well over a century, with segregation existing in living memories, and with considerable evidence of continuing discrimination against African Americans and other minority groups.

Those examples show how nations typically have a sense of identity; yet what justifies that identity and how it can be so readily claimed, given the mishmash of groups within many countries, may baffle. We should certainly have some quibbles – if not some major challenges – regarding what constitutes that 'self' in the self-identity of a nation. Still, let us see how self-determination works in justifying (or not) a nation's treatment of outsiders, keen to settle in the nation's territory.

Self-determination covers a nation's cultures, social values and ethos. Physical borders could have contributed; the land, the climate, may affect the society, its cohesion and values. One's sense of any group identity – be it a nation, tribe or class – can affect how one behaves, dresses and the values espoused; they in turn can affect how overall that identity evolves. The concept of class, for example, can lead people into seeing the world as a ladder which needs to be climbed, otherwise they are deemed failures.

We should distinguish between a collective, a group of people brought together, almost accidentally remaining so, and a collective that has developed into a community. A community is more glued. The nation may have a 'national story' to which people adhere; there may be respect for the traditions of a monarchy, for ancestors who fought in the wars, for certain customs. 'Which cricket team you would support' was once offered by a British politician as a test for whether you are British. The national identity also makes reference to the economic, political and social features, already discussed, but the nationals may be attached to them 'from within', rather than impersonally. Recall the attached/detached distinction first encountered in Chapter 5.

Consider that odd entity, the United Kingdom. There are well-known myths linked to the English: those of St George and of Robin Hood. Robin Hood steals from the rich to give to the poor – repeatedly. St George kills the dragon, a one-off event, allegedly freeing the people from its tyranny. Lovers of A. E. Housman's poetry speak of its English character: its melancholy, understatement, 'stiff upper lip', appreciation of the countryside. That character may now be lost – in any case, may be largely mythical – but still features in the narrative, a nostalgic narrative, of England, a narrative that gains an association with Britain, then Great Britain, then Great Britain and Northern Ireland, then the United Kingdom. It is a narrative with which those citizens who lack the characteristics may yet associate, having grown up with it – and, of course, some citizens determinedly do not.

The 'identity' of the United Kingdom holds together the disparate nations of Scotland, Wales, England and, oddly, a portion of Ireland, namely Northern Ireland's six counties. We may wonder what those nations have in common. We may certainly wonder about the 'nation' of Northern Ireland given its history of violence between Catholics and Protestants, with the latter's gerrymandering of constituencies that ensured decades of significant discrimination against Catholics.

That people do identify, 'from within', with a nation's culture – with certain elements and features – is easily seen. They have grown up within the nation and are attached to its identity 'within', rather than being supportive of its features and values in a detached way, as outsiders may. Some people may argue that the best way to understand such commitment to a nation is by the markers that rule others out; outsiders, if allowed in, may 'pollute' the insiders – thus their entry should be restricted. That attitude towards national identity can adversely affect those living within who are seen as borderline nationals through, for instance, having immigrant parents or 'immigrant looks'.

We have here 'identity politics', with the concept of a nation and hence national sovereignty to the fore. The 'nation state' can be seen as a political institution, to avoid controversies over discriminations grounded in race, 'blood brothers' or ethnicity. Citizens of the nation state – its people – can legitimately express loyalty to that State while accepting that within, there exist different classes, cultures and creeds with differing interests. The reality and importance of the nation state, however understood, is, though, downplayed by promoters of cosmopolitanism. We should be wary; many of those promoters are not moved by cosmopolitanism's 'citizen of the world' humanitarianism. The most vocal may be pulling wool over humanitarian eyes, being mainly interested in encouraging international trade and international freedoms – and allowing the wealthy to transfer capital to less transparent jurisdictions.

Using Britain as an example, let us remember that *some* who call for open borders – at least for free movement of peoples within the European Union – and who ridicule the small-mindedness or alleged racism of nationalists have the luxury of being well-off, of residing in desirable areas, owning homes with large gardens, their children attending fee-paying schools. They would probably have very different attitudes were they living in high-density social housing, their children in some overcrowded and underfunded State schools where most cannot speak English, and where their way of life has been much altered – and all that without local consultation. Interestingly, in Britain, the highest proportions of asylum seekers, a BBC report (February 2019) established, are housed in some of the poorest areas of the country – and often in squalid conditions. Of course, some people in deprived areas enjoy the diversity – many are generous in welcoming strangers – but that does not justify liberals' smug dismissal of the disruptions to, the worries of, those badly affected.

It is worth our deploying imaginative resources here. Just picture – feel, sense, breathe in – a scene where what is familiar life for us is radically and adversely upset. How rational and calmly welcoming would we – should we – be? Indeed, it is notable that migrants to Britain of decades past can sometimes be as strongly opposed to new rounds of immigration as those families with generations of ancestors having lived in Britain.

The significance of national identity and self-determination was much manifested last century in calls for decolonization; people wanted to be governed by their 'own'. Identity-based secessionist movements continue within nations: Catalonia, Scotland, Quebec. Their aim is to secure or enhance self-determination, even if economically things could get worse. Those examples show how a large and diverse nation state, politically grasped, may be fragmented or fragmenting. Within a nation state, some even fear cultural appropriation; members of one cultural group feel threatened when another group uses their ideas, customs or – an example from Britain – even hairstyles. That styling desire to retain a separate identity can sit uneasily with the insistence that yet they are all British.

Let us, though, pretend that we are working with a nation state that is bound as one – at heart, one culture, one religion, one community, though with no doubt some internal differences and disputes. Although Chapter 8's economic and sociopolitical considerations failed to justify tightly closed borders, perhaps national identity and self-determination do the trick. Even if migrants would not upset the economic, political and basic social relationships – they may enhance them – may not a nation be justified in keeping itself as it is, without permitting entry, without even risking cultural dislocation, a fractured self? Many increasingly give the answer 'yes', even in countries that are typically thought of as humanitarian and internationally embracing.

Denmark has developed hostility to migrants, akin to the United Kingdom's hostile environment mentioned earlier. The Danish Minister for Immigration, Integration and Housing, Inger Støjberg, initiated the 2015 'asylum austerity' law whereby the police can strip-search suspected 'illegal immigrants', confiscate cash exceeding £700 or so, and compel them into refugee centres. The aim is to assert Denmark's 'Danishness'. In Sweden, many now see migrants as pitted against Swedish society. In the Netherlands, there is disquiet with Muslims and Moroccans; some call for their enforced sterilization. In such cases, the migrants are on the territory, but not accepted as existing within the society. Assimilation, it seems, is often undesired, but often so is promotion of multiculturalism.

CLOSED OR WELCOMING ARMS?

'National identity' could manifest connections weakly akin to the bonds of the family at home. The nation, likened to a 'self', should be at liberty to determine how it seeks to develop; it should be autonomous, self-governing. A nation's identity, as does a person's or a family's, rests on its continuity with a past and developments into the future. Some highlight the thought of a great eighteenth-century Irish statesman Edmund Burke, whose name is now associated with modern conservatism and a reverence for tradition: people will not look forward to posterity, who never look backward to their ancestors.

That a nation has a narrative – witness France's grief at Notre-Dame's fire and the determination to rebuild – is highly important to its identity. A prime example is that of the Jewish people who see themselves as continuous with struggle over thousands of years, culminating in the Holocaust horrors, leading to modern Israel as explicitly Jewish. The term 'holocaust', by the way, is etymologically associated with religious sacrifice; the Nazis could be perceived as making burnt offerings to God. Some Jews understandably prefer the term 'Shoah' – 'destruction', 'devastation' – for it lacks theological undertones. 'Holocaust', though, is so much better known than 'Shoah'; thus, I reluctantly use it in this work, sadly perpetuating its use.

Consider again a family in the family home: in this version, the would-be intruders – champagne-loving Clarissa and Justina who is just wanting a better life – are on the doorstep, the door slammed shut.

'Why won't you let us in?' Clarissa and Justina ask. To show respect for them as people, possessed of a common humanity, they merit an answer, one with at least some plausible relevance. Here is an answer: 'Our family may close its home, its garden, its domestic borders, to you who seek entry and residency, for there are valuable attachments within any family that others outside lack. You – to express it paradoxically – possess that lack.'

Defenders of the nation state may thus continue: 'So too, albeit not so obviously biologically so, there are attachments between compatriots that justify them discriminating against outsiders. A nation has evolved traditions, laws and infrastructures; it should be free to decide how things should continue, without intrusion of others, unless it so decides.'

Preference and great regard for my compatriots – for 'my family' – is grounded in a commonality regarding way of life. Even when a nation is culturally diverse, many identify with a national identity as just mentioned, despite being unable to express quite how it is constituted. Two questions now arrive. Does the value of 'this' identity, this attachment, carry weight? How does it stand with regard to change?

Which identities have we in mind? Few people today would argue for the merits of a Nazi identity – or of a culture that enforces female genital mutilation (FGM) or slavery. Curiously, millions apparently support nation states that insist women should be veiled in public. We do thus recognize some cultures, some ways of life, as superior to others. That is hardly surprising; some individuals, including those in powerful positions, have disgraceful beliefs – and cultures derive from individuals, their attitudes, beliefs and rituals. Let us not pretend otherwise. It is highly reasonable to protect a better culture or identity from a worse.

To give national self-determination a fair run for its money, we need to consider those nation states that have concern for the well-being of their nationals and do not offend what are taken to be typical human rights – and so forth.

NATIVES FIRST?

Suppose we have a nation – hereafter Nation – that has sufficient space and a thriving economy, one that would not be damaged by significant numbers of immigrants. Suppose Nation is possessed of a reasonable culture, grounding its people with a sense of identity.

Does that identity justify giving pride of place to its compatriots over strangers? The answer is: not obviously so. Freedom to associate (and hence exclude) may apply in the private world; but some roles, public roles, lack that freedom. Doctors usually are not permitted to choose whom to treat, within their competence, if offering a public service; photographers in the public world apparently, as noted in Chapter 3, cannot rightly refuse to work with homosexuals. Our Nation exists in the public world of nations; morally, should it be permitted to give preference to its nationals over others? Or should it have a detached stance?

Now, Nation could happily embrace outsiders – just as a family could choose to adopt children – with resultant risks. It is surely, though, morally permissible for Nation to retain its identity as it is by excluding others. It needs impartiality regarding its citizens – that is, those individuals within Nation – but not thereby an impartiality between those within and those without. Even if there is no national sense of identity, save for nationals respecting democratic procedures, those nationals surely have a right to determine for themselves whether to allow in others. That is Nation's right to self-determination. Of course, strangers seeking entrance could sincerely be in tune with Nation's way of life. If Nation firmly identifies itself as Catholic Christian – its citizens overwhelmingly rejecting abortion, supporting modesty in dress and keeping Sunday as special – can it have any good reasons for barring entry to migrants of the same beliefs and attitudes? Well, the answer may be 'yes'.

The answer may be 'yes' because Nation perhaps values the particular historical links and narrative of its nationals with the land, its developments and 'roots'. Compare with a couple's relationship, that of Stan and Samantha in love. As years move on, they change, yet they may change together. The history of their togetherness helps to bind them. Someone else with all the same features as Samantha would not be Stan's Sam, 'my Sam'. So, too, with the migrants; even though they hold similar beliefs and attitudes to Nation's nationals, they lack the historical development. Think of the significance someone may give to keeping the pocket watch in the family, passed down over generations: a replica however much the same 'wouldn't be the same'.

Suppose a group sets itself up on a small island, as self-sufficient, with membership limited to five hundred. Should the group be compelled to permit membership to a greater number? Could not a nation state be allowed to set itself a number, a total population? Such numerical limits may be highly irrational; but should that irrationality trump the group's freedom, the nation's freedom, to set the limits? Here we should remind ourselves, though, that there is no clear justification for the nation to claim ownership to its land; perhaps that should weaken its insistence on the numerical limit, space permitting, unless other factors come into play.

Consider a different island group, one that has been founded by people with similar values. They live harmoniously: perhaps they are held together by a religious belief; perhaps they have agreements to discuss Plato every day, to smoke cannabis, but never to drink alcohol. Should they be morally obliged to let others join? Further, if they are prepared to allow in others, why would it be wrong to discriminate amongst would-be entrants, favouring only those with similar beliefs and dispositions?

People differ in how they relate to others. Some prefer to confine themselves to the like-minded; others prefer to open up. It is far from clear that one should be considered morally superior, engaged in a better way of living, compared with the other. Paradoxically, they may both value diversity. Those keen to have welcoming open arms are valuing debate, different cultures in their land, yet they then lose encountering such diversities abroad; gradually all lands have their Starbucks and McDonald's, Italian quarters and China-towns, so to speak. Those with closed arms lack diversity at home, but when travelling abroad may be excited, amused, distressed by the differences; they value visiting diversity elsewhere.

BACK TO EARTH – WHERE IT IS TOO LATE

We have been pretending that models of the family, or of groups of friends, can be applied to the typical nation state and its identity. As Spinoza, a Dutch Jewish philosopher of the seventeenth century, emphasized, we should, though, look at people as they are, not as we should like them to be. In reality, our models have but weak application. The typical liberal state, in reality, is neither static nor homogenous.

Here is a temporal diversity: each State is, in one sense, a collection of migrants. Chapter 8 commenced by noting how generations replace generations. Some groups may seek to resist all change in – all challenges from – their future generations; but changes happen. Witness the attitudes of generations today; contrast with those of fifty years ago – in most Western societies. The 'national self' changes, usually gradually so and under influences of existing members. Attempted justifications for closed borders amount to little more than a preference for 'ours' and our future offspring, regarding any changes, over 'theirs' and their future offspring.

Internal dynamism is a particular disturbing challenge to nation states that explicitly ground themselves in race, ethnicity or religion, prime examples being Israel and Iran. Who knows, with generations ahead, whether Jewish Israel will retain any Jewish values? The descendants may all be Jews by the required ancestry, yet have no commitment to Israel as Jewish, maybe no interest in their Jewish history, maybe no respect for Jerusalem's Western Wall.

However extensive generational changes, yes, there remains the causal continuity and narrative of the nation; but, in view of the radical changes, we may wonder why that matters so much – and, indeed, whether it should matter. In the family, there may be some physical similarities over the generations, but would ancestors three generations ago recognize and warm to the values of their offspring these three generations later? It is far from clear that they would; it is far from clear that genetic links and historical narrative alone should count for much.

Keeping with Spinoza's recommendation to treat of how things are, let us note again how many nations lack the homogeneity of a substantial 'national identity', save as myth. Yes, the Texan and Californian and New York-ian may all speak of themselves as American, but think how much they differ. In Britain, we may muse upon how different the lives are for those in the wealthy suburbs of the South East from those in the towns of the North – from the farmers in East Anglia to the Muslims in Bradford and the Turks in North London. Is there really a national identity holding British nationals together, an identity which is more cohesive than that between the British and many outsiders wanting to join in? Well, many believe that there is such an identity – and a stab was made at understanding it earlier on. A narrative, even a mythical one, can develop and be one to which nationals are attached 'from within'. It is a moot point, though, how important such a narrative is – and how important it should be.

With generations coming and going, even within a closed-border nation, change, as already observed, is likely to occur. That it is likely does not justify hastening its happening. On the one hand, opening borders, encouraging international trade and free movement of labour, is often justified on the basis of increasing freedom of choice, yet – as seen – it has led to the same global companies dominating countries, reducing diversity. On the other hand, more openness between countries has also caused some countries with questionable values to change for the better, improving the rights of minority groups.

Returning explicitly to migrations: where we have nations that are already internally diverse, if some immigration is to be permitted, the entrance conditions surely ought not to discriminate against any groups already within the nation; to do so would be to disparage the internal groups – and that does not sit well with the detached stance of the State, a stance not to discriminate. Mind you, with such reasoning, we should conclude that Britain is disparaging the poor, for outsiders may secure relatively easily British residency if entering with sufficient wealth. At times, payment of £2 million can provide residency and £10 million citizenship, if other qualifications are met.

Finances apart, for Britain to refuse entry to Muslims, but to accept entry from Christians, would be, it could be argued, to disrespect the home Muslims. A caveat needs to be entered here: a country may value no one group coming to dominate all others; hence, immigration policies could be set to avoid such domination. Here is another caveat: however diverse, a country may still have some basic characteristics, more or less held by all and that do contribute to an identity. In Britain, the English language is manifestly the nation's language; should not migrants at least assimilate to the extent of learning English and using it in the public world? If they do not, their lives will not touch the nationals'; although within the territory, it is questionable whether they would be within the nation.

Suppose we accept that a nation has a right to determine who should enter – though recall that 'right' is somewhat mythical. The right may yet clash with other rights. We then have usual dilemmas of how to determine which right takes highest priority. Here are some clashes.

Consider the liberal states' love of democracy: would-be immigrants may argue that the approach of the State with borders is undemocratic. What justifies the State taking into account only voices of its nationals? That discriminates against outsiders.

Consider the liberal states' love of liberty: would-be immigrants may argue that their liberty to enter is severely restricted. True, within a country, there are many prohibitions – not to roam on private land, for example – but within public areas, why should not foreigners have that freedom of movement permitted to nationals?

Let us try equality: would-be immigrants may argue that they are lacking equality of opportunities by being excluded, opportunities which are available to nationals. Once again we may respond that internally many lack such opportunities; once again the retort can be, 'But what justifies discrimination on the basis of whether within or without a political border?'

Were we to allow open borders on grounds such as the above, we should remember that there would be open borders for all – not just for those in particular economic or life-preserving need.

CITIZENS OF THE WORLD OR CITIZENS OF NOWHERE?

Cosmopolitanism emphasizes the 'citizen of the world' mantra. The mantra comes to the fore when learning of people desperate to escape from oppressive regimes, poverty or war. Cosmopolitanism does not slip off the tongue so readily when thinking of those wealthy enough to buy citizenship as they please or global companies arranging affairs to avoid paying taxes. Support for cosmopolitanism is distinct from support for globalization. It has moral foundations: we have duties of respect towards all human beings; they have equal moral worth, regardless of attachments. That leads some to denigrate cosmopolitanism, making the silly claim that to be a citizen of the world is to be a citizen of nowhere.

The truth is that being citizens of the world does not mean that we may not also be citizens of elsewhere. 'Citizen of the world' is wrongly taken – maybe knowingly so – to imply that one ought not to possess greater loyalty to that State over this State. That is as foolish as saying that if you maintain respect for all human beings it follows that you cannot prefer being friends with some rather than with others.

There are 'strong' and 'weak' versions of cosmopolitanism. Strong versions may claim that, in our political stances, we should have as much worry for foreigners, thousands of miles away, who are starving or being tortured, as if our compatriots were undergoing such horrors here. That version can harmonize with calls for world government. In theory even strong cosmopolitanism may accept particular attachments to some over others; that is, a division of labour could be recognized. I look after my children; you look after yours. My State provides welfare benefits for its inhabitants; your State does likewise for yours. Of course, the reality is that not all parents – and, for our discussion, not all States – behave in that acceptable reciprocal way.

Weak cosmopolitanisms reduce our obligations towards those who are external to our State. There are negative duties – for example, not to pollute waters that will flow on to others – but, with the weakest, palest version of cosmopolitanism, no positive duties at all to provide water. A medium-to-weak version would insist on the existence of some positive duties, perhaps to make some minimal provision to satisfy basic needs, perhaps to provide adequate opportunities for others across the seas, even if not equality of opportunities.

The old, old question once again arises: how much morally ought we to sacrifice of our own lives – our own nation's good – to help others? Let us not, though – to deploy a well-worn slogan – allow the best to drive out the good. That we cannot, or will not, do everything that is morally required is no good reason for doing nothing at all.

Suppose we stay with nationalism, with nations possessing the right to choose who may enter and reside; suppose there is the perspective of a weak cosmopolitanism. Morality surely still demands that those nations help desperate migrants where they can – though where they can may sometimes best be 'over there', providing facilities, rather than entry 'over here'. That demand is a duty of care for the vulnerable. That demand also means that, when such migrants are on a nation's borders (within or without them), the government ought to allow entry and not deport. It is to follow the principle of *non-refoulement*; that is, refugees should not be returned to a place of persecution or ill-treatment, as per the 1951 Geneva Convention.

Even if we recognize that compassion and a sense of fairness point to our needing to grant entry to asylum seekers and refugees, there are well-rehearsed problems of unintended consequences. Others living in the source countries may be encouraged to flee, seeking refuge, possibly worsening things for them – the choppy seas – and probably for governments and some citizens of the receiving countries. Further, in our compassion for those fleeing, we are discriminating in favour of those able to reach our shores, against those who lack such wherewithal. To pretend that there is equality of opportunity to reach safe countries is akin to claiming that, in the United States, people are free to buy a Rolls-Royce, when that is no effective freedom at all for most people.

We cannot rescue all those in need and who are desperate. We choose how many and whom. We may even pay other countries to take responsibility for some; witness the deals done between European countries over the migrations from North Africa. Such payments smack of commodification of people; but are they any different from parents paying for others to look after their children – or grown-up children paying care homes to look after their parents? Such financial deals may be the best solutions available – though maybe still with some shabby motives. Countries may also engage in cherry-picking: one country opens borders to well-off, professional migrants, while paying other countries to take the poor and dispossessed. In 2018, Hungary's Prime Minister Viktor Orbán was explicitly prepared to cherry-pick, rejecting most refugees as 'Muslim invaders'.

In discriminating between entrants, we may offend the International Covenant on Civil and Political Rights, which prohibits discrimination on numerous grounds 'such as race, colour, sex, language, religion, political or other opinion, national or social origin, property, birth or other status'. Presumably it must mean when such features are irrelevant, for it may well be sensible for countries to discriminate on, for example, grounds of language spoken. In any case, the prohibition against discrimination is regarding all individuals 'within its territory and subject to its jurisdiction'. That gives considerable scope for argument over migrants who have entered a territory illegally and it is saying nothing about those attempting to enter. It is worth reminding ourselves, though, that what is morally right is not determined by what is legally permissible. Even though the law, national or international, does not oblige us to help people in distress, it may still be that morally we ought to help.

In considerations of open and closed borders, we see, as ever, values in conflict. There is a respect for other human beings, their human rights, their liberty, their opportunities – their autonomy, their self-determination. That is at the level of individuals. There is also recognition of the value of self-determination at the group level, whether it be thought of as a 'national', ethnic or community determination, with a shared past and shared aspirations – or just a motley collection. At both individual and community levels, there are dilemmas of what counts as fairness to outsiders and insiders.

Let us recall again: much of the discussion has assumed that nations possess rights to their territories, but that assumption is just that – an assumption, even a myth, a fable. To the extent to which there are no strong grounds for territorial rights, we may hesitate at any conviction that a nation state has rights to maintain closed borders. Borders should at least become pretty porous the more tenuous the territorial so-called legitimacy.

There is a poem 'Waiting for the Barbarians' (1898) by C. P. Cavafy, a perceptive, reflective and sensual Greek who spent most of his time in Egypt's Alexandria. In that poem, he writes of how we wait for the barbarians outside to come – and may then realize that there are no barbarians outside. What are we to do? he asks.

We may wonder whether it is part of the human condition always to see some others as 'other', as threats, as barbarians. In another Cavafy poem, 'Walls' (1897), it dawns on us that we are imprisoned; we slowly realize others – maybe we ourselves? – have built walls around us without our noticing. Those thoughts lead us into this chapter's coda.

WHICH IDEAL?

Suppose the world has no major tragedies, by way of earthquakes, wars and famine. Here are two versions of that world that deserve our reflection, our musings.

In one world, there are distinct nations, distinct races, with their own characteristics, stereotypes. Let us not investigate how they came about. The Italians are recognizably Italian, with excited arms flailing, speaking Italian; the Finns are polite and somewhat formal; the French speak glowingly of their cuisine and sense of culture – and so forth. Some countries, of course, are theocracies. People visit and find the diverse countries fascinating.

The international ethos is to keep the countries distinct; there is no globalization, no McDonald's in every country, no Google spread across every land, no wars of conquest. Maybe these nations, because they do not integrate much, tend to be unadventurous; maybe generations after generations do not, in fact, change things much. These nations may merit the undeserved quip, courtesy of Graham Greene's novel *The Third Man*, about Switzerland. The character Harry Lime comments: 'they had brotherly love – they had five hundred years of democracy and peace, and what did that produce? The cuckoo clock.'

Perhaps some countries remain completely closed. Within each country, people are basically getting what they want. No country judges itself superior to others; people are patriots, but do not treat other nations as barbarians.

In the other world, people have interchanged and integrated between nations so much so that distinctive cultures have been lost, diversity is radically reduced – and all nations are, so to speak, one. There is no racism, no ethnicity conflicts, no nationalism, because there are no distinct races, no ethnicities, no nationalisms; there are no clashes of cultures because, at heart, all is one culture. Perhaps all countries are akin to Switzerland.

How should we judge those two worlds? Do we have good reason to believe that one must be morally better than the other? How could we tell? Of course, if diversity, cultures, differences are to be valued – over the homogenous – as some of us believe, then the first world is much to be preferred. Regarding that world, it is, though, very difficult to believe that inhabitants would not in fact value some cultures more than others; once that arises, we have the beginnings of disrespects, of envy, of offence – leading to conflict. If we have differences, can such attitudes and evaluations be avoided? Ought they to be avoided? As Nietzsche commented in *Beyond Good and Evil* (1886):

> Isn't living assessing, preferring, being unfair, being limited, wanting to be different?

10

What's so good about equal representation?

Let us own up: height matters. We can tell that is true by some simple questions. How often do we hear the expression 'short and handsome'? Do many women, in search of romance, seek men shorter than they are? When are children urged not to walk tall, but to walk short? Both in language and in practice, we disparage the short and praise the tall. Metaphorically, psychologically and physically, the short look up to the tall; the tall look down on the short. The much-mocked Neanderthals were stooped and short. Black slaves (any slaves) would stoop before their owners; former slaves such as Harriet Tubman and Sojourner Truth would sit or stand very straight, in postures of defiance.

Typically, we are heightists. Short people are belittled.

On average, those taller than average do better than those shorter on average – and not just for reaching top shelves. The tall stand head and shoulders above others. Without a care, the tall may sit in front theatre seats, blocking views of those behind, especially the short. Even if, as some claim, heightism is on the wane, heightism as an historical example or as thought experiment – a 'let's pretend it holds' – serves as a provocation for questioning which discriminations, regarding gender and minority groups, should be neutralized when seeking 'equal' or fair representation.

Of course, even with heightism, matters are more complicated than suggested by the simple outline. We need to take into account that the average female is shorter than the average male – and that a few exceptionally tall women would prefer to have been shorter. We should recognize that some tall people are tall solely because of leg length, so even if in front seats, they pose no viewing problems to others behind. Indeed, they may suffer through lower limbs curled to fit within cramped spaces. Let us place such caveats to one side.

Although it is believed that height is mainly genetically deter-mined, nurturing over the many generations has probably had something to do with that determination. The higher the economic and social classes, the taller on average are members of that class. Perhaps one day differential factors could be evened out; but until that happy day comes, we need paradoxically – and let us note the paradox for future reference – to become 'height blind', while also ensuring that shorter heights receive fairer representations amongst the powerful and successful. Only then will the world be fit for all, regardless of what nature and nurture have delivered by way of stand-ing and sitting distances of heads from the Earth's surface.

WHO SHOULD REPRESENT US?

In democracies with constituencies, counties or other designations of areas – with representatives to be elected – there is no good rea-son to believe that a resulting legislative body would contain a wide spread of expertise or awareness of different ways of living; there is no good reason to believe that the elected representatives would be in the same proportions and groups as members of the electorate. It is highly likely that most of those elected would have silver tongues in common; many perhaps, as discussed in Chapter 2, would have motives solely for political power. We cannot easily rid politics of such tongues and motives, but at least we ought to seek a rep-resentational structure that is *fair* – so many argue.

For fairness, relevant parliaments, congresses, senates – the legislative chambers – need memberships that mirror the people represented. How detailed that mirroring should be – to extend to heights? – is moot. Later, we shall see how equal representation works – indeed, fails to work – with the democratic ideal; but we need first to be clear about the aim.

Fairness, it is argued, is not just to do with the franchise and voting procedures, but also with how distributions of differences amongst the represented relate to differences amongst the representatives. Using our heightism tale, surely we need short people in the chambers to represent short people – and, for that matter, tall people to represent the tall. Only the short can truly represent the short, for only the short are aware, through direct experience, of the social problems in being short; only the short have a proper interest in overcoming those problems. The same can be said with regard to the tall, though their problems are minor compared with those of the short.

⫸

Suppose we took seriously the above demand for equal representation for those of different heights. Suppose that currently in the American Congress and the British House of Commons representatives fail to represent fairly by way of mirroring the various heights in the populations; suppose, as is probably true, that relatively there is a greater proportion of the tall in those institutions. Should we fret? Should we be calling for 'short-only' candidate lists or encouraging the selection of the short, *because they are short*, as candidates?

That proposal, to deal with short-ist under-representation, would strike people as bizarre – as bizarre as demanding mirror images in the legislature of the general population's proportions of the red-headed, whisky-drinkers and lovers of yellow socks. The demand is manifestly silly; there is no good reason to believe that such groups have any significantly distinctive relationships, experiences or expertise with regard to public policy and life in general. True, the worry about short-ist under-representation is not quite so silly as those examples; perhaps the tall have an unfair slight advantage over the short in being selected as candidates.

That we can group things in different ways, and hence need to determine the relevant groupings for any project, is well shown if we reflect upon an ancient Chinese classification of animals, a whimsical taxonomy within the 'Celestial Emporium of Benevolent Knowledge', playfully 'discovered' by the Argentine writer Jorges Luis Borges, the distinct groups including: belonging to the emperor; embalmed; those trained; suckling pigs; mermaids; fabulous ones; stray dogs; those included in this classification; those that tremble as if mad; innumerable ones; those drawn with a very fine camel-hair brush; et cetera; those that have just broken the flower vase; and those that, at a distance, resemble flies.

At least the whisky-drinkers do have a distinctive and recognizable commonality in one small area, one that could bring to bear an interest in how taxation policies affect whisky production and consumption. The whisky-drinkers, as whisky-drinkers, though, are unlikely to have distinctive wider contributions to make to public policy; indeed, concerns over whisky taxation could perhaps be better represented by those without any personal whisky-drinking bias.

The above silly suggestions are to remind us that we need to assess the (alleged) sensible cases of proportionality requirements amongst representatives; and that requires us to identify which populations or domains are the relevant reference bases.

Consider the United Kingdom. Should we be outraged by the vast over-representation of white people (about 87 per cent) in the United Kingdom compared with the 18 per cent of white people in the world's population? Or should we be outraged by the vast under-representation of white people in the world's population compared with the United Kingdom? Should we be worrying about the disproportionately large number of non-white people compared with white people, full stop – or the vast number of North Americans compared with Estonians? Consider married men: perhaps we should be distressed about the huge over-representation of women amongst their marriage partners compared with men.

The numerical inequalities just cited do not worry people, for the nation United Kingdom and 'the World' are unlike bodies, such as governments, formed to represent members. Worries arise when we have in our sights parliaments and congresses that expressly exist to represent people. There is roughly a 50:50 proportion of men and women in Western societies and so, it is argued, in political power there should be roughly that same division. In Britain, as noted, roughly 87 per cent are white, with a mixture of Black Minority Ethnic groups (BMEs) labelling the remainder. People conclude that there should be similar proportions in Parliament. That conclusion immediately brings forth a couple of worries.

'BME' applies to a wide range of disparate groups. The very term 'BME' strikes some as pejorative or dismissive because it lumps together the groups; one group's interests do not necessarily coincide with another's. Appropriate proportions, within the BME group, could lead to an insistence that there should be in Parliament, say, just one Pakistani, one Indian, perhaps two West Indians, but one third of a Peruvian. Some minority groups' representation could be 'rounded up' to one member each. Of course, any minority groups, allowed only a few representatives, could well have feelings of grievance: 'We only merit a teeny bit of political concern.' Further, if BMEs need such representational subdivisions, then the population of white people would need subdivisions into Polish, Welsh, Czech et al. Should we divide further and in different dimensions – religious belief, age group and sexual orientation?

The frequent focus on representation to ensure gender equality can distract from debate over how coarse or fine a grain is needed for fairness more generally, though even with solely the gender worry, new problems are arising as transgender matters come into view – as discussed in Chapter 14.

DIFFERENTIALS OF REPRESENTATIVES

Putting the fineness of the grain to one side, we return to the question of why we should be so concerned about mirroring in political representation certain diversities in the population represented. Here come some reasons.

The first is that possession of particular areas of knowledge, understanding or skills can be valuable amongst representatives. Summarize them as 'talents'. In the United Kingdom, it is currently bemoaned that there are no elected MPs with significant scientific backgrounds; that some MPs are medical doctors is praised. Were that a consistent line to adopt – of bringing distinctive talents into the chambers – we should aim to have some architects, manual workers and even philosophers amongst elected representatives, assuming that they bring talents relevant to passing good laws, holding governments to account, and promoting a flourishing society. Members of certain ethnic groups, because being of those groups, could bring distinctive knowledge. If, though, right proportions also matter, we should at best hope for one-thousandth of a neurosurgeon as MP.

It is reasonable to think that women on average (and assume the 'average' caveat is implicit hereafter) have distinctive talents, different from men's. That justifies objections to parliaments dominated by men. The reasonable belief that men and women differ in talents has at times been opposed as sexist: men and women, it has been argued, should usually have equal numbers present in parliaments (and indeed in most occupations) because they have the same abilities and talents – apart, presumably, from child-bearing ones.

Reasoning grounded on talent differentials differs from the

reasoning that different groups have different interests requiring different representations. That is surely true: compared with most others, the disabled may be more interested in transport access; mothers in child-rearing; Jews in synagogue security.

To underline the two different lines of reasoning – the 'talent'; the 'interests' – consider the call for more scientists as MPs. That may be to bring their scientific expertise in the evaluation of evidence to the relevant chamber or it may be to promote the interests of scientists by ensuring that their voice is heard – perhaps when calling for increased funding of scientific research.

Although there are distinctive interests of groups, it does not follow that they can *only and best* be represented by people with those interests. Legislative bodies can act in the best interests of a diverse society without needing to be similarly diverse; they may listen to the relevant groups – to the scientists about underfunding, the disabled about lack of transport – and may even be better advocates for them. A reasonable response, though, is that the interests may not be sufficiently well represented without the vivacity of direct experience – of, for example, getting around when mobility allowances have been cut or walking home, scared of street gangs. Direct experiential evidence can be a strong component of the required 'talent'; only someone who has been sleeping on the streets in the rain could bring that experience to the fore.

Tying in with the 'interests' line of reasoning, even if a group's interests could be well represented by members outside that group, the general belief may be otherwise – and not to have the relevant group self-represented could alienate members of that group from the legislative chambers. Increasing the representation of under-represented minorities may signal to younger members that their voices can be heard, that there are pathways to political power.

The above is a consideration that looks to the future. A further consideration, oft cited, looks to the past; past discriminations against women and certain minority groups account for the current under-representations. Past customs and laws encouraged the belief that only certain occupations were appropriate to women and that, once married, women should relinquish certain employments. Many myths have, indeed, been encouraged: witness the Rodgers and Hammerstein 1951 musical *The King and I*. The King sings of how a girl should take on the quality of honeyed blossom for one man; the man is not to be confined in such a singular way.

As well as the customs and assumptions that manifest prejudice, there are unconscious prejudices. For decades, Western orchestras were dominated by male players; but, it is said, when new applicants were heard behind screens, gender hidden, the number of women considered fine players for prestigious orchestras quickly increased – though, interestingly, harpists are still usually women and trombone players men. Although biological differences no doubt are relevant in many arenas, cultural context and learning environments can alone determine some significant differences between men and women. With regard to mathematics scorings, the gender gap is greatest in Turkey, with men on average doing far better than women; yet the position is reversed in Iceland.

Returning to legislatures, even if there are no prejudices against women, some would point out how certain features of the work, features unnecessary for good legislation, lack appeal for many women. In Britain, the House of Commons may still have the atmosphere of a 'men's club', with difficult working hours and conditions for women who are bringing up children.

In as far as positive discrimination is deployed to overcome historical unjustified discriminations or to combat feelings of alienation or disempowerment within under-represented groups, new problems come into sight: the approach may undermine the confidence of those benefiting ('I wasn't selected on my merits'). The approach, although seeking fairness between groups, can be unfair to individuals within the majority dominant groups, some individuals being discouraged from seeking the positions in question. As ever, competing considerations have to be weighed; it is a myth that there is a clear-cut 'right' answer.

᪥

Let us deal a little more with the 'proportionate' feature. Were it really held that elected MPs should be representative of the general population, with the requirement being that overall they fully give voice to the population's diverse interests, then the vast number of current MPs whose main occupation has been politics would need radical culling to make way for the non-political. We should certainly need some serving criminals, some unemployed and some of the extremely poor as representatives. In those cases that would become self-defeating, for they would then be released, employed and reasonably well-off. Perhaps we could settle for, as being good enough, those who have once had direct experience of being imprisoned, unemployed or poor. That may not help; those representatives may quickly forget their past and identify with their privileged new colleagues.

Even when we do believe that members of the represented groups need to be among the representatives, it is odd to demand that they be so in the same proportions. Why assume that the talents or direct experiences of a group, important for the legislative chamber, have an importance that matches their proportions in the population? Why assume that to overcome a group's feeling of alienation, its representation should match the relevant proportion in the population?

DEMOCRACY, DISTORTIONS AND DUETS
What of democracy? There are the obvious difficulties of ensuring that groups of appropriate individuals stand as candidates in the

right proportions – even that relevant groups have at least some members standing. Further, a candidate is likely to belong to many groups that merit representation. Are we to say that – to offer a fictional character – Erskin MP is in parliament to provide the right representation for male gays, but not to be representative of those other groups to which he belongs: say, the West Indians and single parents?

That silliness should remind us that it is a mistake to encourage electorates to believe that they can only be properly represented by members of their group. The inarticulate would need, for example, to be represented by the inarticulate. If mirroring is thought essential, then it would seem to be, as mooted earlier, on the basis that different groups have different interests, but paradoxically that they do not differ with respect to how their interests should be represented. It could lead to the bizarre conclusion that someone starting with dementia should be represented by someone starting with dementia rather than by a doctor with knowledge and experience of how best to treat such individuals. Further, representatives being elected to represent the interests of their particular group may be in tension with the aim that representatives should be working for the common good.

Whatever mirroring may be thought desirable, it sits uneasily with the democratic ideal that people should be free to stand for election and voters should be free to elect whom they prefer. To put it controversially, how could it be ensured that the electorate gets matters 'right' by electing an appropriate diversity of representatives? Mirroring representation, be it minimal or proportional, comes into obvious conflict with the democratic ideal of outcomes in some way being determined by majority votes.

Consider a thought experiment, based on the worries about women's under-representation, not yet 50 per cent, in the British House of Commons. Avoiding complexities of party affiliation, suppose in every constituency there were a variety of individual candidates, many men, many women. Would something have gone wrong if only the women were elected? Or only the men? That, after all, would be via a majority democratic vote. Even if each individual voter wanted the eventual 'right' gender distribution in Parliament, each can only determine one vote. Compare: no individual wants to be crammed standing on the train, yet the behaviour of individuals ends up with that outcome. No car is a traffic jam, but the collective may be such a jam.

Before going along whole-heartedly with that reasoning, we need to consider to what extent conditions for the input of the democratic vote may already be unfairly distorting. Historically, for many voters in Britain the choice has often been solely between men as candidates. To what extent does that manifest an unfair distortion and one that continues to influence which candidates stand today? One voiced claim is that the current position results, in part, from times when women were excluded in various ways and by various means from public life. Women-only shortlists, therefore, are deliberate but justified distortions to combat previous distortions.

Suppose, though, that a typical democracy, with roughly 50:50 women and men, has a parliament, senate or congress with representatives also in that 50:50 proportion. Do we have any good reason to believe that the country would be better off – lives overall would go better – compared with a country where the representatives did not mirror the male/female proportions in the population? The answer may be 'yes', if only because (it could be argued) the 50:50 representation is fairer. To return to an earlier challenge, how, though, can a democracy stand as a democracy if such fairness is required from voters who, say, vote such that more men get elected than women?

◦||◦

Pretend that we could have, in some way, an equal starting point between the sexes, such that the outcome may justifiably be understood as reached by fair processes. How could such processes operate? Here is one version, a revision based on the current party system in Britain. The revision is the following. Within each constituency, every party that is standing needs to offer a duet. Each party, instead of having one candidate – who (usually) will be either man or woman – always has two candidates: one man, one woman. Voters still have a single vote, but at least they have the freedom, whatever their party affiliation, to vote for their preferred gender. The winning party is the one whose overall vote (votes for the man and woman combined) is the highest. Which candidate of the winning party is elected is the one with the higher vote within that duet.

Although the proposed system above would give every voter the chance to vote for their preferred gender, it would not remotely guarantee right proportionate numbers in the parliament. In that position of fairness between the sexes, there is still no guarantee of the desired proportionate outcome. Should that worry us?

That guarantee of equal representation by way of output could be generated – by doubling up. Of the winning party, both members of the duo secure election. That would lead to a new set of unfairnesses: because party X wins (having the total duet vote), the man of the X duo is elected, even though he has fewer votes than each member of another party's duo. Voters would be ensnared within the dimension of having to vote for a gendered duet package and not just the usual package of a party's manifesto.

Obviously the duet proposal is both impractical and theoretically dubious. Further, if such manipulations caught on with regard to gender, other groups could surely rightly demand attention; each voter should always have the opportunity to vote for Muslims, the transgendered – and even analytical philosophers.

Returning to how a legislative should take into account the different interests, talents, direct experiences of different groups, it is folly to look to bodies that consist of members voted in by elections across the population. Where British democracy potentially has the edge over, for example, the United States is in its possession of, strange as it may sound, an *unelected* second chamber, the House of Lords. That observation is not to defend the current ways in which the Lords membership is determined, though, as it happens and by some degree of luck, quite a few of its members bring distinctive expertise to bear that has often improved legislation, or at least prevented some disasters. That valuable feature suggests that a second chamber should be deliberately designed whereby different groups have a right to be represented – from the medical profession to the business community to unions to the academic to the unemployed to the poor – to the religious. Within those groups, there could be elections regarding who should represent them, but ultimately – as we encountered with Plato's considerations in Chapter 1 – good government is not guaranteed by the operation of a democratic universal franchise. To put it paradoxically, the legislature of a democracy requires significant non-democratic inputs.

BURDENED WITH BIOLOGY?

The above arguments and reflections have cast doubt on the value of mirror representation within elected chambers and, even if once achieved, have cast doubt regarding its stability, unless democracy is manipulated in undemocratic ways. Calls for mirror representation, though, are often motived, as has been touched upon, by the recognition that many features of today's society – be they to do with gender inequalities or poor representations of minority groups – derive from past injustices, injustices that demand correction. Let us not, though, pretend all such differences are *bound* to be the result of injustices such as those of unfair discriminations. There existed no social manipulations by different power bases which ensured that for millennia only women could become pregnant.

Many injustices do, though, arise through social conditions, cultures, the ethos, and they, it is argued, should be changed. The motivation is to overcome sex and racial discriminations. In the United Kingdom, the 'sex' terminology arises from the Sex Discrimination Act 1975, but through subsequent legislation the term's meaning would seem at heart to be that of today's 'gender'. Gender and race, it is said – as opposed to biology and genes – are 'social constructs'. The difference is between the nurture (the social side) and nature (the biological side). That way of looking at things exhibits a strange belief that cultures and societies and ethnic groupings do not derive from human nature and its interaction with environments. The prejudices against women, their lack of political power over the centuries, presumably arrived through the nature of men and women and environmental impingings – just as the attempts to overcome those prejudices arise through the nature of men and women and environmental impingings. From such obvious truths, it should be emphasized, nothing follows about how, 'therefore', women are in part to blame for their historical subjugation or that women ought not to seek to effect changes.

To whatever extent outcomes result directly from biology, cultures and environmental impingings – be they social constructs or physical reality – we can rightly argue that such outcomes are not how things ought to be, morally, socially, politically. We should then work on those that we can change for the better, though tempered with ensuring that any instruments deployed to effect change are morally acceptable. Suppose a drug were to be developed that would give women and men all the same characteristics, even if maintaining their reproductive differences. Who would think that a good idea? Perhaps societies could aim to reproduce and modify in such a way that no differences exist between people regarding skin colour and ethnic looks. Would we really believe that to be a good idea? Recall the discussion of such anguishing matters in Chapter 6.

There is a puzzle here, for of course our reasonings about such matters and what we believe to be morally justified – and not – are also outcomes of biology and the impingings of the environment. That gives rise to the deep metaphysical perplexity of how anything can be justified as the result of a moral awareness or, indeed, 'good' reasoning. In Chapter 5, we encountered a related perplexity, when considering a person's identity and responsibility. Those mysteries pervade our lives, though our eyes usually remain closed. We continue, then, to assume that we can make use of 'good' reasoning, even here – and raise one more worry about equal representation.

BURDENED BY FAIRNESS – OR BY GDP?

Just as legislative chambers are apparently missing out on considerable talent because of the lack of women – and minority groups – so too is business. To what extent that is true depends on the business. A company's boards, higher managements and so forth typically aim for the company's success. To maximize relevant talents within the company is obviously sensible, but that has nothing directly to do with wanting the boards, higher management or workforce more generally to be representative bodies of the population with regard to gender or minority groups. In fact, who or what are the corporate boards meant to represent? If representation is important, then ensuring sufficient representatives of a company's workforce on executive boards might secure better results than ensuring a 50:50 gender division.

Boards that have increased the number of women as members have led, some claim evidence, to the businesses doing much better. Hence, it is argued, other boards must also appoint more women and they will do much better. That, of course, is a fallacious argument – and not just with its generalization – for in some cases it may be a 'zero-sum' game. One company, by appointing more women, does better than competitors; but if competitors also then appoint more women, both companies may be back to square one.

Of course, diversity in executive leaderships may have an intrinsic value, as it may amongst mathematicians, engineers and physicists. Yes, diversity may be good, though we should again wonder why gender diversity requires a 50:50 division. Further, let us reflect: there are few demands that there should be equal numbers of women and men amongst street cleaners, on building sites and, indeed, in prison.

The argument for equality of gender representation is not just for this or that woman to be fairly treated in her attempts to climb the greasy pole, but has as basis the belief that if women more generally are not attempting it much, then 'something must be wrong' and 'something must be done'. A paradox here – at the group level – is that, on the one hand, highlighting women's differences from men, some people claim that boardrooms, politics and the media are missing out on women's distinctive talents, yet on the other hand, any suggestion that other differences between men and women might justifiably explain why women do not have similar positions to those of men is typically rounded upon as sexist.

Given the biological differences between men and women, it might just be the case that on average more women genuinely prefer bringing up their children, in preference to business careers, than do men. If that is so, while we may argue that men just as much as women should have opportunities for raising children, we do not therefore have grounds for insisting that, if fewer men than women take up those opportunities, then something has gone wrong and we must 'correct'. If – if – some women genuinely prefer their own-child-minding, why object – unless we think such own-child-minding is unworthy and it would be better to employ someone else to mind the child, while the woman worked in, for example, a call centre or, let me mischievously suggest, took a job minding someone else's child?

To say that is not to imply that women who want careers should be discouraged or that girls at school should have subject choices different from those of boys. It is to point out that the ethos that women with young children should have paid employment can be oppressive.

An economy is deemed to be flourishing when GDP is increasing, when more people are in work, producing more goods and services. Its calculation is complicated, but scepticism of it and the related Gross National Product (GNP) is displayed by those who instead measure a country's well-being with a Happiness Index (also dubious). A scepticism was shown by Robert F. Kennedy, when running for the United States presidency in 1968. He noted how the GNP includes the production figures of

> air pollution and cigarette advertising, and ambulances to clear our highways of carnage. It counts special locks for our doors and the jails for the people who break them... It counts napalm and counts nuclear warheads and armored cars for the police to fight the riots in our cities. It counts Whitman's rifle and Speck's knife, and the television programs which glorify violence in order to sell toys to our children. Yet the Gross National Product does not allow for the health of our children, the quality of their education or the joy of their play. It does not include the beauty of our poetry or the strength of our marriages, the intelligence of our public debate or the integrity of our public officials... it measures everything, in short, except that which makes life worthwhile.

The ideal sought should be that of flourishing lives for all. A requirement for people to flourish is not that women and men must have the same inclinations for child-rearing, high-flying careers or political power; of course, it also does not mean that women and men should therefore have unequal opportunities. People do, though, seek to flourish, to live well, in different ways.

Consider parenthood. Parenthood is often promoted through maternity and paternity leave; the doubtful assumption must be that both parents have similar wants. Suppose a family with one parent earning and one parent lacking paid employment, yet happily bringing up the children. Policies in Britain encourage both parents to be in paid employment, both receiving taxable earnings. They now need to pay childcare providers; more taxable earnings are generated. Are the policies aimed at what is best for family life? May the motivation be – dare I cynically suggest? – to increase GDP, tax revenues and employment figures?

Further, should special provisions for parenting take priority over, say, special provision for the childless, man or woman? The childless, to flourish, may require careers undamaged through taking long breaks for travel, voluntary work, even champagne drinking. We flourish in different ways; different groups, for various reasons, typically secure more opportunities and more flourishing than others. Societies muddle through, selecting some groups to promote over others; but which merit that promotion? Which discriminations are fair? Which equalities are worth seeking – be they sexual, educational, or even by way of monetary income and outcome regarding quality of life?

Demands for equal treatment sit uneasily with free markets. As seen, if people are to be free to vote as they want, then that conflicts with any patterned gender equality amongst representatives. So too with wealth. If people are to be free to choose which entertainment they most prefer, then it just may happen that the highest paid are women – not particularly because of special talents, but just because a larger proportion of the public buys tickets to see them. Arms would go up – well, the celebrities would be up in arms – if the State intervened to prevent such wealth discrepancies.

If – if – free markets should be allowed to act in that way, such that people are free to purchase as they want, however irrationally, then why should not boardroom choices also be on the basis of free choices? Neo-liberalism, with its free markets, has no inbuilt intrinsic preference for fairness. That lack of fairness may be a good reason to challenge the myth of the goodness of neo-liberalism – to be seen in Chapter 15.

11

Human ~~duties~~ – *oops* – human rights

The movie opens with celestial scenes of blue skies, fluffy white clouds and heavenly music. From those clouds, speech bubbles bubble forth, turning into the mouths of eminent leaders of religion, State and international bodies, voicing stern pronouncements, over a background of repeated whispers of 'Life is sacred':

> *Everyone has the right...*
> *to life, to life, to life, to life;*
> *to liberty, liberty, liberty;*
> *to security, security, security;*
> *to freedom from slavery, slavery, slavery...*

A male choir sings over the scene:

> *No one shall be subjected to torture;*
> *No one to cruel, inhuman or degrading treatment or punishment.*

A female choir, in harmony, sounds to the fore with:

> *All are equal before the law;*
> *All are entitled without any discrimination...*
> *to equal protection of the law.*

This is no discordant cacophony – the words and music hold in a beautiful harmony – but as those words and music continue on a loop, the camera slowly scans across and down to here on Earth, zooming in upon individuals, their faces coming into focus, displaying distorted lips, sunken cheeks, pleading eyes. Discord arises.

Here is a family, cowering under an umbrella, as the whines of nearby war planes increase; the umbrella proclaims: PROTECTING THE RIGHT TO LIFE. The camera pans across to another land, thousands suffering from malnutrition, with weakened cries of, 'But we have the right to food and water.' The view swerves and we are face to face with some prisoners shrieking from torture, their captors mockingly waving banners sporting in big letters: THE RIGHT NOT TO BE TORTURED.

From those scenes of desolation and despair, burst forth shining cities. There, the camera's eye peers through windows of a medical centre, revealing vast arrays of technology – all in the service of keeping some babies alive, including some in pain, with no chance of meaningful lives. Then we encounter an elderly woman, her face distraught, pleading for the right to die, yet a banner flutters across the screen, swirling around her fragile body with the words, 'There is no right to die.' Gradually, we become aware of excited voices of a boisterous party, popping champagne; the scene then glides us, as if in luxury cars, away from streets where people are sleeping rough to a countryside estate. There we find corporate leaders, government ministers and upper-quartile celebrities, laughing and chatting about the latest wheezes for investing offshore, the next fashion show from Gucci and the quickest way to get work permits for their staff – or staff without permits – as more bubbly flows.

᪶

What should we make of those incongruities – so many incongruities – that could be multiplied across the Earth? Although the above introduces incongruous types of incongruity, reminding us of how widely the concept of incongruity applies, this chapter's attention is directed at those that explicitly relate to 'human rights' and especially the political and global dimension to such rights.

There are numerous international declarations, government policies and statements by worthy bodies that set out human rights, both at international and national levels. The existence of such statements, policies and declarations is not in dispute. That most governments commit themselves to abiding by human-rights proclamations is not in dispute. What also is not in dispute is that millions of people suffer, seemingly in violation of those rights. What is not in dispute is that umbrellas and banners sporting 'right to life', 'right not to be tortured', as protection are no protection at all for the families cowering from bombs, torture, hunger or disease.

Have the fine words of 'rights' helped the suffering millions to escape their suffering? The 'human-rights' declarations, some cynics point out, have led to well-heeled government-sponsored groups flying between conferences, giving birth to more and more policies, statistical reviews and wringing of hands.

Philosophers debate the nature of rights; earnestly do they debate, discuss and analyse. A hundred years ago, the discussion might have taken place while sipping glasses of sherry or port in ivory towers; today the imbibing is probably straight from bottles of craft beer in towers not so ivory. We overhear some comments: 'Of course, of course, when we say that people have a right to life, we mean not that it is wrong to kill, but that it is wrong to kill unjustly; and when we talk of killing unjustly, we are saying nothing about letting people die. There is a big conceptual distinction: killing differs from letting die.'

They would agree that the outcome is the same, whether killed or allowed to die: the results are dead people. With killings, though, there are agents, the killers, who must take responsibility for their actions, if intended. When people are allowed to die, it is not so obvious that there are agents who are responsible for the deaths.

Here is a related discussion, when a nation is pursuing war or intervening against an oppressive regime. 'Yes, we know that there will be many deaths and injuries to numerous people – "collateral damage", as politicians and the military deem them to be, somewhat insensitively so – but we the perpetrators are not intending to kill; we, rather conveniently, merely foresee that deaths and injuries of innocent civilians will occur as unfortunate side effects of our intended actions.'

There the observation relies, in part, on a distinction between innocent civilians and combatants, the latter who may be accepting their liability to be targeted. The intervening nation intends to defeat the opposing regime by harming the regime's combatants; it does not intend to harm the civilians – though much civilian harm, it is known, will result. The outcome of suffering and death is the same, whether intended or foreseen.

Another philosopher, in a different discussion, without any unease, insists that prisoners being tortured is a great pity. 'Yes, the prisoners certainly possess the right not to be tortured, but that does not entail a duty on us to prevent such torture from occurring; it does not even entail that we should refuse to hand over prisoners to countries where torture is likely.'

Another philosopher, swept along by his own thoughts, chips in, contemplating those in considerable pain, wanting to die: 'True, individuals have a right to life and liberty, to live their lives as they want, so long as not harming others, yet it fails to follow that they have a right to choose when to die. Even if it is morally permissible and legal for individuals to take their own lives, it is not thereby morally permissible and legal for others to aid them.'

Such distinctions may cause cynical reactions by those under the threat of bombs, malnutrition or torture – or, indeed, of having impotently to live on in pain because no one is permitted to hasten their sought-for death. They suffer amidst the chatter.

Here is the basic reflection: it is all very well to speak of human rights, but how does that help, if there is no pressure by way of human duties? That is usually read as pointing to how those who proclaim their rights should recognize their duties – and that is, indeed, true – but here we are talking of the duties that others have to enable those with the rights to exercise their rights. 'Rights' talk is easy, if there is relative silence about the duties to protect those rights – and to whom those duties belong. In fact, in the Universal Declaration of Human Rights (1948), the sole reference to duties occurs in Article 29, with the rather obscure and unhelpful, 'Everyone has duties to the community in which alone the free and full development of [each person's] personality is possible.'

WITCHES, RIGHTS AND RICHES

Once people believed in witches and witchcraft. Some still do; witness the Nigerian children maltreated, even killed, for being witches. Witch-finders of the past may have argued about the most reliable means for spotting witches and, when spotted, what should be done. No doubt today's seekers of witches have similar discussions. We can readily imagine – and it may well be true – that witch-doctors would discuss and debate how their cures worked against witchery. In Nigeria, Tanzania and elsewhere, probably they still do. We – non-believers in witches – may be interested in those witch-laden practices, their sources and continuation, without any commitment to the existence of witches. We see no sign of witches. We, with no axe or axes to grind, may treat the talk of witches as but an interesting use of language, a way of looking at the world, yet bearing no more on the reality of witches than our discussions of the Greek and Roman gods bear on the reality of those gods.

Now turn to human rights. People suffering poverty, torture or other cruelties of life hear talk of 'human rights'; but they see no signs of such in their lives. It would be understandable for them to be as sceptical of the existence of human rights as we are of witches. We, the fortunate reflective ones, we with riches compared with those desperately suffering from famine or war, may engage in linguistic manoeuvres with the words 'human rights', yet some of us – or those government ministers that issue policy statements on human rights – may have no serious belief in their existence. Looking around the world, many of us, even speakers of 'human rights', may be as sceptical of the existence of human rights as of the existence of witches.

Let us peer more closely. The expression 'human rights' has the air of matters extremely grand, suggesting that all human beings are cloaked in shining armour, cloaked in virtue of being human or with an umbrella shield that deflects injustices. Human rights are, of course, distinct from those rights that people may freely grant to others. I may grant you the right for a month to use my laptop, drink my wine or take my goat for a walk. I should normally then be in the wrong to stop you from doing those things during that period. That wrong suggests that there is a right to justice; now, that was not a right I granted to you. That is a right of morality.

Legal rights often differ from rights grounded in morality. Legally, I may be within my rights to take court actions against retailers who sell me out-of-date chocolates, yet morally I have no such rights and morally I ought perhaps not to exercise that legal right because they are small businesses teetering on the brink. That the moral and the legal are distinct – and that moral rights and legal rights are distinct – does not mean that there lacks overlap. In most countries, it is against the law to kill another person, save as the sole means of self-defence; and most people acknowledge that such killing is morally wrong.

Domestically, we have a vast range of legal rights: employment rights, welfare rights, rights to be forgotten and so forth. Those rights obviously derive from laws enacted by relevant parliaments, congresses, senates. Whether those laws are morally acceptable is a distinct question, concerning, in part, how they came about – for example, whether by some form of democratic consent – and whether some such are necessary for society to flourish. At the domestic level, the law often institutes rights as instruments of social utility to help with social cohesion.

UNIVERSAL HUMAN RIGHTS

Once the emphasis is on *human* rights we enter the realm of universalism and the most basic requirements for all human beings. How, though, should we attempt to justify the existence of such rights? Karl Marx would point out that, although 'rights of man' was presented as universally applicable, it typically focused on interests of specific groups – for example, in property ownership – a point also made by the prominent capitalist Adam Smith (to be met in Chapter 15). The rights are of 'egoistic man', says Marx, of individualistic, self-interested individuals, separate from others and the community, in capitalist competition – 'egoistic man withdrawn into himself'.

Marx has some history on his side. Rights talk in the seventeenth century was much concerned with contract and commerce. Within John Locke's political philosophy, as seen earlier, the right – a universal right – to property ownership is emphasized. Human rights are, in fact, presented as being essential to *all* human beings, universally, across nations – and not in just one group's own interests. By the way, a caveat should be added over Locke, typically perceived as tolerant, liberal and defender of rights, for it is far from clear that he opposed all forms of slavery.

According to some theorists, the existence of human rights is grounded solely in nations having contracted with each other for reciprocal benefits. Others understand human rights, as did Locke, as grounded in God or in Nature – in the natural law or in what it is to be a human being. The 'contracting' account has the obvious disadvantage of weakening the 'human-rights' shield: what of the citizens of those nations that decline to contract as above – or when international agreements break down? The 'God or Nature' account has the disadvantage of apparently insisting on, for example, the right of free speech as belonging to the cavemen (cave people?). There is also the basic mystery of how we know what the rights are.

Whether we understand human rights – those absolute, universal and inalienable rights – as grounded in divinity or the natural world, or the result of international contracts, they are treated as overwhelmingly important and to be resistant to trade-offs. A nation ought not to violate the human right not to be tortured, even when such violation, it is judged, may help to prevent a terrorist attack.

Let us remember that, despite the fine words relating to human rights in the American and French constitutional declarations, many supporters of those declarations saw no inconsistency in continuing to permit slavery – as earlier noted with Locke. Members of France's National Convention spoke of fraternity and benevolence; Chateaubriand, in effect observing a trade-off, wrote of how 'these devotees of philanthropy had their neighbours beheaded for the sake of the greatest happiness of the human race.'

Since the Universal Declaration of Human Rights, many international laws, treaties, covenants have arrived, although with little regimentation. The basic aim is the protection of individuals with regard to health and dignity as well as, of course, life. International Humanitarian Law (IHL) has specific articles with reference to the conduct of hostilities between nations and requiring respect for the Red Cross and Red Crescent. International Human Rights Law

(IHRL) deals with more details of how individuals should be treated in peacetime: freedom of the press, the right to vote and to strike.

Many human rights are explicitly labelled 'humanitarian', presumably helping to leap over the mire of conflicting religious commitments. There has also been the development of the concept of 'crimes against humanity'. 'Human rights' and talk of humanity do possess the aura of the grandest of moral matters. That is why some disquiet can arise when specific items such as paid holidays (Article 24) come into play in the Universal Declaration.

Appeals to humanity link with the thought of a solidarity existing between all human beings – a cosmopolitanism stretching beyond one's own community, nation or State. That harmonizes with ideals of fellow-feeling, compassion and cooperation, though they typically weaken the more distant the sufferings and the more commonplace they have become. Cultures, of course, vary with regard to how strong are their fellow-feelings, comradeship and preparedness to sacrifice for others, as they also vary with how outstretched their arms are to those outside their groupings, their family, village and culture. There is, it seems, a stronger sense of community in, for example, China, Korea and Indonesia than in the United States and Great Britain – but whether that stronger sense points to a sense of community much wider, embracing all of humanity, is open to considerable doubt.

Morality receives a voice through the talk of rights, yet also through people having appropriate feelings and dispositions – philosophers deem them 'virtues' – to be compassionate, generous, courageous and so forth. The expression 'rights' detracts rather from 'feelings', possessing the colder and more detached sense of 'justice'. Morality grounded in our biology, our feelings for each other, is in the spirit of Aristotle, whereas morality grounded in rationality, abstract rights and duties is Kantian. That manifests theoretical conflict, but one can secure resolution, at least pragmatically, when comparing responses of individuals with those of governments.

Most individuals, at personal levels, are largely motivated by feelings for family and friends, and then their town, their country; it is a widening circle, the feelings usually growing more fragile the further away the victims. Disaster appeals showing people suffering, with the immediacy of the 'now' and on-screen here in our homes, can, though, give rise to considerable charitable donations. They would not be so successful, if, without the pictures, the appeals were solely on the basis of human rights. Once at a governmental level, responding to the public's feelings, the talk typically turns to upholding human rights or abiding by international-aid commitments; a government, the State, does not have feelings.

The universality of 'human rights' has given rise to the following understanding. To have a human right to X means that a State's failure to provide X is a serious moral violation or, at least, it will be if there is no serious aspiration to provide X. The State's failure, in some cases, may mean that its sovereignty could rightly be intruded upon by other countries. We should add that such intrusion could be a duty. The moral question here, in the international scene, is how to combine what many see as rational egoism, self-interest, with rational benevolence or altruism.

HUMAN RIGHTS – FOR THE BETTER?

Let us open eyes to global poverty; it is vast and clearly offends human rights. The World Bank, referring to 2016, estimated that around 900 million people exist below the international poverty line. We need only to reflect on how millions of people lack basic sanitation, clean drinking water and nourishment – not out of choice. In being aware of their own plight – and the vast wealth elsewhere – they are conscious of their lack of autonomy, of the humiliation in desperately needing help from others. We could try to picture how we should feel in such circumstances. The suffering of the world is a scandal permitted by those living well – by us.

Now, wealthy countries, far from recognizing their moral duties and their former explicit exploitations of other countries' resources, have done little to deal with such poverty. Their priority, they sometimes argue, should be helping their own poor; that is the position often encouraged by the media – 'charity should begin at home'. Of course, it is usually somewhat disingenuous, for the local poor are often left to languish in their poverty. In 2018, Philip Alston, the United Nations Special Rapporteur on extreme poverty and human rights, issued a statement exposing the poverty and misery in one of the world's richest countries, namely the United Kingdom. The report noted that the British government was 'in denial' of the extent of that poverty. Needless to say, the government denied it.

In fact, wealthy countries could typically do far more to help both their own dispossessed as well as those of struggling countries. That some of those struggling countries have dubious priorities – preferring, say, the development of nuclear weapons over improvements in healthcare – is not sufficient for the wealthy lands to turn away and do nothing. Indeed, those dubious priorities, to some extent, may simply be matching the priorities of some wealthy countries.

Sometimes government policies of rich nations have stood in the way of alleviations; they have enabled oppressive and corrupt governments to borrow from international bodies, with the recipient countries trapped into having to fund repayments – while their corrupt leaders build up their private wealth in New York and London real estate or in opaque accounts of tax havens. Bank loans to the impoverished countries have sometimes been tied to the privatization of State assets, in effect transferring them to prosperous international corporations at knock-down prices.

When rich countries do provide development aid – and sometimes that aid is effectively a means of improving the donors' business – it is often presented as charity; it could, though, be better understood as a moral duty, particularly bearing in mind how economically powerful countries have manipulated and continue to manipulate international trade structures to their advantage. We should add how the economic and strategic interests of wealthy countries can have disastrous results for other countries. Consider the encouragement by the United States, United Kingdom and others of arms sales and provision of military expertise to Saudi Arabia; the sales and expertise assisted Saudi's military intervention in Yemen, which commenced in 2015, the results being famine and disease, as well as injuries, for millions of innocent civilians.

These days, citizens having their rights violated, particularly by oppressive governments or war, may well look beyond their borders for protection. Certainly, many nations and international bodies grow particularly exercised about human rights when they are being violated by a nation – though that is when it is usually exceedingly difficult to enforce them. In practice, when nations have intruded upon the sovereignty of others, the appeal to individual human rights may well have been a cloak, covering other motivations, namely those of self-interest. Ethnic cleansing in a country may lead to vast migrations and geopolitical destabilization; that danger could be sufficient to justify the intervention, whatever the international humanity status. Whether that is a moral justification, solely in terms of consequences, is another matter – though our Machiavelli, of Chapter 2, would have approved.

Have the words of human-rights discourse, the statements and commitments, succeeded in reducing the amount of suffering, of unequal treatments and so forth, compared with what would have been without them? Presumably, human sufferings overall are vastly greater than, say, two hundred years ago, but that is down to the size of population. As a proportion, we cannot tell – and the answers may be different whether we are describing deliberate sufferings or those resulting from a wild Nature. In lucky countries, such as the United Kingdom, there is radically less suffering that is deliberately and directly instituted by laws – and that reduction results from social reforms linked to the growing respect, in some quarters, for human rights.

Despite the numerous violations of human rights, the proclamations of 'human rights' have probably increased awareness of how nations ought to behave. The proclamations sometimes inspire governments to do better. Unsurprisingly, at times they are ignored or actively violated. On occasions the United States has got away with 'murder' – literally – being actively involved in overthrowing elected governments and the assassination of leaders that threaten its business interests. In the 1980s, President Reagan backed death squads in El Salvador. For another example of how money, business and trade can come before justice, witness British Prime Ministers Cameron and May blocking later investigations into the 2006 murder of Alexander Litvinenko in London, ordered, it is thought, by the Russian State. That quietist approach to Russia only changed years later, in 2018, with an attempted assassination of another Russian in London authorized, also it seems, by the Russian State.

Talk of our possession of human rights is perhaps today's deceit, yet the talk could manifest an aspiration – for the reality of human rights, in application, tomorrow. Violations today of human rights understood solely as aspirations would be constituted by lack of serious intent, domestically and internationally, to do better, to realize the aspiration. Let us, by the way, not complicate matters by taking into account how such rights should apply to future generations and hence the regard we should have now for those currently non-existent people.

LOGIC CHOPPING – EXCUSES FOR DOING NOTHING MUCH

Once we have the list of basic human rights – and, let us pretend, a list upon which most nations agree – is that an end to the matter? Obviously not. We are brought back to the relationship between rights and the duties, if any, of others to protect those rights of people when under attack. Consider the following: *If there are rights, there must be corresponding duties to protect the exercise of those rights.*

Even if we accept that plausible claim, it does not take us far – for what are the corresponding duties? Children have a right to health; does that mean that the United States, Britain et al. are under a duty, an obligation, to provide the clean water for that health, in countries that are too poor to make the provision themselves? The 'we' also gives rise to its own questions – all nations, the nearest neighbours, the better-off in the country in question?

Is there a duty to provide the clean water facilities, however inconvenient it is for us to do so? Is it merely not to get in the way of children trying to secure clean water themselves through whatever means? Is it to prevent others from restricting that water supply, perhaps others who do so through supporting a regime that prioritizes nuclear-weaponry development over welfare of its poor? Those questions bring us to interpretations, meanings and trade-offs.

Here are some worries. They raise serious questions to which, typically, no generalized answers can be given. They need reference to particular cases, some of which involve disreputable 'logic chopping' – convenient moves to avoid duties – while others point to important distinctions.

First, what is the meaning of the central terms deployed? Interpretational matters arise with liberty, free speech and the right to the basic necessities for life, but let us consider torture as a specific example.

The United Nations' Convention Against Torture came into force

in 1987. Torture is understood as an affront to a human being, usually because of the excess pain caused, be it physical or psychological. Torturing someone can also consist of the actual or threat of
such pain to others, such as the person's children. Torture violates a
person's dignity, a person's autonomy and rationality; it is designed
to break the subject's will.

Now, the United States had frequently announced that it 'did not
do torture', but in 2002, when interrogating terrorist suspects, the
techniques deployed – for example, waterboarding, where captives
suffer experiences of drowning – were thought by many people to
be blatant torture. The United States, needing semantic cover for
its techniques, decided that the phrase 'severe physical pain or suffering', which occurs in various rights declarations against torture,
should be understood as 'an indicator of ailments that are likely to
result in permanent and serious physical damage in the absence
of immediate medical treatment... and such damage must rise to
the level of death, organ failure, or the permanent impairment of a
significant body function.'

In as far as countries could get away with such politically inspired
interpretations, the 'right not to be tortured' was of no help to
victims of waterboarding in Guantánamo Bay and elsewhere influ-
enced by the US. Some may point to the judiciary for guidance over
such matters. Yes, the US Supreme Court may rule on what counts
as torture, but let us not pretend that the judiciary is immune from
the political; after all, US presidents largely determine who sits on
the court.

Secondly, in addition to deliberate interpretations given, we – as
ever – have the problem of grey areas. In the case of human rights,
we may argue that we should err on the side of generosity, in the
spirit of the 'human right'. Just because there are grey areas, that
does not suggest the distinction between, for example, torture and
harsh treatment is non-existent – and hence that 'torture' can just

be seen as some slightly harsher treatment. We should remember that there are clear cases of red that are distinct from clear cases of orange, even though there are 'grey' fuzzy areas that are indeterminate.

Thirdly, a further distinct question is whether there can be a morally acceptable trade-off between rights and violations. The United Nations' Convention Against Torture permits of no exceptions to the right not to be tortured. Despite the well-known aphorism that 'ought implies can', we may well be in situations whereby we ought to do something, yet cannot do that something because we ought also to be dealing with another problem. Principles can lead to clashes, when trying to follow them – and so too can human rights. Stories have been told such that, for example, a proposed torture may be seen as nothing but a justified exercise of the right to self-defence. Indeed, many may simply reject the claim that the right not to be tortured ought never to be violated. Some, following Alan Dershowitz, a prominent American lawyer and academic, recommend the institution of 'torture warrants', the warrants being issued when national security is at risk. Clearly, that recommendation goes against the Convention.

Associated with questions of trade-offs is whether human-rights violations may receive the go-ahead on the basis that later on, if need be, compensation will be made. When the human right to liberty is deliberately violated – to uphold another human right – the victim can rightly demand compensation. Contrast with the individual, properly found guilty of an offence; his subsequent imprisonment does not justify a demand for compensation. Accepting that future compensation claims may be permitted runs the risk of governments treating likely compensations as fees for being allowed to violate human rights – just as some corporations build into their calculations the fines that they will suffer if they are caught offending anti-pollution regulations or exceeding decibel limits. The fines are understood as just another business expense. That understanding, one suspects, would radically change if corporate punishment involved imprisonment of relevant executives or forfeiture of the business. The reinterpretation of fines as fees arises again in Chapter 15.

Returning to the logic chopping, we meet 'fourthly'. Fourthly, there are questions of whether unmentioned caveats to the human rights are assumed implicitly to hold. Compare with moral principles: people may well casually assert that one 'must never' lie – yet 'white lies' are allowed and, as noted earlier, in past times there may have been the assumed caveat, 'save to save a lady's honour'. The human right 'to life', for example, is empty until we have cases showing how it is meant to operate.

Even when it is agreed what the 'human-rights' declarations mean, and instances accepted, with caveats covered, there remain puzzles about quite what is logically entailed by commitments to the declarations. Consider the human right to dignity; suppose we all agree that having to sleep rough on the streets is an offence to dignity, what follows? The key question, to which we are now returning, is which duties, if any, do rights impose on others?

Consider the individual level. There are negative duties: if people have a right to dignity, then I ought not to prevent individuals from exercising that right; but am I under any positive duties? Does a positive duty to provide food for the starving outweigh a negative duty not to steal? Are the pleas of the hungry, the homeless, which put pressure on me to do my duty, violations of my freedom? Arthur Hugh Clough, a nineteenth-century British poet, wrote a Ten Commandments satire, 'The Latest Decalogue'; it includes a much-repeated couplet: 'Thou shalt not kill; but needst not strive / Officiously to keep alive.'

That reflection manifested a worry about whether it is in an individual's interests to be kept alive; but it also asks whether morality, human rights, may make demands on us that are too heavy for us to bear.

The so-called Doctrine (excuse?) of Double Effect comes into play here, touched on earlier. It is famously associated with medical matters and war. Political leaders make difficult decisions to go to war; they foresee the resultant sufferings of innocent others, but merely as side effects. Does the psychological difference between on the one hand foreseeing with certainty and, on the other hand, intending, make a sufficient moral difference? We may well feel that it is certainly a piece of logic chopping if the pilots dropping the bombs know full well that civilians will be injured or killed, but soothe themselves by musing that they do not intend, but merely foresee, that outcome.

Consider my going to the opera, buying champagne or, for that matter, contributing to a musical charity. That has the effect, let us suppose, of my lacking the funds (in my eyes) to help the destitute. The continuing suffering of the destitute is not intended by me, but is an unfortunate side effect of my opera-loving luxuries. Does that psychological difference make all the difference or is the explanation to do with the proximity and specificity of undesired and undesirable side effects? A nation's government, perhaps elected on the relevant policies, prioritizes drawing medical staff from abroad to improve its health services – thus adversely affecting the countries losing their medical staff. Is that morally acceptable?

Most of us personally avoid involvement with the rough sleepers on our streets – we may deploy some logic chopping ourselves – so we may wonder what hope there is for those people thousands of miles away, suffering even worse conditions in other countries. In fact, people do help, on a personal level, those 'afar' – for, as already noted, people can respond when a tragedy is great and is brought safely into homes through television and social media. That disposition to 'feel' for others in such circumstances leads some governments to rush aid to crises points resulting from famine, tsunamis or earthquakes. Whether that is a sensible way of helping is another matter now to be questioned.

Empathy is not always good; it can lead to vast donations because of media coverage of a single attractive child in need of expensive medical care, when those donations would relieve far greater suffering elsewhere. We need, though, to reflect on what human life would be like if we were unmoved by immediacy and emotions, but always engaged rational calculations. Further, rational calculations can involve errors and, to some extent, random choices, as well as unforeseen consequences. Because of the vast suffering and numerous deaths from malaria, insecticide-coated malarial nets were supplied to Zambia – that was surely for the good. It is reported, though, that they were quickly put to more practical use: namely, for fishing in Lake Tanganyika. Their use was extremely effective, for the nets caught plenty of fish of all sizes; the results, though, have apparently been the severe depletion of stocks with potential problems of food provision.

As ever, we muddle through, with rationality, mixed motivations and empathy. Sometimes the emotions distorted by closeness, by proximity to us, may have longer-term benefits. In late 2018, in Saudi Arabia's consulate in Istanbul, there occurred the gruesome murder of a respected Saudi journalist, Jamal Khashoggi, who challenged the ways of his government. That event caused Western governments, notably the United States and United Kingdom, at last to speak up a little against Saudi Arabia, despite knowing for years of that State's horrendous treatment of protestors and abuse of human rights – and despite that, as mentioned earlier, supplying weapons to Saudi which have been used to violate the human rights of those in Yemen. Indeed, starvation of Yemeni civilians appeared to be the aim; and that is a method of warfare prohibited under various international laws and protocols related to human rights.

AFTER LOGIC CHOPPING

Even if we – as citizens, as a nation, as the government – recognize that some serious abuses of human rights are occurring in another country, we have one more card to play to save ourselves from feeling that we must interfere, other than the obvious card: namely, that matters would be made worse. The card involves the extent to which we should respect the sovereignty of the country of abuse. While that sovereignty can at times be rightly violated – according to the international human-rights declarations – there are judgements to be made about proportionality, risks and likely results.

That a few people were being tortured in the United States may justify other liberal democracies making representations, urging cessation, but hardly to invade the United States. That the black population suffered from fierce anti-discrimination and mistreatments in apartheid South Africa fifty years ago probably did not justify military intervention, yet justified various boycotts which maybe aided the collapse of that apartheid regime. Contrast with the military interventions in Sierra Leone and Bosnia, where, at the time, it seemed likely that some genocides could be prevented or at least halted, though some innocents would be harmed or killed in the process. Probably, they turn out to have been relatively successful interventions, in terms of current consequences, whereas doubts may well exist with regard to the invasions of Iraq and Libya. In assessing such actions, one has not merely the difficulty of assessing outcomes – outcomes which are continuing – but also of how things would have developed without intervention.

Regarding continuing deliberate governmental violations of human rights, suppose Western governments had no need for the relevant oil, trade and security agreements, should they then consider violating the sovereignty of Iran, Saudi Arabia and China with the intention of halting the numerous human-rights abuses in those countries? Once there are human-rights violations, is it just a matter of calculation of likely consequences and how beneficial they will be, depending on various likelihoods?

Whatever the answers to the questions raised, and they require 'case-by-case' reflection, we must recognize that in democracies voters typically are resistant to voting in governments with policies to help to protect human rights abroad; in various ways, governments give priority to their citizens and their citizens' preferences. Analogously, parents typically give priority to their family life flourishing rather than to helping others; possibly that is morally the right thing to do – though we may wonder, as we did in Chapter 6, why people are usually so sure of that.

As already mentioned, we need not look across the seas from liberal democracies for human-rights abuses. The United Kingdom government in 2017 was found, for example, to be in violation of the UN convention on disabled people's rights, to which the United Kingdom had been a signatory since 2007. The United States is the only country uncommitted to the UN Convention on the Rights of the Child; it is frequently challenged over its detention of immigrant families and for its mistreatments and discriminations of citizens in violation of various basic rights – un-logic-chopped, of course.

Returning to overseas aid, Britain gives 0.7 per cent per annum of GDP. The percentage is probably not as pure as it sounds, for it is often tied to trade deals, loans and the military – to benefit Britain. That money could instead have been used to provide housing in Britain for the homeless and the rough sleepers, people who can scarcely be described as being treated with dignity. Of course, the choice is not remotely as simple as that may suggest; the British government could still provide the aid, yet also help the homeless and others dispossessed, if not spending money on prestige rail projects of doubtful value and nuclear weapons, also of doubtful value as well as of dangerous value and, arguably, of a corrupt morality.

As ever, there are difficult questions of priorities; as ever, whatever is said, governments – as with individuals – deem much luxury spending and projects as more important than saving lives and reducing suffering even within the home country, let alone abroad. We may warm to Montaigne's description, in his 'Of Cannibals', of those surprised individuals:

> ... they had observed that there were amongst us men full and crammed with all manner of commodities, whilst, in the meantime, their halves were begging at their doors, lean and half-starved with hunger and poverty; and they thought it strange that these necessitous halves were able to suffer so great an inequality and injustice, and that they did not take the others by the throats, or set fire to their houses.

Once nations have serious aims of doing at least something, and something more, for those abroad, how should it be determined what is to be done and for whom?

PRIORITIES: GENOCIDES OR MALARIAL DEATHS?

It was in 1859 at Solferino, during the Second Italian War of Independence, that the Swiss banker Henry Dunant arranged assistance for injured soldiers, irrespective of the side for which they fought. He was horrified at what he saw; he was moved by compassion. Thus came about agencies such as the Red Cross.

Much of the international language, as noted, is in terms of 'rights' even when the accompanying interest is humanitarianism. An earthquake, though, does not violate people's rights – only people can do that – but, as a result of the earthquake, people's right to life is in jeopardy. The outcome, whether through deliberate rights' violations or through natural disasters, is suffering, suffering that prevents people from exercising their right to dignified lives.

We, as individuals, are bystanders to all manner of ills. We, as nations, as governments, are bystanders to all manner of ills. Some create urgencies for both individuals and nations to help, though sceptics of international aid are always eager to question what the help is used for, whether it gets to the people in need, and whether it is the most effective way of helping those people, especially when abuses are shown to be perpetrated by some aid workers: for example, exchanging aid for sexual favours.

Suppose there is, in some justified way, a certain determined cash amount, the X-factor, that a nation has available to help promote the exercise of human rights elsewhere. Should one seek to maximize the numbers that can be helped? If so, which ones should be selected – and should the effects on future generations be taken into account? Also, to what degree of help – just to some basic level of existence or a greater level of flourishing? Should one help only those most deserving of help?

We have no good reason to believe that those suffering from famine are any less 'worthy' than those who are, for example, suffering from wars. In fact, there is considerable evidence that money, the X-factor, spent on improving water facilities, on local programmes of farming, would achieve far more than the greater money spent on wars pursuing dictators, such as Saddam Hussein or Bashar al-Assad, wars that themselves have led and are likely to continue to lead to suffering and deaths of innocent millions.

There is also considerable evidence that more lives would be saved, more suffering would be averted, were the X-factor to be directed at eradicating malaria than, say, intervening to prevent an attempted genocide – or than attacking Syria in 2018 because of some chemical-weapon use. Typically, though, there is far more outrage at killings and harms deliberately brought about than at similar outcomes of natural disasters. We have some people clearly to blame in the case of genocides and the use of chemical weapons, but not in the case of volcanic eruptions, other natural disasters or the spread of malaria. Suppose the X-factor money could be used either to prevent a genocide or to bring an end to malaria. Suppose, taking into account likely consequences, the amount of suffering prevented overall is the same. Some may still prioritize dealing with the genocide for, in doing that, not only have we reduced the suffering of innocents, but also stopped a deliberate evil – and maybe even achieved some retribution in punishing the leaders.

In general, by reducing extreme poverty, far greater numbers would be saved from suffering and death, it seems, than by interventions to prevent massacres. Poverty reduction could in fact be radically aided by changes in the rules of international 'free trade' where wealthy countries dominate the terms of trade. That to one side, there would be big strides towards human flourishing if, in poor countries, women's subservient roles could be overcome. Contraception programmes would undoubtedly help, but their supporters need to deal with accusations of racism and disrespecting certain religious beliefs. Such worthy projects, though, ignoring the difficulties of implementation, lack the immediacy, the media frenzy, of planes setting off, in 2018, to bomb one side or the other in Syria – or, indeed, the immediacy of sending out aid parcels to people suffering from tsunamis, their desperation appearing daily on social media – well, appearing while news and newsworthy.

⫙

Every day, as well as the horrendous violations of human rights, with people imprisoned and tortured, there are millions of people who are lacking the ability to exercise even the most basic of rights listed in the Universal Declaration. If – if – nations are truly committed to those basic rights, then they should surely avoid the 'logic-chopping' excuses and at least do something to enable people to have secure lives of dignity. That 'something' moves us away from the glamour and excitements of war-like interventions and the immediacy of planes setting off with food parcels. Here are a couple of examples of glamour lack.

Menstruation in various poor areas of Africa, India and South East Asia has the effect that women stay away from school and work, through pain and embarrassment – through lack of dignity. It is estimated that many girls usually receive 25 per cent less school and college education than they ought. Apparently, in some parts of India, 70 per cent of girls stay away from school because of periods; it is 50 per cent in Kenya. They cannot afford to pay for sanitary hygiene and painkillers. In effect, women's periods contribute to the poverty. International aid projects dealing with that would not be particularly appealing to the mainstream media of many countries, though there is sometimes some local mainstream coverage of such matters regarding women and poverty – as, for example, in Britain.

Here is another example of a valuable project: the research into technologies for desalination. That could eventually lead to millions having easy access to clean water. Another example, already mentioned, would be greater research into combating malaria. Such research – and related educational and social projects – would increase, with likely successful outcomes, were governments to direct pharmaceutical companies into areas with the greatest benefits for humanity instead of leaving companies to aim at greatest profitability – usually research areas with most relevance to the well-off. Appreciation of the distorting effects of corporate profit motives on people's well-being is developed in Chapter 15.

Western governments, liberal democracies, know all this, but are mainly silent. As we know, in democracies, politicians nearly always have eyes on the short-term electoral advantage. That recognizes that people – the voters – are more affected by the immediacy of a crisis abroad rather than by long-term projects, even though the projects are more effective. That also recognizes that people are overall more concerned by what happens at home than elsewhere. The mainstream media connive in all that.

'Human-rights' talk may at least embarrass nations into making efforts in the right direction of helping human beings universally to flourish. And perhaps, human as we are, that requires promotion of some of the immediate-results interventions – to keep people on side. Also, being human, we cannot deny how we are moved by sights and sounds of sufferings before us, on screens. Human as we are, we may blame governments for not dealing in longer-term projects; but we could all do our bit, by pressing them to do so, instead of succumbing so much to self-interest.

At times, those of us who worry about these matters – of the millions suffering right now, to whom we blind ourselves so easily – lapse into despair over the international inactions, despite the proclamations of human rights. Certain buildings, treasures and ideas of identity shine in greater glory than do lives. Witness how the wealthy can suddenly make hundreds of millions of euros available for Notre-Dame's restoration after the 2019 fire damage; 'cathedral rights', so to speak, trump human rights. We nearly all prefer our luxuries over the lives of the destitute. We logic chop. 'Surely, the existence of pre-eminent human rights is as much make-believe as is the existence of witches.'

Yes, human-rights talk is indeed largely glossy rhetoric, but at least it is a rhetoric that may help to advance the good; contrast that with the talk of witches.

12

Free speech: the Tower of Babel; the Serpent of Silence

The Tower of Babel is described in Genesis, though not by that name. It is a magnificent creation, a city of storeys – no doubt, more to be added – a city that stretches higher and higher to the heavens, to God. The inhabitants were once all of one voice, one language, one faith. All, it would seem, were in harmony in the quest of reaching up to the divine – until, courtesy of that divinity, they were cast into confusion, into chaos, finding themselves speaking different languages, in conflicting tongues. They failed to understand each other; they heard only babble. God, it is said, had taught the people not to be so arrogant in aspiring to reach Heaven.

Thus it was, some argue, that the Tower became that of 'Babel', for the term, deriving from the Hebrew word *balal*, means 'to jumble', 'to confuse'.

We have a Babel of today. Through social media – through Facebook, Twitter and much more – through urgent online debates and instant reactions in the media, there is a cacophony of speech, of texts, of shouts and shrills, pronouncements of anger, of retorts, of rebuffs. Of course, it is not all like that and not even all like that within the social media. Within some Facebook groups, there is considered discussion; some tweets offer useful information of local events, traffic jams – and, more importantly, can provide instant evidence of terrorist attacks or police brutality. Further, well before the presence of social media, broadcasters would often demand immediate political reactions to events, with politicians only too eager to oblige. The days are long gone when a politician would act as did British Prime Minister Clem Attlee, interviewed in a 1950s election campaign. Attlee, having said very little, is asked – the interviewer desperate for something – 'Have you anything to add, Prime Minister?' Attlee, with no concern for spin, soundbites or image, simply replies, 'No, I don't think so' – and is no further badgered.

Without much reflection, we may yet think how splendid it is that people from across the globe are interacting, engaging in discussion. Let us note, though, that many people tweet and post only within pockets of the like-minded – they are in echo chambers, tweet bubbles – and, as such, there is no stimulation for understanding, merely an addiction to repetition of soundbites, of mantras. When others from outside enter, deviating from those tongues, the communication is often nothing but shouts and shrieks, abuse and nastiness; such communication would paradoxically be unheard of and unspoken by many of the participants were they face to face and in each other's direct hearing.

Clashing communications are not necessarily manifestations of misunderstandings; rather, there is often no desire for understanding. There is little eagerness for engagements to reach the truth or to reach reconciliation of competing views. The 'true or false' division may, in fact, mislead. We need scope to allow for those linguistic acts that are nonsense, waffle, vacuous, guff or 'bullshit', though some writings on the latter may well be self-referential.

There are, of course, exceptions.

Our Tower of Babel is not restricted to the social media and cyberspace dealings. Witness how rarely interviewers are seeking the truth or reasoned debate; news programmes are described as 'shows' or, at least show themselves as attempts at entertainment.

Witness how rarely those in power address questions or produce reasoning or evidence relevant to the questions. Witness, indeed, how often they begin 'let's be absolutely clear', continuing with obscurity, distractions or platitudes. Exactly how the interplay between social media and mainstream media interactions operates is a moot question, but what is not moot is that the vast number of interactions on social media enables Big Data collection, unheard of a decade ago. Moneyed parties, be they political or corporate, target individuals, voters' groups and groups under celebrity influence, with aims of affecting consumer or voter behaviour, downplaying reflection.

It can be easy to forget that corporate aims are often intimately linked with the political. In Britain, an independent report on the 2015 election of Jeremy Corbyn as Labour Party leader established that high percentages of newspaper articles, designed to damage him amongst the mainstream electorate, were misleading. It is hardly helpful for democracy, where an informed electorate is required, if such media powers deliberately conflate commentary, conjecture and facts – and, in many cases, with mis-facts.

Picture our Tower of Babel, as a modern city, or modern country, or indeed the global village, with the babble and 'baa, baa's which, despite the millions of instant communications – or maybe because of them – ensures little communication by way of understanding. 'Baa baa' – the sound of sheep – is the supposed ancient Greek source of the term 'barbarians', the barbarians with their 'blah, blah' speech, lacking the language of civilization, of the Greeks. Our Tower of Babel is the Tower of Blah Blah. The blah blah is not to seek the truth, to follow arguments where they lead; it is not a spread of understanding, though it can and does change behaviour.

Kurt Gödel, a twentieth-century Austro-American, considered

one of the greatest logicians of all time, claimed that reason never errs. We may doubt that claim – well, certainly, reasoning can err – but he is right that error is typically due to extraneous factors such as emotion and poor education; we could add: and simply poor eyesight or poor intellectual-sight. Vested interests, be they political or corporate or a combination, rarely seek to argue their case, providing good reasons; rather, they appeal to emotion, with reliance on 'alternative facts', contributing to the noise of the blah.

Vulnerable groups, minorities, often find themselves attacked, or so they feel, in today's Babel – attacks based, for example, on race or sexual orientation. When in colleges, at meetings, in seminars, such groups can feel exposed, uneasy, offended – or too easily offended. Lovers of 'free speech', even when away from the mass of mindless blah and when keen for engagement, have little regard for such feelings – well, so some vulnerable groups apparently experience. Mind you, majority groups are sometimes much disparaged by minorities.

HATE SPEECH: THE UNITED STATES AND EUROPE

Our Tower of Babel is built on free speech – well, that is the tale – though we should not ignore the commercial foundations. Free speech, some argue, is a precious jewel to preserve, even if we have to suffer offended feelings and considerable nonsense. Does that mean we should leave our Tower of Babel untouched by constraint?

The great political philosopher Thomas Hobbes, in his 1651 work *Leviathan*, expressed the central problem for arranging a justified State: 'For in a way beset with those that contend, on one side for too great Liberty, and on the other side for too much Authority, 'tis hard to passe between the points of both unwounded.'

Hobbes, having lived through the seventeenth-century English Civil War, concentrated on the need for stable government. The State of Nature – a state without government, without society – is, he argued, a state of war, where the life of man is 'solitary, poor, nasty, brutish, and short'. Of course, the obvious reply is, 'It could be worse, dear Thomas; it could be solitary, poor, nasty, brutish – and long.'

That reflection to one side, this chapter is dealing with a particular problem of authority and liberty – that of passing unwounded between censorship and free speech. This is where Western democracies divide. European governments try to contain and restrain elements of the babble by law, social pressure and regulation; the United States does not – well, not as keenly so. The United States is hostage to its First Amendment: 'Congress shall make no law respecting an establishment of religion, or prohibiting the free exercise thereof; or abridging the freedom of speech, or of the press; or the right of the people peaceably to assemble, and to petition the government for a redress of grievances.'

The Tower of Babel, American-style, flourishes because of the Amendment's protection of the freedoms of religion, speech and the press – though on American campuses there are increasingly calls for safe spaces, to protect members of vulnerable groups, members who feel under attack from the blah. Those on the political right tend to be keen to invite controversial speakers to campus, while many of the liberally minded seek, paradoxically, to prevent – well, so it is anecdotally reported. That liberal response is more typical in Europe, at both college and national levels.

In Europe, in contrast to the States, there is a variety of anti-discrimination legislation, legislation that in part is designed to prohibit 'hate speech'. The European Court of Human Rights upholds the principle of freedom of expression – views may be expressed that 'offend, shock or disturb society or sections of it' – but the court makes illegal the expression of 'hate speech'. European countries, through their own laws, also maintain such restrictions:

In Great Britain, the 1986 Public Order Act declares: 'a person who uses threatening, abusive, or insulting words or behaviour, or displays any written material which is threatening, abusive, or insulting, is guilty of an offence if: a) he intends to thereby stir up racial hatred, or; b) having regard to all the circumstances racial hatred is likely to be stirred up thereby.'

Sweden prohibits hate speech, and defines it as publicly making statements that threaten or express disrespect for an ethnic group or similar group regarding their race, skin colour, national or ethnic origin, faith or sexual orientation.

Denmark's Criminal Code makes it an offence to use threatening, vilifying or insulting language against a racial group or religion.

The Netherlands has a Criminal Code that prohibits making public intentional insults, as well as engaging in verbal, written or illustrated incitement to hatred, on account of one's race, religion, sexual orientation or personal convictions.

France criminalizes incitement to racial discrimination, hatred or violence on the basis of one's origin or membership (or non-membership) in an ethnic, national, racial or religious group.

In Britain, the 'protected characteristics' designated in the hate-crime legislation are race, religion and sexual orientation; the coverage is much smaller than that of the Equality Act (2010), regarding equal opportunities, as encountered in Chapter 5. There are, though, proposals for extension, to include hostility towards women as women, men as men and the elderly as the elderly. We may wonder how far that should go: should not hate crimes include coverage of hostility towards punks, hippies, intellectuals? Why not against Conservative voters, the unemployed, the poor or the wealthy?

The underlying thought is that hate speech reduces the standing of whole groups and attacks the dignity of their members; hence, it should be prohibited. We see, though, how it is far from clear what determines which groups merit inclusion and which do not – and also what counts as disrespecting a group. Here a paradox, or at the very least a tension, hovers on the horizon. According to certain fundamentalist Islamic groups, for example, Muslims who reject their religion or dishonour Muhammad merit punishment, even death. In many European countries, the law, at the very least, restrains the expression of such beliefs – and that smacks of the law disrespecting those groups. Contrary to what is often casually proclaimed in liberal societies, not all views should be respected. Disrespecting views is, though, compatible with tolerating their expression. Liberal societies are, then, muddled in their glib comments about encouraging respect, while upholding laws that aim to prevent the expression of certain views from even being tolerated.

Some countries ban the public denial of certain truths, notably those relating to the Holocaust. Some countries criminalize groups that express commitment to the Nazis, whether or not that commitment is a denial of the Holocaust or an approval. Such countries include Austria, Belgium, the Czech Republic, France, Germany, Switzerland – and Israel. By the way, let us ignore questions of defamation law, though in that arena, the American slander and libel laws tend to be more defendant-friendly than those in other countries such as Great Britain.

Overall, in Europe, insulting certain groups of people is much condemned and has various associated laws that restrain it, but, curiously, insulting individuals, though not in terms of such group membership, is – legally at least – acceptable. Insults aimed at political stances – apart from Naziism and terrorist-based ones – are usually legally permissible. Trouble by way of inconsistencies and conflations, inevitably, can arise because politics and stances on ethnic groupings and religion intermingle. For example, anti-Semitism and anti-Zionism are clearly distinct positions, but a frequent way of discrediting anti-Zionist positions is by claiming that they are a cover for anti-Semitism, conveniently forgetting, for a start, that many fundamentalist Jews object to Israel as a Jewish state.

The cacophony of the European Tower of Babel or Blah Blah seems, from the above, to be matched by the cacophony of laws and conventions against hate speech. From the citizens' perspective, there is a reasoned distrust of those who would restrict free speech, yet also distrust of allowing free rein in view of the prevalence of speakers whose sole aim may be to manipulate, offend or cause trouble.

In 2018, Boris Johnson, before becoming British prime minister, referred to the burqa as ridiculous because women who wear it look like 'letter boxes and bank robbers'. Instead of just casting doubts on the closeness of that similarity, people demanded investigations, deeming him manifestly Islamophobic even before those investigations. Christian hoteliers Ben and Sharon Vogelenzang were accused by a Muslim patron of calling Muhammad a 'warlord', leading them to be formally charged, though they were ultimately acquitted. Some politicians in Britain who point to Hitler's one-time interest in the Jews having their own State in the Middle East are deemed anti-Semitic – and so it goes on.

Although there are the European attempts to limit free speech in certain arenas, free speech is sometimes heralded and praised. In 2015 there was outrage at the French satirical magazine *Charlie Hebdo*; the magazine had published cartoons of Muhammad, leading to the murder of some staff. The big 'I am Charlie' protest in Paris that followed, with many political leaders marching, spectacularly supported the freedom to publish. Bizarrely, a Saudi Arabia representative also marched; 'bizarre', of course, because Saudi

Arabia is a country where protestors against the State and Islam, even mildly protesting, are thrown into gaol for years and flogged – or worse.

Banning words, in certain contexts, is nothing new. In 2017, there was a banning of Harper Lee's novel To Kill a Mockingbird, this time by the Biloxi School Board in Mississippi: 'there is some language in the book that makes people uncomfortable.' Once, the Church, philistines and morality defenders were major condemners of freedom of expression; these days, many of those well committed to culture, and far away from religion, seek to cut free expression down to size. Lee's novel, in fact, has often been banned by school boards: it 'represents institutionalized racism under the guise of good literature'. In 1981, North Carolina parents objected to Lord of the Flies on the curriculum because it implies 'man is little more than an animal'. Yes, as noted at the time, the truth can get banned.

There was – and still exists – the 1989 fatwa, issued by Iran's Ayatollah Khomeini, against Salman Rushdie, then living in Britain, calling for his murder because of The Satanic Verses. Virtually all Muslims who supported the fatwa – and, for that matter, non-Muslims who criticized Rushdie for writing the book – had not read the book and were under no obligation to do so. 'Do not open if likely to be offended' is an impotent recommendation; it is impotent for, it seems, just knowing that something exists may be offensive enough. Many argued that Rushdie should have been sensitive to the feelings even of those who would never read the book. Canada initially banned the work; sensitivity – or fear? – stopped many bookshops from holding copies or at least from displaying them. The then Chief Rabbi in Britain, Rabbi Jakobovits, condemned the publication; he proclaimed that it is wrong 'to tolerate a form of denigration and ridicule which can only breed resentment'.

In Britain, as seen, there is a mishmash of laws limiting the right to free speech. We may be committing a crime if using abusive words likely to cause harassment, alarm or distress or cause a breach of the peace. There are laws against indecency; any incitement to racial hatred; to religious hatred; incitement to, or encouragement of, terrorism; or the glorifying of terrorism. There exists treason for advocating the abolition of the monarchy or imagining the death of the monarch. Pressure groups and fashions of the day can, of course, restrict speech, even song. Frank Loesser's 1944 'Baby, It's Cold Outside', very popular and much covered, is now frowned upon by some, with stations refusing airtime. Men, it is said, may hear it as encouragement to inveigle women into seductions undesired. The objectors apparently are unaware that another verse has the woman inviting in the man.

The list of attempts to restrict expression could go on.

The Tower of Blah Blah is, of course, a challenge to those restrictions, for it is currently highly difficult to monitor and control. One reason for that difficulty is that it forms a vast commercial and successful enterprise, so there are powerful vested interests at work, unconcerned about what actually goes on. There is a similar conflict with regard to pornography available online. Family-orientated politicians and others in authority keenly condemn pornography's easy availability, yet permit it for, again, it is lucrative business – and business that one way or another often helps to fund political parties keen on free markets.

THE SERPENT OF SILENCE

Dangers of physical attack, as with the murders related to *Charlie Hebdo* and those of some Danish cartoonists, together with legal and social dangers through anti-discrimination legislations, can lead to self-censorship. Various plays, works of art, publications – and political engagements – have not, it seems, seen the light of day; understandably, many people have preferred to play safe.

Just raising questions about or criticizing certain groups can lead to a flurry of complaints. In Britain, mainstream Jewish organizations promoted the International Holocaust Remembrance Alliance (IHRA) definition of anti-Semitism and its examples, eager to deem those who question it, be they Jews, academics or lawyers – be they from families who suffered in the Holocaust – as anti-Semitic. People who challenge Islam, criticizing the Islamic treatment of women, doubting whether it is intrinsically a religion of love, often receive the charge of being Islamophobic. Later, we see that those who question whether trans women are really women are deemed transphobic. There is a lot of the 'phobic' around – well, accusations of such.

We may picture such moves, and the legislation against hate crimes, as unfurling a serpent of silence. The Serpent of Silence winds through the Tower of Babel, ever growing, ever expansive, leading, perhaps one day, to a Tower of Silence – well, silence with regard to everything deemed controversial by those with certain power or authority. A day may arrive when people are so scared or numbed that they dare not challenge the status quo for fear of offending this group or that group – or perhaps even themselves. That may appear far-fetched, but the value of picturing the far-fetched, bringing it vividly to mind, may alert us to dangers of travelling much in its direction. Of course, some people use such possible dangers in bad faith – to justify their disregard of hate-speech restrictions. Others, also in bad faith, may use fears of 'hate speech' accusations to smother debate, at least public debate.

Once there was a great worry about blasphemy and how to prevent it. Blasphemous speech, it was thought, could offend God, bringing the whole community into disrepute. For liberal democrats, blasphemy no longer matters with regard to upsetting God. What matters is whether freedom of expression gives licence to upset certain groups, be those groups identified by their religion, race, gender, sexual orientation or disabilities.

The worry about causing offence and the desire to avoid giving offence can paradoxically lead not merely to some silences but also to 'compelled speech'. A nice example occurs with the court rulings in the United States regarding the Masterpiece Cakeshop: the owner argued that his having to create an iced wedding cake for a same-sex marriage ceremony offended his sincerely held religious beliefs about marriage, thus violating the Free Speech or Free Exercise clauses of the First Amendment. Ashers Bakery of Northern Ireland was at first deemed to have broken British anti-discriminatory law because it declined to supply a gay customer with a cake iced with the slogan 'Support Gay Marriage'. Did that manifest the owners' support for such a message – and hence were they being compelled to assert what they deeply rejected? The eventual Supreme Court ruling, in 2018, happily found them not guilty of illegal sexual-orientation discrimination: the ruling noted that the Ashers would have refused to make such a cake for any customer, irrespective of their sexual orientation; their objection was to supplying the message on the cake, not to the personal characteristics of the would-be purchaser.

Imagine the Tower of Babel transformed into a Tower of Silence, of silence on controversial matters. No longer would people feel sufficiently confident to make any jokes or serious observations – for fear of upsetting this or that group. Utter not a word against this or against that... Because of the absence of the relevant words – absence of the relevant deeds – there could be no justified accusations of racism, anti-Semitism, Islamophobia and so forth. Of course, it is rather difficult to imagine the scene, for many Muslims would need to go quiet about their views of Jews, while traditional Christians would be unable to say what they really thought about same-sex relationships. Certain Orthodox Jews would not dare to announce their belief that a Jewish Israel created by man ought not to exist. Palestinians – and Daniel Barenboim, to name but one Jew of many – would keep quiet about how in their view the 2018 Basic Law: Israel as the Nation State of the Jewish People is akin to the introduction of apartheid, given its explicit statement that the Jewish people have an exclusive right to national self-determination in Israel.

All would be silent; well, we could no doubt comment on the weather, the storms and floods, so long as not attributing them to the wrath of God upset by the existence of sexual promiscuity and greed in the world – a claim made in Britain by the Bishop of Carlisle in 2007.

'Lock up your libraries if you like; but there is no gate, no lock, no bolt that you can set upon the freedom of my mind.' Thus wrote the novelist and leading member of the Bloomsbury Group, Virginia Woolf, in her 1929 *A Room of One's Own*. Well, we may question whether there can be such freedom of mind – certainly, its having much value – without expression of that freedom by way of public speech. We may warm to Spinoza's view in his 1670 *Tractatus Theologico-Politicus*:

> No one can surrender his freedom to judge and think what he likes; everyone, by the utmost right of nature, is master of his own thoughts. From this it follows that if the sovereign authorities of a State try to make men (with all their different and conflicting views) always speak according to what *they* prescribe, they will get only the most unfortunate result.

Mind you, the work was first published anonymously to protect both Spinoza and the publisher from political retribution and was written in New Latin in the hope of avoiding censorship by the Dutch authorities.

ılı

Although we have encountered the odd example of prescribed speech by way of the Masterpiece Cakeshop, the focus here has been on the envisaged Tower of Silence where the customary prescription has been for silence. We may envisage things getting much worse. Recall Anonymous, from Chapter 3.

By way of attire – 'A-ttire' as it was called – Anonymous sought to protect herself from intrusions, from being observed, her movements noted, her purchases made – her identity publicized. With the development of technologies, there may well come a time when not merely physical movements can be registered globally, but also thoughts. And let us not immediately ridicule or dismiss such an idea; after all, think how amazed the ancient Greeks would be at today's communications. The Serpent of Silence may invade minds such that we dare not even think what we should like to think – and we dare not even think of what it is that we should like to think.

That possibility moves us into much worse scenarios; after all, once technology arrives to detect thoughts, it will be a small step to move to inserting thoughts – and a small step into collapse of any sense of how these are *my* authentic thoughts rather than ones deliberately imposed from outside. We, indeed, suffer this already in a mild way through the media and subtle means of advertising and marketing, as seen in Chapter 4.

'OFFICIALLY, FINE'

There used to be a quip in Romania, when under the old so-called communist regime. If someone in the street came up to you and asked, 'How are you?', the wise reply – in a sense the only reply – would be, 'Officially fine.' It summed up the idea that one ought not to say anything against the official line. And that is, in effect, a generation of the Tower of Silence. That silence maintains the status quo, whatever that happens to be, when the Silence descends. We may be lucky in that status quo; it may accord with our desires. One aspect of human life, though, as distinct from robotic life, is that our freedom to express ourselves is essential to flourishing lives. Think also of how protests and demonstrations, publications and pamphlets, have helped in promoting social justice. Without them, who could honestly be sure that any such changes for the better over the decades would have occurred? Some supporters of parliamentary democracy vehemently object to extra-parliamentary influences by way of protest marches, civil disobedience, and certainly unlawful activities, as being undemocratic, conveniently forgetting how they have sometimes led to beneficial outcomes – and may do so again.

In France, for instance, regular and significant protests by the 'Gilets Jaunes' (the 'yellow vests') in 2018–19 brought about some easement of the economic plight of many citizens. The force deployed against the protestors by the State, though, was such that the United Nations Human Rights Council called for investigations. Indeed, President Macron has supported policies to limit demonstrations and prohibit dissidents' networks. When protests turn into riots, it is worth reflecting on reasons why many people stay away; one reason was highlighted by Benjamin Zephaniah's cutting poem of the 1980s. There he drew attention to those who do not riot, observing that people 'don't riot' if with comfortable homes, good jobs and secure futures.

Freedom to speak – as opposed to the 'Officially, fine' speak – has a long history of defenders. In 1644, Milton published a speech for the Liberty of UNLICENC'D PRINTING, to the PARLIAMENT of ENGLAND, which includes: 'And though all the windes of doctrin were let loose to play upon the earth, so Truth be in the field, we do injuriously, by licencing and prohibiting to misdoubt her strength. Let her and Falshood grapple; who ever knew Truth put to the wors, in a free and open encounter.'

Milton believed that free speech would enable truth to triumph, for truth could never be shown to be worse. Many years later, Mill, as noted, strongly defended free speech, even speech that offends, and insisted in his 1859 *On Liberty*: 'If all mankind minus one, were of one opinion, and only one person were of the contrary opinion, mankind would be no more justified in silencing that one person, than he, if he had the power, would be justified in silencing mankind.'

For Mill freedom to speak is essential to our liberty, our autonomy – and, as with Milton, it is also a means of reaching the truth. On the autonomy consideration, many of us can recognize how a flourishing life requires our being free to express ourselves, to say what we think; it involves a freedom to know our minds by speaking our minds. Further, as mentioned, there is the value of reaching the truth.

What is spoken may be true – and that is an obvious benefit, unless one wants to lose touch with reality – but even if what is spoken is false, it should benefit by way of being tested, challenged and eventually overcome. That latter 'overcoming' may be wildly optimistic – just as may be the defence of free speech more explicitly in market terms: namely, its providing a marketplace of ideas to be probed. In 1919 Justice Oliver Wendell Holmes's defence for supporting the United States' First Amendment was based on the claim, 'The best test of truth is the power of the thought to get itself accepted in the competition of the market.'

Understanding the presentation of ideas, beliefs, morality as taking place in the marketplace, though, ignores questions of how truth should be discovered and transmitted, how to select truth from falsehood and how to distinguish fine valuable ideas from the trivial and frivolous. It also ignores the power discrepancies between the players in the market. The marketplace of ideas, if taken on the economic model, generates gatekeepers whose motives usually are not to maximize access to truth or serious debate. Witness the power of media groups, where newspaper proprietors typically seek advertisers and readers, not to inform, but to generate profits directly or indirectly through promoting free-market governments. As Tawney observed, the media's activities seem largely to be to sell pieces of paper with nonsense on one side and advertisements on the other – and these days, we should add, the news, advertisements and commentary can be difficult to distinguish.

The mainstream media and politicians, those who benefit from such, talk up the freedom of the press and other media, conveniently forgetting how these gatekeepers are owned by a wealthy few who, in the case of Britain, mainly live offshore with their own political motives. Let us not, though, think of the past, when Mill was writing, as some golden age. Yes, there were papers that gave space to heavy debate, with full reports of parliamentary proceedings, but they were available to, and appealed to, only a few – and probably did little directly for democracy.

Plato was sceptical, with good reason, of the marketplace analogy. He tells us to beware the sophists, the teachers, in the marketplace, in the agora. Only if you are already a knowledgeable consumer can you safely buy teachings. If you are not, 'Do not risk what is most dear to you on a roll of the dice, for there is a far greater risk in buying teachings than in buying food.' When you buy food, Plato reflects, you can take it back home, see if it is stale, taste it and so forth, before eating. Teachings are different. 'You put down your money and take the teaching away in your soul by having learned it.' We may understand Plato's objection as that, when confronted by newspaper commentary, advertising and similar, we may be in no position to make a rational assessment of what has been said.

The Tower of Blah Blah may be seen as offering some degree of correction to the marketplace model, where there are powerful gatekeepers, but the Tower has no structure for understanding, for selection, for truth. After all, the noisiest, the most noticed, the most *believed* are not thereby communicators of truth or inspirers of cultural progress.

We may remove the commerciality implied in the 'marketplace of ideas' and understand the marketplace, rather optimistically, as one where the aim of the participants is to reach the truth through the cut and thrust of debate, of university seminars and erudite papers in leading journals, of scientific research and theory testings, on conjectures and refutations, of examinations on the model of law-court proceedings. Note, though, none of that just mentioned coheres well with a 'free-market' idea in the sense of an unregulated 'free for all' where anyone can contribute. There are academic qualifications needed, entry requirements, structures of debate, peer reviews, institutional support and much more.

Both the Tower of Blah Blah and the Tower of Silence are uncomfortable towers in which to reside. As ever with matters of the real world, we have to find compromises. We put up with some Blah Blah; we accept some Silence. The underlying question here is how to assess the dangers of 'hate speech' compared with the dangers of 'hate-speech laws'. It is, though, a myth to think that there is a clear means for determining where lines should be drawn between prohibited speech and speech permitted.

CONFLICT, CIVILITY AND CONTEXT

There have to be some limits on the chatter, on the blah blah and on serious free speech; however great the advocacy of free speech, there are good reasons for restrictions. As the well-known quip goes, from Justice Holmes: 'You ought not falsely to shout "fire" in a crowded theatre – for that is likely to lead to an unnecessary stampede with consequent injury.' Mind you, the observation often omits the 'falsely'.

A much lesser-known example is that of the 'corn-dealer'. Mill, in his 1859 work *On Liberty*, told of a mob outside a corn-dealer's house being incited by a speaker to burn it down.

No one claims that actions should be as free as opinions. On the contrary, even opinions lose their immunity when the circumstances in which they are expressed are such that merely expressing them is a positive incitement to some harmful act. The opinion that corn-dealers are starvers of the poor ought to be allowed to pass freely when it is simply presented to the world in print; but someone can justly be punished for announcing it orally or passing it out on a placard to an excited mob that has gathered in front of a corn-dealer's house.

Mill made the point that acts of any kind which harm others without justifiable cause may be – and in the more important cases absolutely must be – brought under control. Unless such likely harm, maybe direct harm, can be shown, people should be free to speak and, indeed, to express themselves, as they want; and, sceptical as some of us are, we may readily observe how there are many cases where the demand to repress, censor or close down has nothing to do with preventing harm to people.

We may be reminded of various 'non-disclosure agreements' – gagging clauses – where the 'agreements' can be challenged, for they have often been made when powerful and wealthy individuals have sought to silence apparent victims of abuse. We may also be reminded of how corporations proclaim, rather too readily, 'commercially sensitive information' and how governments, despite insisting on their love of democratic participation, resist calls under the 'freedom of information' legislation. When outsourcing, governments often add clauses to prevent contracting parties from revealing embarrassing motives or unwanted truths.

We may, then, certainly question the motives of some who seek to curtail free speech, just as we may question the motives of some who offer it strong support. In the main, powerful groups flip between sides as it suits their interests. On the one hand, corporations demand the freedom to publicize their products and services; the public has a right to know what is on offer. On the other hand, corporations resist revealing their internal business machinations and complex structures for tax avoidance; the public has no right to know what goes on behind the scenes.

As ever with social matters, there are grey areas. Mill gave us the excited mob being incited to burn down the dealer's house there and then; we need to recognize, though, that there are degrees and degrees, nearer and further proximities to dangers. What may be said here ought not to be said there.

Other elements that swirl within the maelstrom are, as mentioned earlier, those concerning anti-discrimination restrictions on free speech, such restrictions being common to European countries and their laws. That mishmash of laws could of course be regimented. There is then the conflict with countries such as the United States that resist those restrictions. The conflict can be seen thus: free speech in terms of what can be said takes priority, as with the United States' First Amendment, but for the Europeans, free speech in terms of who gets to speak comes first. If the vulnerable are to be able to speak freely, the privileged, the majority, may need to embrace some degree of silence.

In 2009, for example, Daniel Férct, a right-wing Belgian politician, distributed leaflets advocating the policy of 'Belgians and Europeans first', saying that non-European job-seekers should be returned to their countries of origin and that we should stand up against Belgium's Islamification. He was convicted of breaking anti-discrimination law and was disqualified from running for election. We may wonder whether that serves democracy and whether it is helpful to try to maintain such views under wraps rather than openly debating them. Defenders of free speech may, indeed, insist that such advocacy should not be banned, but tolerated. That liberal attitude of toleration could well be disingenuous. We tolerate views with which we disagree and which we feel will have no impact. Once the views gather support, then we cease to tolerate.

In ancient Athens, there were two concepts that may be understood as giving voice to different ways of viewing free speech. The Greek *parrhesia* is the freedom to say what one pleases, as and when one pleases; that chimes with the First Amendment. The Greek *isegoria* pointed to the freedom expressed by citizens having an equal right to participate in debate in the democratic assembly; that may chime with the European approach, where 'hate speech' is seen as disrespecting individuals and deterring them from entering debate – as well as having the danger of inciting violence.

For the ancient Greeks, it seems, spoken truth lacked the value we theoretically give it today; but what was valued was speaking out. That 'speaking out', in our times, is often presented as 'speaking truth to power'. To do that, one may need to be outspoken, to whistle-blow – and for some to manage that, they need the space of safety.

Civility relates to 'our ways of doing things' and those ways are usually ones established by the civilization. Presentation may trump content. What may be said and how it may be said can be a means for maintaining those in power. Aristotle, in his *Constitution of Athens*, commented critically on the demagogue Cleon who was 'the first who shouted on the public platform, who used abusive language and who spoke with his cloak girt around him, while all the others used to speak in proper dress and manner'.

An underlying and philosophical question here is how people should come to believe. Philosophers seek good reasons and evidence – and politicians, when it suits them, maintain the same aim – yet we may wonder whether rhetoric and emotion is not at times just as good, if not better, when the outcome is good. We may have sympathy for those speakers who lack the knowledge or awareness of how 'one ought to speak'. On the one hand, the negative hand, demands for civility may be demands for a certain conformity; that may silence dissent, for it prevents those who lack the necessary rhetorical skills from joining in. On the other hand, the positive hand, demands for civility may be out of respect for people engaging in public discourse, encouraging that engagement.

The call for civility surely comes, and rightfully so, when we read, for example, a newspaper commentator of Britain's *The Sun*, Katie Hopkins – well-known, it seems, solely for outrageous remarks – announcing with regard to the desperate people crammed on boats in the Mediterranean: 'Rescue Boats? I'd use gunships to stop illegal immigrants. Make no mistake, these migrants are like cockroaches.' Being poor, desperate or fleeing are not, apparently, 'protected characteristics' regarding hate speech; were they to be so, speech disparaging individuals on those grounds would be illegal. 'Protected characteristics' is, of course, a curious concept to deploy here; the world would be a better place if the poor were not poor, the fleeing were not compelled to flee. The need is not to protect the characteristics, but to protect people being abused because they possess those characteristics.

Hopkins continued with how towns are 'festering sores, plagued by swarms of migrants and asylum-seekers'. In that spirit, David Cameron, when Britain's prime minister, spoke of 'a swarm of people coming across'. Such descriptions, of people as akin to insects, of certain people, 'illegal immigrants', as automatically criminals, offends civil discourse by offending people. That rhetoric is nasty and is intended to silence those who would seek to defend the 'cockroaches'.

In a liberal society, supportive of free speech, we should accept ridicule, mockery and vivid language, but – as ever – there are degrees and degrees, matters of taste and the context of the speaking. In the seventeenth century, the theologian Roger Williams was much exercised by the 'persecution of the tongue'. Williams is little known today; he was born in London, educated in Cambridge, with much of his life spent in Massachusetts. He founded the American colony of Providence Plantation and co-founded the First Baptist Church in America. His works, such as *The Bloudy Tenent of Persecution, for Cause of Conscience* (1644), argued for religious freedom; he was eager to loosen tongues, accepting that toleration and disagreement may well be disagreeable yet remain immensely valuable. Of course, whether disagreeable or not, there is the basic worry, much aggravated by today's social media, that free speech can give rise to blatant falsehoods spreading across the population – as apparently in the case of alleged dangers of the MMR vaccine (for measles, mumps and rubella). Should the defence of free speech include a defence of deliberate deceit being circulated through, for example, false identities where some may parade as Democratic Party supporters, urging people not to vote? That happened in the United States congressional elections of 2018.

Minimally, one should expect that in the regulated media, errors ought to be corrected with greater prominence given to the corrections than the errors. After all, is freedom of speech so valuable that speakers must not be deterred by requirements to correct and make amends, if what they broadcast is false, misleading or without evidence? Would we – should we – seriously believe that there is considerable value in the media being at liberty to seek to indoctrinate people into believing that drinking highly-sweetened drinks is excellent for health, that if they vote for left-wing parties they are traitors to their country and that extramarital sexual activity leads to eternal damnation? Those are cited because for commercial, political and religious reasons respectively they have at times been promoted one way or another.

⊣⊢

There are ways of saying things without saying – well, recall how the cake-makers and bakers worried regarding what they would be taken to be saying. There are times and places when truths ought not to be said – out of courtesy, sensitivity and diplomacy. There are also times and places when truths ought to be said – and often they ought to be said when authorities, conventions or vested interests conspire against the saying. With that in mind, this chapter ends with a touching example.

Some years ago, a young man, an intellectual, someone who wanted to change the world, mimed in a city's public square. People could tell what he was miming. His mime was of someone giving a protest speech; it was, though, a speech without words. People drew round to watch and 'to listen'. They saw the expressive gestures, the flicker of tongue, the mouthing lips; they listened to – silence. The authorities also watched and listened, but did nothing; after all, he was not speaking out loud. Had he done so, he would have been arrested and silenced. To protest, he had paradoxically silenced himself.

The incident occurred in 1986, Zagreb, Yugoslavia, when under dictatorial rule. The incident, although silent, said much and says much. It is a tribute to humanity – to the young man's ingenuity, courage and commitment to free speech. It may also be a condemnation of humanity: the authorities' desire for power, conformity, repression. The incident displays human absurdity – a protest speech without words. A protest was being made, as all could tell, yet the law – *the law* – remained unbroken. The protestor obeyed the law's demand not to speak, yet spoke. The police were dutiful in stopping protest, yet allowed protest.

13

Regrets, apologies and past abuses

Should we regret the Pyramids, the Panama Canal and the Sydney Harbour Bridge? How about St Peter's Basilica in Rome, Paris's Notre-Dame or, in England, King's College Chapel, Cambridge – the choir of which, at Christmas, is enjoyed by around 30 million listeners worldwide? Let us think, instead, of the motorways, the sewage systems and power plants. With a moment's reflection, we may realize that all those items share a commonality beneath: abuse and abuses. They are the abuses from which most of us benefit.

Here, when I speak of 'most of us', I speak certainly of people who lead at least reasonably acceptable lives in Western democracies. Many other people in other countries also benefit. Whether within democracies here or in countries elsewhere, the lives being considered are those of people who are getting by not too badly to those of the pretty well-off to the splendidly wealthy to the excessively rich. Many, though not remotely all, may be deemed 'bourgeois lives' in that they are comparatively privileged, with material prosperity and social advantages: they are often professional lives, with the advantages of privileged education and valuable opportunities successfully engaged.

Whether professional or with more minimal status, many people in Western societies typically have lives that may involve holidays abroad, secure homes, cars and eating out; these people find time for activities much valued, be they attending the opera, playing the piano, visiting art galleries – or going to baseball, cricket, football or watching movies followed by late-night drinking. They are lives that usually engage with celebrations, birthday presents, with children and grandchildren being taken to zoos, exhibitions or, at least, for an ice cream or three. There are also lives that revolve around religions, be they grounded in churches, mosques or synagogues.

Of course, there are vast differences between those lives just mentioned; so, the extent of the benefits received courtesy of the abuses that are shortly to be highlighted vary considerably – but even at the lowest levels, though not all, the benefits are great, if only through the presence of a stable social structure, with the workings of law, health provision and some degree of security.

Look around. That is, indeed, what we do when we delight in the splendours of the Vatican, the Pyramids of Giza and San Francisco's Golden Gate Bridge. We take selfies – well, some do – and praise the magnificence of the buildings, while, in practice, looking at ourselves and how we are so much enjoying the sightseeing. More mundanely, but even more importantly, we rely on infrastructures – from drainage to highways, from electric lighting to clean water 'on tap'; from trains and planes to internet access and digital cameras for the selfies – and on spectacles. Yet more mundanely, we use electric toasters, hair shampoos, washing machines and irons; well, washing machines and irons may be mysteries to some, to those who rely on others to work for them.

Trace the history of all those buildings, facilities and consumer goods – and somewhere along the line, we see that they are built, in part, on sufferings, coercions and related injustices. We could look to the distant past for the treatment of the slaves who built the Pyramids. We could recall the atrocious factory conditions in the nineteenth century – children sent up chimneys – that created the wealth and hence the means for scientific progress, engineering feats and today's grand museums, universities and research facilities. There are the appalling years of slavery, with racial discriminations actively supported for decades in the United States, the British Empire and elsewhere.

In Germany, there are many memorials to victims of the Holocaust; in South Africa, there is the Apartheid Museum and memorials drawing attention to the terrible sufferings under the apartheid regime. Only in 2018, through the Equal Justice Initiative (EJI) in Montgomery, Alabama, has a museum opened explicitly to document and highlight the history of slavery and lynchings in the United States and the subsequent repressions, violence and humiliations wrought upon African Americans because of their race. The EJI seeks to overcome the tendency of the United States towards amnesia.

We should remember the historic animal testing that went into today's shampoo and cosmetic products. We could look to poor countries' current working conditions, many unsafe and squalid, some verging on slavery, that give rise to the 'competitively priced' garments in the West. Turn to our laptops and mobile phones: battery supply chains lead to sources in the 'Democratic' Republic of the Congo – to mining miseries of cobalt production. Children and parents dig with shovels, live in toxic hazes, with land and water polluted. The international corporations are highly profitable; the families scarcely scrape a living. For that matter, we could turn to the current working conditions of the very poor in the wealthy countries.

In this chapter, we concentrate on the easily forgotten historical abuses, instead of the more often discussed immoralities of, for example, major wars and today's miserable working conditions for millions.

⊪

Over the centuries, people have been much abused; they have been abused in ways that today most of us would deem appalling. Those abuses have, as a matter of fact, been involved in the means that generated today's Western societies. As already hinted, we should move our considerations wider still – to how laws and their applications, how our democracies and ways of living, have developed via numerous horrors and outrages.

Our comments merit subdivisions, into quite who did what, when, how freely and how directly or indirectly the abuses arose. We could look at the options then available to workers, what then were considered the norms and how readily they were accepted. Those elements, though, should not detract from the fact that most of us would believe that such injustices – working conditions, coercions and sufferings – were appalling. Our welfare, security, and what gives value to our lives, rest upon those sufferings, even if those sufferings were accepted at the time as inevitable.

Two thoughts need to be emphasized. First, even were this society, today's society, perfectly fair – whatever would constitute that (we have encountered that mystery) – it would still have arisen from the historical horrors mentioned. Thus, we are looking at how the past affects us. Secondly, the focus is not on the washing machine and so forth, but on the realization of our values. Washing machines are valued instrumentally, solely as means to what people value in themselves – health and well-being, maybe the leisure to discuss literature, to travel the world, to have children with fulfilled lives or simply to tend a garden or feed the pigeons on a window ledge.

OPENING EYES

Particularly in the United States and Great Britain, activists of various ilk have been opening our eyes a little to the considerations above. They have directed us to the statues of the 'great and the good' of the past, a past where those great and good were much involved in, and beneficiaries of, the fruits of slavery, people's deprivations and blatant injustices such as theft – whereby, paradoxically, they enhanced their reputations as the great and the good.

Look around: we see residences, streets and landmarks named after past eminences. Certain activists call for statue removals and streets to be renamed. In the United States, Yale University in 2017 deleted the name 'Calhoun' from a hall because Calhoun strongly supported slavery. In Britain, Oriel College, Oxford, underwent the 'Rhodes Must Fall' campaign: Cecil Rhodes' statue must be removed because of Rhodes' South African dealings – though little publicity arose over how best to deal with distributions of the Rhodes Scholarships' funds. Jesus College, Cambridge, removed a bronze cockerel – the Okukor – looted in 1897 from Benin City, now part of Nigeria.

Were we to become consistent about the inappropriateness of certain names continuing to be used, then, given today's apparent standards, we should be renaming King's College, Cambridge; the relevant King Henrys who built the college engaged in much abuse. For that matter, even if institutions have not been founded directly by those named, some may feel uneasy at the mere association; colleges with religious names (Jesus, Christ's), some could argue, are linked to individuals and institutions that have caused considerable suffering over centuries.

Examples of removal of statues and renamings could be viewed as attempts to hide the past of which we now feel ashamed, be it because of the past suffering or the past injustices. Some may be associated with ideas of 'making amends', of contributing funds to help the later generations of certain abused groups. There are other examples where correcting apparent historical injustices is resisted. For many years, Greece and some people in Britain have been demanding that the British Museum in London return to Athens the exquisite sculptures, the 'Elgin Marbles', from the 2,500-year-old Parthenon temple; they claim that Lord Elgin took them illegally. For that matter, Russia has now and then pointed out how the United States unfairly acquired Alaska.

There is also an unease these days – well, amongst some – for all the wrongs the nation, 'our' nation, has done. We could add 'and will do'. 'We', in Britain, apologize for past actions – mind you, only a few of them. We pardon Alan Turing, a major figure in the development of the computer and in defeating Nazi Germany in the Second World War, for his homosexual 'crimes', yet keep quiet about the hangings of sheep stealers or British involvement for centuries in slavery. Britain has offered sincere regrets regarding the torture of Kenyans in the 1950s under British orders. Maybe no British citizen, alive at the time of the apology and regrets, had been involved in that mistreatment and torture – yet Britain as a community, in some sense, felt responsible for its past actions. In the Kenyan case, it paid compensation, the money for which came from current taxpayers who had nothing to do with the torture.

There are, of course, oddities in those apologies. One oddity is the determination of which apologies and regrets get given: apologies and regrets currently flow over past injustices to do with sexual orientation, yet not for those sheep stealers who were hanged or, in the United States, those protest marchers against racism who were shot. Some may argue that highlighting past injustices does not show any concern for the past sufferers or our shame today of what was done, but rather is a means of drawing attention to, and trying to overcome, current closely similar sufferings and injustices. Exploitation of the poor and of many ethnic minorities continues, but not the hanging of sheep stealers; that is why attention is paid to individuals such as Rhodes and Calhoun, but not those past hangers of stealers.

Another oddity is grounded in a logical point: it does not make sense to apologize for something that we have not done. That illogicality may be overcome if we can operate with a strong sense of community identity and some idea of collective responsibility; a community can apologize now for what 'it' did decades ago, even though no member of the community now apologizing existed during those decades ago. Further, the individuals who suffered then no longer exist, but the community to which they belonged does. The apologies effectively are of one community to another, rather than to individuals. That is not to imply that, once individuals are dead, whatever we do is irrelevant to us and irrelevant to them. Even assuming that death is complete annihilation, what we do, certainly soon after the death if not more distantly, can be a mistreatment, or correction of former mistreatments, of that deceased person. Respect for individuals can extend beyond their lives; witness how most people accept that it is wrong to kick around corpses, ignore last testaments or speak ill of the dead.

OUR IDENTITY

How we deal with the past, as has been shown, hits matters to do with community identity and responsibility; such matters also arose in Chapter 9. One useful analogy to reflect upon here is one's own individual identity through time.

Each one of us has a history, such that we remember and regret – or smile or feel embarrassed at – things that we have done. We forget lots; we remember lots, some of which we wish we could forget. We feel more distant psychologically from certain features of our past than from others. We still, though, accept responsibility – to varying degrees. We could not live a life in which 'I' referred only to a momentary self. Yes, there are problems with our sense of identity over time – maybe we have to live by a myth of a continuing identity – but we do identify with a continuing self, for better or worse.

The connections, through similarities and causalities over time in one's life, ground talk of a person's identity. They also ground justifications for the recognition that there are degrees of responsibility, depending upon temporal distance from the events in question and extent of the psychological similarity, between us now

– and us then. After all, am I really the same person and hence with a high degree of responsibility for something that 'I' did thirty years ago, something which I can scarce remember doing and when 'I' held very different values?

The above comments on personal identity may be played as an analogy to make some sense of our identifying with a nation, a country, a community; we speak of our nation, our country, our community. The similarities and entanglements between us and other members of the group by way of common interests, projects and commitments bind us within the group. As a result we identify with this group's way of living but not that group's – with these values but not those.

This way of living can no more be a matter just of this moment's living than my sense of self can just be for this momentary 'I'. Once I recognize some form of identity with the group – the nation, the community – that identity is bound to extend into the past, paradoxically even into a past that pre-dates my existence and even into a past of values that differ from those of the community today. Of course, we typically feel our identity holds more closely in some respects than in other respects regarding responsibilities and commitments of the past. Perhaps we identify with a political class that upholds certain values – maybe even, to some degree, with a nation's values – though not at all much with 'mankind' in general and what it has got up to. We may understandably feel far, far away from the life of a nation that imposed hanging of sheep stealers, but close to trade unions in their past and present, fighting for improved employment rights and working conditions.

A distinction now comes to the fore. On the one hand, there is a personal responsibility in as far as we identify with the national responsibility and maybe feel embarrassed at our being part of a nation once committed to, for example, the repressions caused by its imperialism, even if we have not benefited. On the other hand, we may simply be recognizing that we are enmeshed in the causal chains that have benefited us with regard to, for example, the wealth of colleges derived from imperial exploitations – yet we accept no responsibility.

IMPERSONAL REGRETS

Casting to one side where our community identity may embrace responsibilities for injustices and sufferings in the past, we find that we have sufficient trouble, sufficient worry, with simply being enmeshed within the causal nexus. As noted in the Prologue, there is an ancient mantra 'All things conspire'. What we value in our lives has been realized as a result of historical causes, contingent causes – that is, the way the world has been. We cannot be – or, at least, ought not to be – *unconditionally* pleased, then, with our lives, pleased without caveats; we ought not to be, for the very fact that what we realize as valuable in our lives is enmeshed in sufferings and injustices of the past, conditions that are lamentable and that warrant rejection. We regret – or ought to regret – those social conditions.

Some may reply that we need to take into account conditions at the time; certain people in the distant past were better off suffering in the way that they did than in alternative ways. Even if that is true – probably it was better to be working long hours in dreadful factory conditions than to be in debtors' gaols or locked workhouses – it is still a bad and hence regrettable that those were the options. If we are insensitive to such ways of the past, then, it may be suggested, we are either emotionally blind or inconsistent – and that is no good way to live.

To bring out what is going on here, let us compare with agent-regrets. Agent-regrets are personal ones; we may look back and regret what we did. What we did is clearly relevant to how we should feel today, when we take responsibility for what we did. What we did, though, should also affect how we feel today, even when the deeds were 'not our fault'. I may regret how I (mis)handled a situation with colleagues – all my fault – yet someone may also regret being the man who, in 2006, tripped and smashed three historically important Qing dynasty vases when visiting the Fitzwilliam Museum, Cambridge, even though it was not his fault; he neither deliberately tripped nor was reckless.

The above are cases where we are personally involved. We also, though, have impersonal regrets about past situations; the situations are regrettable. We are distressed that they arose. Of course, that distress relies on our having values such that we treat such cases as regrettable, but those values are unlikely to be exclusive to us. We, as a group with those valuations, may experience the same regrets about the history of slavery in our community. Contrast the agent-regret, when we are directly involved, wittingly or voluntarily.

With regard to impersonal regrets, we were not there; we did not order the building of the Pyramids or the highways that take us to the airport and the planes that fly us to Egypt. We can, however, regret that something happened – it was regrettable that the associated sufferings occurred – even though we were not involved in the happenings. The disquiet is that what we may take as valuable in our lives – that makes them worth living, that gives meaning to life, such as appreciation of great buildings and works of art – as a matter of fact rests on those events that are indeed highly open to regret.

The benefits, resulting from past horrors, to many of us are extensive. We value research, universities, opera – some of the associated institutions control many material resources with objectionable histories. No doubt, our engagements in such activities are better than trading on stock markets – or should it be 'gambling'? – yet we cannot be unconditionally pleased. We are not the agents of the history, but we have the benefits still. We are implicated; we could not do what we value now, but for the objectionable events of the past. The 'all in all it has been for the better' does not sound so plausible when so many others – when any others – have suffered. Try telling that to those who suffered; try telling it with a straight face.

HOW TO VIEW

With some of our preferences, we can just shrug our shoulders; satisfying them would not have been worth living for. For instance, given that I am alive, I find myself enjoying, say, football, basketball or chess; I have a preference for it. My preference is not such that it gives me an unconditional ground for being alive. I would not 'live for it', just as I would not die for it; football is not a matter of life or death – though Bill Shankly, a successful and respected British football manager, once quipped, 'It is far more serious than that.' Yes, those conditional preferences are also enmeshed in sufferings of the past – to be regretted – but those sufferings are not contaminating something highly important to me.

By contrast, saving the whale may be a sufficiently worthwhile project that I value my existence to do; it is valuable, not conditional on my existence. University research, freedom of information, reading books, a respect for free speech are not valuable, as I grasp them, only on condition that I live. We see no intrinsic value in washing machines or even the sewers, but they have instrumental value to help us to lead lives that we value.

Some plays and performances displayed on stage or screen may be enjoyed merely as entertainments – musicals, say – while other plays and performances possess 'high' intrinsic value: for example, certain productions of Shakespeare's plays, Greek tragedies and Samuel Beckett's bleak renderings. Many in the audience are now well aware of various scandals, screen and stage, that, since 2017, have been growingly revealed; powerful directors and producers have, it seems, abused their positions, taking sexual advantage to varying degrees of (mainly) female actors, causing considerable distress. Of course, we may be surprised at the surprise; for decades jokes and nods have existed about the director's casting couch, be it in show business or more elevated productions. That surprise to one side, now that such scandals are acknowledged in the industry, ought not that awareness at least cause some unease at enjoying the industry's fruits?

Minimally, one should regret that such exploitations have taken place in an industry from which one gets pleasures; but such exploitations should be more upsetting for those who see the artistic as possessing intrinsic value and not just as a means of entertainment. Similar questions and thoughts could be directed at those actors who still benefit from being within the industry as well as those who, to further their thespian careers, played along with the abuse, perhaps aware that 'consent' is not always a black-or-white matter. No doubt, it is despicable that actors needed to kowtow to powerful directors and their directorial whims, even dictatorial whims, to secure desirable parts. We may, though, surely wonder whether that merits greater outrage than that merited by many other cases where, just to survive, men and women have been forced into great dangers and indignities, be it working down the coal mines, joining the army or scraping a living as a hospital cleaner.

Once we are attending to what people see as intrinsically valuable, we should note how, at a very fundamental level, most people value their lives and simply being alive. Now, how we came to be, how we came into existence, results from a vast intermesh of actions and accidents over centuries, many of which are bound to have involved numerous sufferings of many others.

Some may propose the way to solution, to prevent our values enmeshing us in regrets, is via calculation – as if: 'if only I could work out that the values in my life exceed the disvalues that brought them about, then all would be well.' The past sufferings, though, are so vast that they swamp what little of value we may now find in our lives. Even if the calculations, though, worked out in our favour, our lives have still been tarnished by what was required for our flourishing. Even if the sparkles of the jewel easily exceed the grubby chip, the jewel is still chipped. Even if poison is in a pretty bottle, it is still poison.

Take the Pyramids again: we have to acknowledge that we disapprove of the conditions that have given rise to the astounding sights of which we approve. We may operate this at a recognizable individual level: an individual has suffered hardship, yet as a result fine works are composed. That may be open to personal calculation, but contrast with those individuals who committed some wrongs (perhaps theft), yet as a result, years later, their lives now have meaning. Those lives should not be unconditionally embraced: to do so would require those wrongs to be embraced. Hardships and struggles may be needed for success – witness again the quip against Switzerland that invented only the cuckoo clock – but not necessarily immoral hardships, hardships imposed on others.

A particularly haunting case is that of Jews and the horrors of the Holocaust. In the nineteenth century, the Austro-Hungarian Jew Theodor Herzl, a political activist, well aware of the anti-Semitism rife in many countries, argued that Jews would never be safe until they had a land of their own. Strictly Orthodox Jews viewed such Zionism as a pernicious heresy. Initially, most Jews were indifferent, but gradually the Zionist movement grew, with Britain's 1917 Balfour Declaration calling for a 'national home for the Jewish people'. The Holocaust strongly reinforced the belief of Jewish people that they needed Israel as a safe haven and, it is argued, gave the impetus such that the major international powers and the United Nations actively supported the creation of the modern Jewish Israel. That homeland, now valued by most Jews as essential to their existence, has resulted, in part it seems, from undeniable horrendous sufferings and injustices that they of course deeply regret – and, for that matter, is tangled in existing sufferings and injustices for the Palestinian people.

Most of us value our lives as being within a land that has been reformed over the centuries, developing at least some respect for human rights, the rule of law, welfare provision, freedom of speech and so forth. Many of the reformers were able to fight for the relevant social changes only because they lived lives sustained, one way or another, by the workings of the poor often under wretched conditions. The liberal values of today upon which we depend and which we approve came about through considerable injustice. Consider the role of slavery in Greece and hence the fine achievements that we still value. Here is an example, courtesy of Friedrich Engels, from his 1877 Anti-Dühring, where he defends Marx's stance against a version of socialism by a certain Eugen Dühring:

> Without slavery, no Greek state, no Greek art and science, without slavery, no Roman Empire. But without the basis laid by Hellenism and the Roman Empire, also no modern Europe. We should never forget that our whole economic, political and intellectual development presupposes a state of things in which slavery was as necessary as it was universally recognised. In this sense we are entitled to say: Without the slavery of antiquity no modern socialism.

Nietzsche deserves a look-in here. Nietzsche was haunted by the thought of the interconnection of things, in particular how our lives are intermeshed within the worldly sufferings. We have to affirm the totality of world history, if we can unconditionally affirm our own lives, argued Nietzsche. He wrote of the greatest burden being that of the 'eternal recurrence', of our lives exactly as we have lived them being repeated eternally. Whatever Nietzsche meant, one thought here is how we cannot escape from having to acknowledge our position in the interconnection of things – and that interconnection must involve all the sufferings in the world.

Of course, we are shielded in the main by our ignorance of the

details. We cannot, though, live lives that we can affirm unconditionally – once we bring forcibly to mind such pasts. We, no doubt,
engage in some self-deception or some 'bracketing-off' of the unfortunate events. There is the conflict between 'how much better,
had things been otherwise then' and how pleased we are with how
things are now.

We should remember that this very luxury of reflecting on these
matters – of operas and galleries, of football games and chess – all
require some degree of material prosperity which is grounded in the
sins of the past – and we are affecting others right now. How should
we treat our relationship with past sufferings from which we now
benefit? To repeat: what we most value, in many cases, has been
conditioned by immoralities that we should surely regret.

CHANCES OF REDEMPTION?

Obviously, we cannot help those who are deceased, be they Egyp-
tian slaves or the poor in the workhouse. That is not quite true: we
can acknowledge how badly treated they were; we can show respect
and regrets. After all, as mentioned earlier, when someone dies,
we recognize that we should show some respect, even though the
deceased knows nothing of it. True, some may say that that is just to
ease one's own regrets – or guilt – but the mistake they make is the
'just'. A person's interests extend beyond the grave.

Some of us have the wealth and education and motivation to
seek to make amends – and that is no doubt all to the good – but it
does not free us from the fact that we have that luxurious position,
grounded again in the past of sufferings. We may attempt compensation; we help present members who are suffering and are of the
community whose past members suffered. At least, in those cases,
we are doing something worthwhile for that group. If one sees
one's meaning in that, one is then requiring even more strongly the
existence of the dispossessed for what is valuable in one's life; it is a

conceptual necessity. It is akin to Mother Teresa needing the poor, so that her virtue of compassion may be manifested. Tell that to the poor – and see what comfort it brings.

Paradoxically, of course, whatever we do we are dependent on the sufferings for which we are now expressing regrets. To that extent, it may be argued, we are also victims, albeit mildly so in comparison with those who suffered in the past. We cannot escape; we cannot wash our hands. Of course, we did not choose to be born into this nexus, of surrounding sufferings, past and present – and, no doubt, future ones – but we are hardly that badly off, for we do still value the Pyramids, even though that value is tarnished. We could at least acknowledge that we ought not to squander what others have unwittingly given us. To squander would be like throwing away the venison; the deer has already been sacrificed. We ought then to count our blessings, feel some humility, and have the grace to acknowledge all that upon which our lives rest. We should do – and here is a platitude – the best that we can.

Suppose we recognize the value of equality or at least fairness; our lives are compromised for we are living on the shoulders of those who suffered vast inequalities and injustices. We cannot of course compensate those who are no more, but we can see their kinship with others who are suffering now; we could devote our lives far more to helping the dispossessed.

There are, then, two important features in this discussion that are worth emphasis. For our being in a position to compensate, we are still relying on that prior suffering. Further, we are deploying that 'collectivity' or sense of community, one that embraces members of the past: we cannot help past sufferers, but they are part of the collective or community of sufferers, so we should help these ones now.

In a small way, we may seek to redeem ourselves, even though we still rely on the discrepancy of our lives and the history of injustices.

Yet, however much we do, we cannot make it the case that we are not relying on the sufferings of others. As we cannot change that feature, then (some would argue) it is of no matter to us; we should no more worry about it than we should worry about the number nineteen being a prime number. The mistake there is the assumption that all regrets can only be sustained by an agent who could have done otherwise. Overall, we should face the reality: we are fortunate enough to be able to face the unfortunate.

To quote a gloomy Adorno – Theodor Adorno, twentieth-century German philosopher who emphasized the need to understand society – a wrong life cannot be lived rightly. We are enmeshed in the wrong. To be authentic, we need to recognize our position and express humility – given that our lives have depended upon so much suffering and so cannot fully go well.

As for all the government apologies about previous wrongs, I advise governments to express blanket regrets for all that has happened. Further, do not pull down the statues, break them up or hide them away, but keep them there, to remind us – not to celebrate, but to regret.

We readily can see how we should give thanks to the past, as we walk through parks, visit groves and galleries. When we wonder about life and our relationship with others, it is worth musing upon the ancient Greek adage: 'A society grows great when old men plant trees whose shade they know they shall never sit in.'

There, people looked to the future that they shall never see, yet they do so for others. They owned choices, unlike most of the individuals in history who have been highlighted in this chapter.

14

'Because I'm a woman': trans identities

Allow me to introduce Alice: yes, Alice most famously of *Alice in Wonderland*. She has stepped through the looking glass and engages in conversation with Humpty Dumpty (HD), the great wall-sitting egg.

'There's glory for you,' announces HD.

Alice is baffled. 'I don't know what you mean by "glory".'

HD smiles contemptuously. 'Of course you don't – till I tell you. I mean "there's a nice knock-down argument for you!"'

'But "glory" doesn't mean "a nice knock-down argument",' objects Alice.

'When I use a word, it means just what I choose it to mean – neither more nor less,' replies HD.

Alice is, of course, doubtful whether we can make words mean just what we want them to mean. HD's response is:

'The question is: which is to be master – that's all.'

⫸

Charles Lutwidge Dodgson, a nineteenth-century Oxford mathematics don, wrote about Alice under the nom de plume 'Lewis Carroll'. The tales are sources of many philosophical and logical wonderments. Dodgson created his nom de plume. Such pseudonyms are not unusual, typically with no nefarious intent. True, sometimes they are used to avoid difficulties – embarrassment, even prosecution for blasphemy. Sometimes we meet 'anonymous' instead, as noted earlier with Spinoza.

Proper names, such as 'Lewis Carroll', designate individuals, but not usually through meanings of the words deployed. Dodgson did not adopt the name 'Lewis' because he was like a lewis, a lewis being an iron grip for heavy blocks.

With descriptive terms – such as 'glory', 'woman', 'racist' – matters are different. They rightly apply only when the individuals satisfy the descriptions; further, the terms often possess evaluations. To be deemed 'racist' is to be condemned. To deem oneself a woman implies right to enter 'women-only' spaces.

Applying descriptive terms can have significant consequences, even when applications are misuses. Adages such as 'no smoke without fire' and 'mud sticks' come to mind. We encountered dubious descriptive deployments in Chapters 2, 12 and elsewhere when discussing how politicians and the media seek to affect voters by devious means.

SINCERELY SAYING IT'S SO – DOES NOT MAKE IT SO

What we identify ourselves as – and what others identify us as – is the topic, focusing on the transgender debate, a debate high on certain political agendas. Someone born biologically a male and treated as such insists he/she is a woman – and vice versa. To question that insistence can cause distress, but stressful questions ought not thereby to be out of bounds. Questioners can sometimes be perceived as offensive by the transgendered; questioners themselves, though, can sometimes be offended, if reaping, as knee-jerk reactions, accolades of 'transphobic'. Similar stresses occur when people are deemed racist; dialogues can come down to little more than 'Yes, you are' versus 'No, I'm not'. Sadly, the public domain tends to be no good place for rational reflection; witness the abusive elements within the Tower of Babel.

Not unreasonably, many trans individuals see the argument as one about their rights.

Trans individuals suffer when having to hide their status; they often undergo adverse discrimination when 'coming out' and showing the world how they are. They should have the right to determine how in reality they are – as women or as men – without being disparaged and having to endure unfair treatment. True, in being looked upon as women, they may undergo various unfair discriminations that persist against women, but it is more important to trans women to be true to their identity as women than to calculate advantages and disadvantages of reaping diverse discriminations.

Trans women – and this is not unusual – speak of their identity, their self, as essentially tied to being women. As one of many examples, in 2016 the British physicist Ruth Padmore, a trans woman, wrote of how her very existence was being denied by the outspoken feminist Germaine Greer, when Greer claimed that individuals with male genitalia could not, as a matter of fact, *be* women. Some trans women, in reaction to that claim, adopt the stance: 'Only we should decide our own identity; that is our right.'

Let us first run through some basic points. Returning to our eminent egg, HD, people obviously may use descriptive terms – 'glory', 'woman' – privately as code to mean something else, but in everyday language those terms have common meanings, albeit meanings that may evolve. I cannot attempt the HD move and secure a semantic self-certification of a word's meaning for the public world – just like that. Using common meanings, I can, though, seek to show matters in different lights. Earlier, we met the following example.

'Nannying', with the connotation of looking after children, is used disparagingly of the State when it offers guidance on healthy eating. I have drawn attention to one similarity between that so-called nannying and the manipulative ways of the corporate world. If 'nannying' by the State is to be disparaged and warned against, then so should 'nannying' by the corporate world with its enticements to affect consumers' purchasing behaviour. There are, of course, differences as well as similarities. The State's nannying aims to be in citizens' interests; the corporate nannying aims to promote profitability. The latter 'nannying' can at times be more akin to abuse.

Trans individuals are trying to show matters in a new light, opening our eyes to how things are and how certain individuals ought to be treated. They are not usually engaged in HD outbursts about word meanings, but about what the reality is, given existing meanings. Contrast their position with those in the political sphere, as seen in previous chapters, who often seem to have regard for neither truth nor how things are. Those politically-minded individuals are aided by others who shrug shoulders, content to speak of a 'post-truth' society and 'alternative facts'. Because of that 'post-truth' line, let us muse upon some obvious, albeit important, background points for this discussion.

In the vast majority of cases, saying that something is so does not make it so; wanting something to be so does not make it so, and being absolutely certain something is so does not make it so. Those facts need attention, not just when exposed to the silver tongues of political leaders, but also when certain groups are much taken with insisting, sincerely so, how they should be classified, or how others should be classified, the aim being, of course, to justify demands for certain treatments. That trans individuals are sincere in their claims about their identity as man or woman does not establish that they are right.

The emphasis above – about how thinking does not make it so – is much needed. In Britain, the claim by people that they are victims of racism are recorded and investigated as 'racist incidents'. That stance resulted from the 1999 Macpherson Report into the fatal stabbing of Stephen Lawrence, six years earlier. Lawrence was a black teenager who suffered an unprovoked attack, yet initial police investigations were highly inadequate and no charges were then brought. Sir William Macpherson was eventually appointed to head an inquiry; it led to London's Metropolitan Police being described as 'institutionally racist' and to the following definition: 'A racist incident is any incident which is perceived to be racist by the victim or any other person.'

The obvious objection to the definition, rightly made, is that people can misperceive incidents or deliberately claim them to be other than they are. True, the perceptions of apparent victims may be highly relevant evidence for determining whether the individuals are victims as described, but other factors should come into play before concluding that those perceptions constitute sufficient proof. People make mistakes. Morgan says, 'You hate me because I'm gay.' That may be true, but it may be false. Morgan may be hated not because he is gay, but because he is a successful author in contrast to the speaker who provoked Morgan's response. Of course, whether hate is ever a morally appropriate emotion is a different matter. Curiously, 'anti-hate legislation' covers only certain protected characteristics.

With that preamble, let us turn more directly to the trans matters. Should trans individuals be treated as in the best position for determining their gender?

TRANS GENDER AND SELF-CERTIFYING

Many trans people want to self-certify as being a woman or a man. The controversial way of expressing this is the following: a man should have the right to self-identify as a woman – a *trans woman* – and a woman the right to self-identify as a man, a *trans man*. For ease, let us discuss matters in the 'man to woman' direction; similar observations apply to the 'woman to man'. The individuals discussed here are not, for example, the kothis, a much-disparaged group living in India; the kothis are effeminate males, trapped against their will into adopting the female role in same-sex relationships.

The attention here is not directed at those individuals who have intersex conditions where the physical anatomy is neither clearly male nor clearly female. Those individuals may be keen on surgical interventions. In Germany, they may legally adopt the classification 'divers' – diverse or miscellaneous. The trans individuals discussed here need have no particular interest in altering their sexed body. The key point for them is that they believe that their gender identity, as man or woman, does not match their birth assignment. A trans woman was at birth clearly identified as a male, a boy – later, a 'man' – but that individual, at some stage, sincerely and deeply believes (s)he is a woman and has been all along.

Trans women do not see themselves as making words – 'woman', 'man' – mean whatever they want them to mean in the manner of HD. They know, they say, the meaning of the word 'woman'; they know how to apply it. They can tell that they are women because they are relevantly similar psychologically, and in personality, behaviour and attitudes, to those individuals whom we typically treat as women. For the claim to work as wanted by trans women, those similarities need to be akin to the similarities that non-trans women typically have to each other.

Trans individuals sometimes use the terms – unfamiliar to many of us – 'cis' and 'cisgender' to apply to individuals whose self-identity conforms with the gender that standardly corresponds to their biological sex, 'cis' being from the Latin for 'on the same side as' in contrast to 'trans' for 'being across from'. For terminological clarity, 'bio-women' will now be used here for those women who are non-trans, who were originally identified, biologically, as women and who remain so, their gender also remaining 'women'.

For avoidance of doubt, perhaps it is worth reiterating that the trans matters being mused upon in this chapter are primarily to do with those people who have been born male, sported male genitalia, and maybe for years have dressed as men, yet insist that they are women. Some trans undergo surgery or drug treatment to change their biology; some prefer not to do so. Some may dress as stereo-typical feminine women; some may not. Their sexual preferences may now be different, though need not be so. A trans woman may be sexually attracted to a man – or to a woman.

Many trans women speak of feeling 'born in the wrong body'. They may have experienced years of distress over their sex, gender and sexuality. They now realize that 'all along' they were women, despite being biologically male. Trans women say that they experi-ence the world as bio-women do. Quite what that means – and how they know – are fair questions yet to be considered.

The reference to gender – so far used casually – is intended to introduce a level of identity distinct from that grounded in sexual biology. Under British law, in so-called 'transsexual' cases medically diagnosed as such, or when individuals have lived in the acquired gender for at least two years, the individuals can request a Gender Recognition Certificate (GRC), establishing their 'acquired' gender.

Self-certification goes further than that current British law, though proposals are in place to permit it. Self-certification may be justified as extending civil rights and liberties to groups whose members formerly and formally had their true gender identity denied. The claim is that if biological males sincerely think of them-selves as women, then they should have the right to certify as such. Compare with how gays have secured rights; they can now express their sexual identity without fear and they have secured 'gay' as the preferred term rather than the medical-sounding 'homosexual'. Of course, in many countries that expression is still prohibited. Let us not, by the way, live by the myth that all is well in liberal democra-cies; in some areas of the United States, Britain and other European countries, it is unwise to engage in gay expression, despite what the law permits.

As a matter of legal fact, most countries require some medical evidence to support any gender reassignment, if any is permitted at all. A few have fully engaged self-certification for adults; they include Argentina, Greece and the Republic of Ireland. Self-certification avoids demands for medical confirmations or other proofs. Those demands smack of treating trans people as suffering medical conditions; they can be demeaning and invasive. Further, such proofs can be costly, hence they adversely affect the poor unlike the wealthy – as do most attempts at justice, as observed in previous chapters.

The right to self-certify, in this context, is not the right to certify that one has *changed* gender, but to self-certify as being, say, a woman all along, despite at birth being deemed a boy and later a man. If the 'all along' version is open to self-certification, it is unclear why people should not be allowed to self-certify as changed in gender or indeed to chop and change.

SEX AND GENDER

Most people easily switch between the terms 'gender' and 'sex' without recognizing a difference; they may readily speak of one and the same person as a woman, a female, a lady, a girl. A man, a male, heterosexual, may yet accept that he is effeminate or womanly, but may still refer to himself as male, a man, a guy.

The vast majority of individuals whom we have deemed 'female' – 'girls', 'women', 'ladies' – have sex chromosomes XX. Males, boys, men typically have two different kinds: XY. Prior to the twentieth century, that chromosomic distinction was unknown, yet in the main there existed no problem in distinguishing between women and men, between females and males. We should, then, be able to discuss the matter without essential reference to chromosomes.

Those whom we standardly treat as females and bio-women have naturally developed the reproductive organs of ovaries and so forth; for some years, they usually can conceive and gestate – and menstruate. Such individuals have certain cancer likelihoods that males lack and for which, of course, only females are screened. Let us refer to those individuals as 'females' (biologically females) and reserve that term for people usually with such features. With a similar line of reasoning, let us refer to those who standardly sport testicles and penis as 'males' (biologically males) – and reserve use of that term in that way.

That terminological use, based on a reproductive distinction, does not imply that a person cannot be a female if, because of a genetic fault, illness or surgery, she lacks some of the typical features. Further – and distinct from that fact – the terminology does not imply that there are no borderline cases, grey areas, regarding possession of such biological features. That there are borderline areas does not undermine the basic female/male distinction. There are numerous concepts that we deploy perfectly well in most cases, yet hesitate at borderlines – for example, whether an object is coloured red or orange. Traffic lights in the United Kingdom, relying on colour distinctions, typically work well.

Until we encounter what trans individuals argue, we may readily accept that all women are females. That tends to be how language is used. Women, for example, who cannot conceive sometimes speak of not feeling fully a woman. Describing individuals as women – and let us now use 'gender' when using expressions 'women' and 'men' rather than 'females' and 'males' – certainly adds something over and above the female-ness. For a start, it adds being human; while we speak of female foxes, we would not speak of women foxes – well, not usually.

'Woman' typically brings in more than human features of being female. It depends on the society, but normally we can tell who are men and who women. It is by looks – by shape, 'planes and surfaces', by voice, hair or dress. Look along any bustling street: most citizens of the relevant country readily agree who are the men and who the women – and in the vast majority of cases, they are right. A mishmash of criteria is in play with 'woman'. Of course, sometimes we may hesitate; someone does not fit the typical.

Further, some women we may recognize as women, yet not as being womanly; some women may prefer not to appear womanly.

If we see adults who strike us as women, but then discover they are males, we are more inclined to say that they are men rather than that we have women with male anatomy – or we may be unsure what to say. What *constitutes* being a woman is not determined, or not solely so, by the outward appearances that we standardly use for telling whether individuals are women. Possession of a certain passport may be the standard means, the criterion, for telling that someone is a UK citizen – but that possession is not what constitutes being a UK citizen. The criteria for X need not coincide with what constitutes being X.

From the above considerations, a reasonable conclusion is that being female is essential for being a woman. That, though, is not the conclusion of the trans world intent on self-certification. The terminology deployed by trans individuals is explicitly to allow for the following: that not all individuals rightly gendered as women are females. There could perhaps be some HD meaning revisionism in play here. Even if the word 'woman' currently involves reference to being female, our language use would carve up the world more accurately – 'at Nature's joints' – if we accepted that what constitutes being a woman is not essentially tied to the biological female. Once we used the word 'fish' to cover whales; we now know better. When it comes to man and woman, the trans world knows better – so it believes.

⁂

Trans women say that they are women. That has led some to complain that lesbian bio-women discriminate against them. Lesbian bio-women may fairly reply that it concerns them whether a trans woman is eyeing them as a bio-woman would or as a male would – and also whether biologically they are males. That is a reality carving that is important to bio-women. That returns us to the earlier question of what it is that trans women possess that makes them women, given that they are not female.

The trans answer is that 'being a woman' is constituted by having certain feelings, desires, personalities, attitudes and associated behaviours. Let us use 'psychology' as the blanket term. Most human females have that psychology, but the trans claim is that that psychology is not necessarily grounded in being biologically female. Because 'being a woman' is constituted solely by psychology, women – bio and trans – are in the best position to know that they are women. Compare with how you are in the best position to tell whether you are in pain. Doctors adjudicate whether there is physical damage to your fingers, but you are the authority over whether your fingers hurt.

That pain example should remind us that there must be some recognizable pain behaviour, otherwise we should not have learnt how to use the word 'pain' in a public language. Trans women must have learnt how to use the term 'woman' from the behaviour of other women, most of whom are bio-women, and what that behaviour manifests regarding feelings, personality et al.

Whether it is true that being a woman, as opposed to being a female, is solely to do with possession of a certain psychology is open to question. Historically, some philosophers have suggested that womanhood extends beyond being female to some distinctive psychological features. We could hypothesize that those features are not essentially grounded in female biology. Kant, for example, suggested that women have stronger feelings than men for everything that is beautiful, decorative and adorned; compared with men, they have as much understanding, but it is a 'beautiful understanding'.

Dare I mention Arthur Schopenhauer, the philosopher of pessimism? Writing soon after Kant, he tells us that women are 'directly adapted to act as the nurses and educators of our early childhood, for the simple reason that they themselves are childish, foolish, and short-sighted – in a word, are big children all their lives'.

Of course, there is no good evidence for those claims – they are prejudices – but they illustrate a not unusual belief over centuries that what, in part, constitutes being a woman is possession of certain psychological traits different from those of men.

Perhaps that 'womanly psychology', as understood by trans women, is grounded in innate dispositions, separate from biologically being female, though it could, presumably, result from upbringing and be no worse (or better) for that. That womanly psychology, whatever it quite is, must be a subset of those desires, feelings, attitudes and so forth that bio-women typically have. After all, trans women, one takes it, lack the feelings, attitudes and disturbances, 'from within', to do with menstruation, conceiving and breastfeeding. It would be most odd to believe that those psychological features possessed for some time by most bio-women lack biological groundings; it would also be pretty odd to think that other psychological features of typical bio-women are unrelated to biology and, for that matter, resultant interactions within society.

Even if there are some psychological features that trans women and bio-women have in common – and that men (bio and trans) lack – are there sufficient psychological features in common such that a male could be a woman? How should that be determined? The demand by trans women, let us emphasize, is not to be treated *as if* women; the demand is that they be recognized as actually being women. Because they are women – so they sincerely believe – others should recognize them as such. Thus, liberal societies may feel that they ought to accede to self-certification; they ought to grant trans women, on their say-so, all the rights of bio-women.

CONSEQUENCES: RESPECT FOR WHOM?

Acknowledging people's rights has the feeling of being respectful; deciding to 'grant' them certain rights, though, may come over as disrespectful or paternalist. Either way, we should be mindful of the effects on others and on their rights. It is a moral matter concerning which rights take priority, which dangers merit greatest regard. For example, we may, without much reflection, accept that people have rights privately to own drones and supercars; reflection, though, may lead us to urge restrictions for, without restrictions, the rights of others may be adversely affected by way of privacy invasions and noise pollution.

In the late twentieth century, many men 'came out' as gay. That was a form of self-certification – of obvious benefit to them, allowing free expression of their sexual orientation, and to people, more generally, when assessing possible sexual partners. Public rituals that amount to little more than self-certifying are necessary for couples, including same-sex couples, to be deemed married. That has led to some inconsistencies in Britain over the treatment of siblings who live together and seek marriage for taxation advantages; those inconsistencies could easily be resolved. Are there, though, problems with transgender self-certification not so easily solved?

Self-certification, in certain arenas, has had major unfortunate consequences. There have at times been vogues in Britain for self-certifying one's ability to service large loans for property purchases; that self-certification often ended in tears – sometimes literally so. Hence, restrictions at times are introduced. More pertinently, consider Rachel Anne Doležal, an American civil-rights activist; she became famous for insisting that she was a black woman, yet in fact was of white European ancestry. She passed herself off as black, causing anger by many of the black community and, indeed, many of the white. Later, she spoke of identifying with the black community – but that is very different from one's identity *being* black. In the Netherlands in 2018, Emile Ratelband sought permission to self-certify as aged forty-nine, for his psychology, he insisted, was twenty years younger than his sixty-nine physical years; he argued that declaring the sixty-nine years adversely affected his romantic prospects. He lost the case; one's age in a typical Western society is tied in so many ways to more biological factors than those that affect how one feels.

The trans case for self-certification differs from those just mentioned; the transgendered discussed here rest their arguments, as said, on the premise that gender is solely a psychological matter. Now, we may happily suggest that a liberal society should recognize trans women as identifying *with* women – and that can be self-certified – yet not succumb to accepting that they *are* women, purely through self-certification, or, indeed, living *as if* women.

Suppose we accept that biological males who self-certify as women really are women. Women now fall into two categories: bio-women – that is, those people, born female, and treated thereafter as women without objection; and trans women – that is, those people, born male, not initially treated as women, yet now certifying as women. Insisting that both are equally well 'women' could have adverse consequences and lose a valuable distinction. Consider the effects on others if the distinction between bio-women and trans women withers. Here are some.

Many bio-women over decades have fought for 'safe spaces', for 'women-only' areas. Putting to one side whether such spaces are justified, if trans women are legally – morally, socially – women, without qualification, then they should have the same rights as other women to such spaces, otherwise there would be unjust discrimination. An obvious problem is that some males who are men may self-identify as trans women solely to gain access to women-only areas. Trans individuals respond that the possibility is unlikely to be realized and, when it is, 'safe-space' rules would protect against disturbances. Hence, we shelve the concern, even though some bio-women are undoubtedly and sincerely worried – and possibly the trans community dismisses their worries too readily.

Let us focus on those biological males who sincerely believe that they are women, albeit who have no desire for medical interventions. They call for respect regarding their identity and well-being. There is, though, also the need to respect the identity and well-being of those bio-women who value safe spaces for bio-women. Now, some trans women complain vociferously at being excluded from such spaces, but it is unclear why they should be free to enter areas traditionally kept specifically for females who are women. Some, maybe many, bio-women seek safe spaces because they fear sexual pressures or, indeed, feel uneasy more generally in the presence of males and the male gaze. True, trans women may also feel that way – but, from the bio-woman perspective, trans women may be perpetrators of the male gaze, despite having sincerely self-certified as women.

In summary, should the protected 'ladies-only' spaces – changing rooms, shared accommodation, swimming ponds, hospital wards, prisons – be for bio-women only or for bio-women and trans women only or for only 'women' understood as...?

Similar problems, some argue, arose when men 'came out as gay' and hence perhaps felt at ease in approaching other men in men-only changing rooms and men-only prisons, perhaps (unwittingly) oppressing heterosexual men by demands for gay sex. The problems, though, are not so similar, for there is no history of men fighting for heterosexual-only safe spaces, only to have those spaces undermined by gay rights.

Think, too, how if trans women are to be women, then many statistics relating to women would change: average income levels, prevalence of various diseases, eating disorders, men/women ratios in the workplace, representation in parliament and so forth. Trans women being women could also be to the detriment of some bio-women: for example, those of certain conservative religions who need at times to be in the company only of bio-women. Further, trans women, because of their male biology, may, in certain arenas, dominate bio-women. Further still, the inclusion of trans women as women, if consistent, should extend to single-sex women-only sports, the trans women, being with male biology, probably out-running bio-women with the female biology.

As an analogy relating to some of the difficulties mentioned, sup-pose prosperous white bio-men in the United Kingdom were free to self-certify as members of a particular minority ethnic group, a group suffering much adverse discrimination; a result would be an improvement in the income and employment statistics for the group. That could lead to the government declaring how things are now going so much better for the group and hence how various com-pensatory funding programmes should be withdrawn. That would manifestly be to the detriment of the non-self-certifying members of the group.

There perhaps are already unfortunate consequences of the pub-licity given to transgendering. In Britain, there has been an increase (still a small number, of course) in the number of children and ado-lescents saying that they are of the wrong gender; in some cases that has led to irreversible medical interventions by way of surgery and drugs. It is not unreasonable – and not transphobic – at least to wonder whether some children, maybe already psychologically vulnerable for other reasons, are mistakenly latching on to trans-gendering to deal with their problems.

The difficulties, taken together, may not be sufficient to oppose self-certification. Some of the difficulties – for example, those aris-ing from discriminations against women by some religions – should in any case be overcome. It is, though, a myth – a liberal 'we must not discriminate' myth – to think that self-certification is manifestly a right to be granted to trans individuals who want it. In many walks of life, biology matters and cannot be erased by siren voices declaring as discriminatory recognition of the biology.

ON THE ERADICATION OF WOMEN

Some, often designated 'radical feminists', suggest that 'woman' adds to 'female' as follows: women are economically, socially, politically and sexually oppressed on the basis of their being female. Sex – female/male – rests on biology; 'gender' is based on resultant differences between women and men that arise through a culture's differential treatments. The result, it is claimed, is a differential gendered socialization, one in which women, with their female reproductive role, have lower value than men. To avoid qualification multiplying upon qualification, I use 'radical feminism' in that sense – the sense where a female/male biological distinction is upheld in understanding the woman/man gendered distinction. That stance, thus understood, is at odds with the trans' stance: namely, that being a woman rests solely on certain psychological features.

According to the feminist line as just set out, most females are raised to be passive, submissive, weak and nurturing – as women – while most males are raised to be active, dominant, strong, aggressive and superior – as men. Presumably that line depends on claims about typical Western societies, for there may well be some societies where 'women' have the superior role. If that is so, then, following the understanding of 'woman' just outlined, unless marked as relative to a culture, those individuals, as a matter of logic, are not women, though they are females.

The concepts 'woman' and 'man', on the above feminist line, carry obvious evaluations. For both genders, the position is coercive: men are expected to behave in a certain way; women are expected to behave in a different way. Thus, some such feminists may aim completely to remove gender from life. If or when women lose their subservient role, no longer would there be women on that understanding – just as, if slavery is truly abolished, there no longer are slaves. Paradoxically and subtly, once women's subservience is overcome, we may rightly say that these women still exist, but no longer are women, though they remain females. It would strike many as curious language that, if or when women secure equality with men in some way, they cease to be women – and presumably men cease to be men.

That linguistic infelicity to one side, although trans women often suffer oppressive discrimination, if – *if* – the feminist line is right, then trans women fundamentally are not women; trans women lack the biology and hence lack the relevant resultant oppression. That fundamental disagreement is why many trans women and feminist bio-women are in dispute, sometimes heated dispute. The protected spaces for bio-women, the battles for equal representation and so forth, are to do with correcting injustices that women with female biology have typically suffered. Those concerns become distorted if trans women are to be women. The matter is not just a matter of words.

How should we determine which approach – the radical feminist; the trans; the everyday – is right? Is there even a rightness here? The answer is to resist being mesmerized by a word, but to reflect on similarities and dissimilarities, judging which ones are relevant and where, for human lives to flourish. Everyday classifications are sometimes rightly revised: as noted earlier, whales no longer are classified as fish.

COMPETING QUESTIONS; COMPETING DISCRIMINATIONS

Ludwig Wittgenstein, an Austrian-British philosopher based in Cambridge, a genius who anguished about both ethics and logic,

brought to philosophers' attention the truth that searching for defi-
nitions, for the black or the white, is often deeply mistaken. In his
posthumous *Philosophical Investigations* (1953), he famously introduced 'family resemblances':

> Consider for example the proceedings that we call 'games'. I
> mean board-games, card-games, ball-games, Olympic games,
> and so on. What is common to them all? – Don't say: 'There must
> be something in common, or they would not be called "games"'
> – but *look and see* whether there is anything common to all. – For
> if you look at them you will not see something that is common
> to *all*, but similarities, relationships, and a whole series of them
> at that...
>
> And the result of this examination is: we see a complicated
> network of similarities overlapping and criss-crossing: some-
> times overall similarities, sometimes similarities of detail.
>
> I can think of no better expression to characterize these simi-
> larities than 'family resemblances'; for the various resemblances
> between members of a family: build, features, colour of eyes,
> gait, temperament, etc. etc. overlap and criss-cross in the same
> way.

Which similarities and dissimilarities matter between bio-women
and trans women – and the mattering may differ, depending on
whether the trans are simply self-certifying or have undergone
surgery and so forth – depends on context, intentions and consequences. The similarities are obviously not remotely sufficient for
both groups to be treated in the same way with regard to cervical
smear tests, health policies and many medical interventions.

Are bio-women and trans women possessed of the same history of oppressive inequalities compared with men, regarding pay
and conditions? The right answer is probably 'no'; hence, from
a radical-feminist viewpoint, there exist insufficient similarities

between bio-women and trans women for the latter to be deemed women.

Are radical feminists right in grounding that oppression of women on females' reproductive biology? That could be so. A good additional response would be that many of the poorest in society have far more in common in suffering oppression than just those who are female have in common. It could be better to concentrate on reducing the poverty of men and women, trans or otherwise, rather than concentrating on injustices grounded in gender.

Liberal idealists will retort that all injustices should be addressed; the reply is that one needs to direct energies somewhere and, if some success is a viable possibility, then the most egregious violation of rights is that somewhere. Would that exceptionally well-paid media bio-women and trans women, for example, leading very comfortable lives, and rightly objecting to being paid less than men in equivalent positions, devote even more energies to protesting against the very low pay and appalling working conditions for millions of people – women, men, trans and otherwise.

Some may condemn the observation above as 'whataboutery' – as attempting to discredit the justice of equal pay for the sexes when in equivalent well-paid work. That condemnation, though, can itself be used to deflect from important matters of justice. The justice of equal pay between the well-paid is not here being questioned; what is being questioned is whether the well-paid's yearning for justice is untrammelled by self-interest. Here is a small analogy:

> Samantha is vociferously complaining that someone has jumped the taxi queue. 'It's unfair,' she shouts, enraged. 'My son's going to miss the ballet.' Onlookers respond, 'Hold on, *what about* the distraught father who pushed in front of you, getting the taxi first? His daughter's just been knocked down, bleeding profusely, and no ambulance in sight.'

Does that onlookers' response merit easy dismissal as some 'what-aboutery'?

∿

Should trans women be allowed to enter spaces effectively des-ignated exclusively for bio-women – be they swimming pools, changing rooms or safe houses – to protect them from male eyes, male sexual pressures and male genitalia? Many trans women consider that question to be offensive rhetoric; but for many bio-women, it is neither rhetoric nor intended as offensive. To the ques-tion, the obvious answer is that those spaces are inappropriate for trans women who exhibit male biology. Trans women who demand entrance to such spaces are thereby denying the right of bio-women to have such spaces. Of course, it is a fair question whether there should be spaces exclusively for bio-women. Should a liberal society be so committed to anti-discrimination that bio-women's desires over this should be overridden as obviously morally wrong?

Here, we have competing liberties, competing rights. As is often the case, it is a myth of liberalism that there must be definitive 'black-or-white' right answers.

What are we to say about trans women who dress as women and live as women? They probably have sufficient in common with typ-ical bio-women rightfully to attend 'women-only' meetings where public world pressures on women are being addressed.

Different groups demand different rights, treatments, liberties. Sometimes we want wider classification – to embrace more within a group – sometimes we want narrower, to uphold important dif-ferences. Related to that matter is the question whether we should be more worried by the tyranny of the majority (here, the bio-women) or the tyranny of the minority (here, the trans women). Trans women may be distressed at being barred from (bio-) women's safe spaces, but the vastly greater number of bio-women may be distressed if trans women are allowed. Are bio-women who seek to ban trans women from (bio-)women's safe spaces and 'ladies-only' bathing pools akin to those white racists in the Southern States of America who objected to anyone black in colour sitting near them on a bus? That kinship seems to be the implication of certain activist trans women's attitudes against the bio-women's defence of their exclusive safe spaces. Or are trans women as bad as those bio-men who lack respect for bio-women having their own spaces?

In some respects trans women are women; in other respects they are not. For some purposes they are; for others they are not. Also, things change. Some 'trans-inclined' now reject commitment to just two genders. They are non-binary; they see gender as a spectrum, adding to the melee with agender; demiboy; demigirl; aporagender; lunagender – the list goes on. Such transgenderists, it seems, are simply noting how people possess various psychological features, to varying degrees, concerning personality, sexual orientation, attitudes and so forth. Some are more usual amongst females, others amongst males. That there is a spectrum, though, is compatible with a big distinction existing between typical men and women. The existence of the colour spectrum does not undermine the distinction between, say, red and green; further, it says nothing about whether green items are far more numerous than red. By the way, that there exists a big distinction between typical men and women, highly relevant to many relationships, is why the kinship, mentioned above, between the racist bus example and (bio-)women safe spaces is poorly grounded.

Trans may argue that bio-women who want safe spaces exclusively for bio-women are prejudiced; they should be coaxed into changing their feelings – but why the 'should'? Yes, the embarrassments that many people feel in the presence of opposite reproductive biology, when unclothed, may fade away. When in 'all-gender rest rooms', bio-women may come to welcome bio-men and trans women watching them doing their make-up.

It is not easy to see how the male/female reproductive distinction will be eradicated; it is not easy to grasp why it should. Perhaps one day, though, drawing the woman/man distinction will be as quaint and irrelevant as drawing today a distinction between English people with Norman ancestry and those with Anglo-Saxon. Until that happy day comes, if happy it be...

15

Happy Land

Consider the following possible country, a little akin to today's Iran. It is Happy Land. It is a country in which alcohol consumption is illegal, in which women cannot travel outside the home without a man's permission and in which homosexual relationships are punishable by death. People are expected to answer the calls of the mosque. Women in public must always be completely veiled. No one should cast doubt on the existence or behaviour of Muhammad. It is a country of that ilk.

There is an astonishing feature of Happy Land's inhabitants: virtually everyone accepts the rightness of the laws – even those individuals who sometimes lapse and break them. There is no evidence of the population having been brainwashed; generations have come and gone, valuing their society and its ways. The citizens are well aware of how other societies run, of their laws and customs, but they dismiss such societies as corrupt, if lacking Happy Land's ways. Happy Land has the laws and customs by which people ought to abide – so their citizens firmly believe. That 'ought', they may say, can be inferred from... – and here they point to some traditional Islamic texts.

We could modify our Happy Land and delete the Islamic groundings, yet in other respects the land is much the same. Here the citizens do not turn to ancient scriptures to justify the laws. Instead, they insist that their way of doing things and the differential treatment of women and men is what is 'natural'; things cannot successfully be otherwise (one must not interfere with Nature, at least that portion of Nature). Even without regard to Nature or ancient texts, some may insist that it is intuitively true that their way of life is how things ought to be.

Our Happy Land could be presented as democratic, but that is not essential. Maybe it exults in democracy; and generations of people vote for the continuation of its policies. Happy Land may, though, be authoritarian or totalitarian, lacking democratic procedures, but the citizens once again accept that the laws and customs establish how things ought to be. In such an authoritarian Happy Land, many people perhaps would prefer democracy, but paradoxically accept that their preference is mistaken. The people recognize their fallibility – as many Catholics once did, when disagreeing with edicts of popes.

Maybe most people are happy living in Happy Land, happy in the sense of having feelings of pleasure and suffering few frustrations. Even that, though, is an unnecessary condition for the land rightfully to be deemed 'happy'. 'Happy' can be used in the sense of being in accord with how things ought to be. The citizens may be happy in the belief (they deem it knowledge) that they are in harmony with the divine will or with the natural order of the universe. Such an idea is given by Sir Robert Filmer, an early seventeenth-century conservative thinker, who defended the divine right of kings, a position that came under detailed attack by Locke. Filmer observed that God 'caused some to be born with crowns upon their heads, and all others with saddles upon their backs'. That stance, showing greater variety, occurs in the Victorian hymn 'All things bright and beautiful', with the verse – a verse which these days is often left unsung –

> The rich man in his castle,
> The poor man at his gate,

God made them high and lowly,
And ordered their estate.

Things are right and proper when people 'know their place' – and at all times and in all places. Even the lowliest of Happy Land have typically accepted their place.

What are we to say about countries of that ilk? Presumably most readers would be much distressed at the notion that lands with such laws and customs are morally acceptable. Surely, many would vehemently insist, the lands offend human rights of equality, dignity and liberty, and that is so even if the inhabitants firmly and sincerely believe things are as they should be.

When we explain our views to Happy Land's inhabitants, they dismiss us. The dismissal may result from their disputing our understanding of what is right and wrong. In the straightforward 'happiness as pleasure' version, they may simply confirm their preference for how things are without even addressing what is right or wrong.

As seen in Chapter 4, we may, though, be so committed to our knowing what is right and proper for people to have flourishing lives that we maintain that the people of Happy Land must be failing to grasp their true interests. Perhaps, because of their culture, they cannot, in fact, fully grasp the immense value of autonomy or individuality. If we are to uphold our position, we need to claim that we know – just *know* – that the way in which they live is wrong. Perhaps that is indeed what we ought to do. After all, most Western liberals rightly claim to know that female genital mutilation (FGM) is just wrong, whatever its importance within certain cultural traditions.

NEO-LIBERALISM, CAPITALISM AND FREE MARKETS

We shall be gone some time before we return to Happy Land – but we shall return. We need to take a scenic route that allows us to reflect upon our typical liberal-democratic societies, taking Great

Britain and the United States as our models, though we could equally well be looking at Canada, Australasia and other developed economies. Here, 'liberty' is the watchword; the social, political and economic structure is grounded in liberty. It is a liberty understood in terms of free markets and the private ownership of property – of land and the means of production. It is a liberty that is intertwined with capitalism. It is 'neo-liberalism': people, in the main, should be at liberty to trade, to buy and sell, as they think fit. Liberty, thus understood as with the capitalist impulse, leads to bringing into markets what we may have assumed to be outside markets: forests, rivers, minerals, land. As noted earlier, the rise of social media in a sense has now brought our thoughts, feelings and private inter-actions into the marketplace. Vast ranges of what we think of as our data are up for sale; unwittingly, we hand data over to others when we click, confirming that we have read the terms and conditions of the 'free' services.

In praising free markets, it is easy to overlook the question: from what are free markets free? Even the most ardent free-marketeer does not seek a free market in laws of contract, regulations over weights and measures and the dispensation of justice. There is not meant to be a free market in determining which laws should exist, how they are implemented and when judgements should be made that they have been broken. There is, then, a recognition of val-ues other than those of free dealings – values, indeed, that set the framework for the markets.

Neo-liberalism assumes that people, in the main, are motivated by self-interest, including their family interest, maybe extended to close friends. Well, they are motivated by what they consider to be their self-interest; after all, they can make mistakes. Of course, owners or managers of capital – of the businesses, the production lines et al. – are aware of the possible bad effects of competition on their business returns. Hence, they sometimes engage in secret agreements to restrict innovations, to build in product obsolescence and to prevent new competitors entering their markets.

Competition, in any case, it is accepted, does not permeate through all levels of business: employers and employees need to cooperate – plumbers rely on their mates to turn off the water; managers need workers in harmony so that nuts fit the bolts – but, from the perspective of the business, cooperation is usually valued only for the profitable outcome. The free-market economy is expressly grounded in sellers and buyers. Some may disingenuously insist that they are both engaged in the same activity – namely, getting the better of the other – but that is a case of 'the same' not amounting to being the same. After all, they are not pulling in the same direction; what benefits one is at a cost to the other.

Lovers of truly free markets do not value markets so unconstrained that businesses can eventually secure monopoly positions such that, for example, one business completely controls internet communications, another pharmaceuticals and a third a country's fishing business. Lovers of free markets approve of constraints against such positions – unless they themselves are involved in the ownership or success of those monopolies or near monopolies. Witness the wrangling of the great global corporations that seek to control more and more of the market; witness Amazon, Apple, Alphabet (owner of Google) and Berkshire Hathaway. The global powers are pictured here by the American journalist Matt Taibbi; he writes of Goldman Sachs: 'The first thing you need to know about Goldman Sachs is that it's everywhere. The world's most powerful investment bank is a great vampire squid wrapped around the face of humanity, relentlessly jamming its blood funnel into anything that smells like money.'

Despite the glorification of free enterprise, considerable government intervention and investment has been required for the development of technology, pharmaceuticals and environmental-friendly products which the 'free market' would not initially take on. Even free-marketeers may acknowledge that long-term planning cannot rely solely on free markets, where businesses and investors usually have an eye only on short-term profits. That short-termism also applies to many politicians who look only to the next election.

THE INVISIBLE HAND – INVISIBLE BUT VOCAL

The current neo-liberal ethos was promoted by the Mont Pèlerin Society, a little-known group amongst the public at large, created in 1949 at Lake Geneva. It argued for free markets and opposed State intervention. A key figure was F. A. Hayek, a twentieth-century Austrian-British economist, whose work against Keynesianism became a stimulus to the policies of Margaret Thatcher in Great Britain and Ronald Reagan in the United States. The policies were copied in many other countries.

When it is pointed out how the neo-liberal approach has led to gross inequalities in both wealth and income, with the poor exploited by the wealthy, the argument is supplemented with, to put it paradoxically, the observation of what cannot be observed – namely, the 'invisible hand'. Hayek and colleagues brought forth a voice to the invisible hand, hereafter 'Hand'. Hand proclaims: 'People being at liberty to engage in voluntary transactions, even though motivated by self-interest, is the best way for a society to run – for the benefit of all. The free market is the means of coordinating actions, ensuring maximum efficient use of resources.'

Goods, services and experiences, if freely traded, are distributed according to the so-called law of supply and demand. When demand increases for a particular item (and we use 'item' and 'product' to cover services, intellectual property, adventures and experiences as well as physical goods), the price rises; that, theoretically, leads competitors into the market, increasing production, thus prices fall and a greater demand can be satisfied.

Hayek argued that any rational distribution of resources needs to be based on the 'real costs' of those resources, as determined via free markets. The prices at which people are prepared to trade, if trading freely, manifest the relative values of the goods to them. That line of reasoning also applies to people's labour, be it intellectual or physical, for labour – people's abilities, energy and time – too should be bought and sold. Neo-liberalism – at least since the rejection of slavery – draws a line at trading in the ownership of people. People are, though, often referred to as 'human resources'; and, in view of the amount of time and devotion they sometimes need to give to the businesses – well, they may feel little better than slaves.

Adam Smith, the eighteenth-century Scottish intellectual and pioneer in economics, now comes to the fore. He is still revered. Smith introduced Hand to the world of business, though it is mentioned only three times in his writings and has but a single appearance in the seminal The Wealth of Nations (1776). Regarding that use, scholarly dispute exists whether he meant it as fiction or indicative of divine design. Here he talks of the businessman: 'he intends only his own gain, and he is in this, as in many other cases, led by an invisible hand to promote an end which was no part of his intention... By pursuing his own interest, he frequently promotes that of the society more effectually than when he really intends to promote it.'

Elsewhere we meet the more extravagant claim: 'The rich... are led by an invisible hand to make nearly the same distribution of the necessaries of life, which would have been made, had the earth been divided into equal portions among all its inhabitants, and thus without intending it, without knowing it, advance the interest of the society...'

Hand's invisibility may remind us of the invisibility of the mysterious ways of an all-powerful, all-benevolent God in permitting worldly sufferings. That is the puzzle of evil. We may well wonder about the benevolence and justice of Hand, as we do with God, in view of the considerable poverty in countries such as the United States where Hand dominates. As a 2018 report notes, 'hidden beneath fabulous wealth, the United States tolerates poverty-related illness at levels comparable to the world's poorest countries.' In the main, Hand delivers more and more typically to those that already hath – well, those that hath in financial power, if not in spirit. It is a myth that Hand is even-handed; it is a myth that Hand delivers the best that can be delivered for all.

Theresa May, as British prime minister in 2017, claimed that a free-market economy, operating under the right rules and regulations, is the 'greatest agent of collective human progress ever created'. Clearly, on that view, either the rules and regulations are not working as they should for the proper reign of Hand or Hand itself is letting down millions.

Probably Smith was not as optimistic about the workings of Hand as his devotees are today; they speak as if with papal infallibility over Hand's ways. Smith was not as optimistic, at least regarding the financial benefits to the poorest, for when addressing 'the real happiness of human life', he somewhat conveniently announced: 'All the different ranks of life are nearly upon a level, and the beggar, who suns himself by the side of the highway, possesses that security which kings are fighting for.'

Defenders of neo-liberalism, though, do not appeal to sunning as a means of handling any guilt over poverty. They point out how, over the last fifty years, worldwide poverty has decreased; they put that down to the development of free international trade. 'Let us not worry if a teeny number have grown incredibly wealthy – so long as the poor, through Hand, have been helped.'

That line of argument is disingenuous. There are many other factors which could well account for the poverty decrease and life-expectancy increase. There have been many beneficial scientific, technological and medical advances. They cannot all be attributed to free markets and global 'free' trade; many advances have occurred because of deliberate State interventions. Many free markets have held back the developments of the poorer nations, as argued by the economist Ha-Joon Chang in his 2008 *Bad Samaritans*.

Consider the economic transformation of South Korea (not an unusual case) since the 1960s – and Samsung's development from dealing in fish, vegetables and fruit to being a leading exporter in mobile phones and other technological delights. Was that vast economic development through free markets? No. Free markets had a role, often with a ruthless approach towards employees, but the Korean government selected certain industries to develop, engaged in tariff protection and subsidies, owned all the banks, built up some state-run enterprises and controlled foreign exchange. The United States and Britain, decades earlier, ensured their economic development through protection and subsidies, using international free markets only when in their own interests, often to the detriment of poor nations.

Have the most successful deliveries of services been courtesy of capitalism? No. It is forgotten that, in the nineteenth century, leading into the twentieth, in Britain, for example, some large local authorities developed municipal services with impressive performances, providing municipal housing, tramways and so forth. Joseph Chamberlain, a Liberal, as mayor of Birmingham in the 1870s, became known for his 'gas-and-water socialism', when he persuaded the authority to buy out the private gas and then water companies, the aim being to consolidate services and improve standards of safety and health. Basing services on the local has the obvious value of being in contact with what is needed; it has the downside of what has become summed as 'postcode lotteries' – the services that we receive depend on the irrelevancy of our postcode: that is, on the administrative area in which we live.

TODAY'S MYTHS

Neo-liberalism with its free markets needs many laws, rules and regulations, to keep Hand in play. We may question the moral justification for some of those laws. Even Smith was sceptical of some: 'Civil government, so far as it is instituted for the security of property, is in reality instituted for the defence of the rich against the poor, or of those who have some property against those who have none at all.'

Capitalism loves the creation of companies and corporations as legal entities in their own right, free to trade. They are separate from their 'owners' who can then legally avoid various responsibilities. As the American writer Ambrose Bierce defined in his 1911 work *The Devil's Dictionary*, deemed one of the masterpieces of American literature: 'CORPORATION, n. An ingenious device for obtaining individual profit without individual responsibility.'

Corporations can fail, going into liquidation, leaving suppliers and employees unpaid, pension promises lost, while the directors remain unscathed. Indeed, even the shareholders of the company, if private, may have ensured their own security by taking large dividends from the company prior to collapse. A company, so the mantra goes, is legally obliged to maximize profits for the shareholders, the owners. These days, that mantra has some caveats – the company should take into account the effects on the community and other stakeholders such as employees and creditors – but the ultimate aim remains: namely, that of profit for the shareholders, that of self-interest.

Senior executives of major companies are rarely significant owners of the companies, risking their own capital; they could just as easily be running State-owned enterprises, as happens in some European countries, with the remit to act in the consumers' interests. Further, the high-earning levels of senior executives, as a matter of empirical fact, bear little relationship to the success of the relevant corporations. Indeed, what moral justification can there be for the vast discrepancies in remuneration levels between executives employed in air-conditioned offices and those workers on building sites or down in the sewers?

Whatever the matter of morality, whatever the facts of corporate success, Hand tells us that executive pay levels are just the results of free markets, and the markets cannot be bucked. That overlooks the fact that the members of the boards, selection committees and remuneration committees often overlap and move in the same circles; they have generated the ethos of high remunerations for senior executives. It also assumes that the best person for a job would always want the highest possible remuneration.

Contrast the outcome of those remuneration networks with the position of typical lowly employees: increasingly, such workers are in insecure jobs – as part-timers or temporary – be they lecturers or Uber drivers; increasingly, corporate owners take advantage of legal loopholes whereby the employees are magically deemed as 'self-employed', hence lacking many employment rights. They are the 'precariat' – the term derives from 'precarious' and 'proletariat' – those whose existence lacks predictability and security.

Let us also note that much of the income that is received in the 'free-market' economy is received by a small number of people as 'rentiers'. They own the land, the physical assets, and also the intangibles such as derivatives, brands and intellectual property. With the privatization impulse in Britain, initiated by Prime Minister Thatcher in the 1980s, half of the public estate – about 10 per cent of Britain's land – has since been transferred to private corporations, with some of the wealthiest individuals deriving their main income from resultant rentals.

Decades ago, Maynard Keynes had called for the 'euthanasia of the rentier'. Today's rentiers have patents to drugs, own student loan books and digital platforms – where, again, there is little scope for a free market. One corporation sought to patent the use of turmeric for healing wounds; at least the Indian government managed to stop that. In contrast to that approach, Tim Berners-Lee at CERN did not patent the worldwide web. The United States and Europe often complain about the theft of their intellectual property by Chinese companies; they conveniently forget how the West acquired the know-how for mechanical clocks, gunpowder, silk and paper from China.

Today's global corporations seek to determine social policy, bypassing democratic controls. Witness those companies that take nation states to court because various health-protection laws have impeded 'free trade'. The vast size of some corporations enables them to strangle small businesses until they go out of business. Being global corporations, they – of course – ensure that least tax is paid and surprisingly (or maybe not) political leaderships allow that to continue. Let us again note the revolving doors; those in the upper echelons of business and those in government and statutory authorities shamelessly spin between roles.

To summarize, today's capitalism is far removed from the ideal of small businesses in competition, delivering goods and services at the lowest price. It is far removed from the alleged ideal that hard work and entrepreneurial risk should be the sole means to vast wealth. It is also far removed from individuals with capital choosing to invest in businesses in which they work and with which they identify. Once capital was raised for the development of long-term projects to which people proudly committed. That now is rare. Indeed, stock markets of the United States and United Kingdom are, in part, playgrounds and gambling dens for the wealthy and fund managers engaged in ever greater High Frequency Trading (HFT), looking for immediate profits. And let us not forget that when the going gets tough, State interventions are suddenly popular. Recall the massive bail-outs required when major financial institutions, with sleights of hand to enhance profitability, brought about the 2008 global crisis. The audacious response to that crisis by lovers of free markets was to blame the lack of regulation.

'THE NASTIEST OF MEN'

Apart from the myths regarding how capitalism's free markets operate – and the myths of how they brought forth the economic prosperity of most countries – there is dubiety about the underlying ideas. Keynes provocatively summed up the position thus: capitalism amounts to 'the astonishing belief that the nastiest motives of the nastiest men somehow or other work for the best results in the best of all possible worlds'.

Keynes argued that it is better to have the 'psychopaths' in the City rather than in government: '... dangerous human proclivities can be canalised into comparatively harmless channels by the existence of opportunities for money-making and private wealth, which, if they cannot be satisfied in this way, may find their outlet in cruelty, the reckless pursuit of personal power and authority, and other forms of self-aggrandisement.'

He was well aware, though, that while it is 'better that a man should tyrannize over his bank balance than over his fellow-citizens', the bank-balance power would sometimes help owners to tyrannize over citizens. Today, things are worse: the 'psychopaths' running and trading the global corporations now possess vast and significant powers over governments and, indeed, voters.

The self-interest, as promoted in a capitalist society, leads to moral mistreatments. Kant argued that morally one ought never to use a person solely as a means. The capitalist is using both employees and consumers as means. It is not 'solely so', it would be argued; individuals are voluntarily engaged in the activities, for wages or for the acquisition of consumer products. The question then becomes whether those engagements are truly voluntary. How voluntary an action is – how much freedom it manifests – depends in part on the options known to be available and their effects, if taken up. We met such matters in Chapter 4.

Further, self-interest, for many people, is not solely the satisfaction of what they need and want, but involves what Hobbes termed 'eminence'. Competition is not just to ensure that one does well, but that one does better than others – that, indeed, others will fail. We may recall an observation by the American writer Gore Vidal: 'Every time a friend succeeds, a little something in me dies.'

The ethos of the market economy, as well as possibly corrupting our motives, can corrupt what some understand as morality. Nostrum Laboratories, for example, suddenly increased the price of the antibiotic nitrofurantoin in 2018 by over 500 per cent, from $474.75 to $2,392. Nirmal Mulye, chief executive officer, claimed: '... it is a moral requirement to make money where you can... to sell the product for the highest price.'

Here follow some other examples, showing how once the market ethos gains ground, the only acceptable way to value things is, it seems, by the price they fetch in the free market.

Parents sometimes pay others to fulfil their moral duties: they pay the fines for being late in collecting their children from school; the fines are treated not as fines because of committing a wrong, but as fees for child-minding. The market ethos has taken over. The wealthy are sometimes permitted to pay for cell upgrades when in gaol; donations to certain universities ease the entry of the donors' children. Vacant boxes at the opera house and football stadium may indicate that they are being rented by corporations, not because of great corporate interest in the music and game, but for occasional use to impress customers. Membership of distinguished 'gentlemen' clubs in London may be gained for similar reasons, rather than to further an appreciation of the arts, sciences and good conversation. In Britain, schools are increasingly assessed in terms of how many pupils gain entry to good universities; the universities are, in part, deemed successful the higher the earnings of their graduates. The outcome is that provision in schools of, for example, music is reduced; it is far more important to focus on subjects that are most likely to lead to high earnings.

Suppose you want to keep the population growth under control. You could limit the size of families by law – applying to one and all – or you could issue tradeable procreation vouchers to each couple. With the latter approach, the poor have an incentive to sell their vouchers and not have children, thus reducing overall inequality. Does that financial benefit justify, in effect, trading children as commodities? When people feel what is valuable ought not to be traded, blatant attempts at commercializing can sometimes fail; the commercial world, therefore, may favour creeping commercialization. Witness how in Britain gradually (with the odd exception) each day has become a trading day and with trading hours extended.

Corporations make charitable contributions – good – but the boardroom discussions are in terms of how contributions fit the corporate image and the likely corporate benefit rather than the value of the charity. The market economy can, as Smith argued, corrupt our moral sentiments, generating a 'disposition to admire, and almost to worship, the rich and the powerful, and to despise, or, at least, to neglect persons of poor and mean condition'.

In sum, free markets can corrupt social bonds; they become little more than monetary transactions, transactions that encourage motivations of self-interest. Paying high prices for something, though, is neither a necessary nor a sufficient indicator of that something being appropriately valued.

Here, another observation by Wittgenstein is pertinent. He was strolling with his close friend, David Pinsent. Pinsent briefly took off to photograph a scene that struck him. On his return, Wittgenstein was silent and sulky. Pinsent reports: 'I walked on with him in silence for half an hour, and then asked him what was the matter. It seemed, my keenness to take that photo had disgusted him – "like a man who can think of nothing – when walking – but how the country would do for a golf course".'

Wittgenstein did not have the free market itself in mind; his anxiety was more embracing. He was depressed by how what is valuable can be corrupted if treated as a means to something else rather than valued in itself. That was a line we indeed find in Keynes – an associate of Wittgenstein – and in G. E. Moore's *Principia Ethica* (1903), deemed by Keynes 'the Bible' of the Bloomsbury Group. Lovers of free markets may fail to appreciate natural beauty in itself, but only as a commercial product. That does not mean that free-market commercialism is bound to destroy natural beauty – though it often does – but that, when it becomes corporately owned, free-market lovers will tend to impose entrance charges, thus blocking access by the poor. Even when people have a sense of the intrinsic value of, for example, the natural world – and not just as a means to an end – they can be persuaded into believing that it must still be valued in commercial terms, how it is a cost to companies which could otherwise exploit it.

Of course, that the market economy is corrupting in some areas does not imply that it is corrupting in others. The problem is that once the market economy is ingrained in the ethos, it spreads. In Britain, what had been considered as properly the provision of the State has been gradually privatized or outsourced on the basis of the alleged desirability of private capital and free markets – for example, prisons, probation services, utilities, welfare assessments. In many cases, the results have been costly and socially damaging. People in need of help, of understanding, of encouragement are often treated as transactional costs to be analysed as elements within business models, entered into spreadsheets, designed to maximize corporate profits. There are, no doubt, odd exceptions.

⁂

Let us return to more comfortable areas for free markets operating for profit – providing typical goods such as cookers, crockery and croissants. That is, where consumer satisfaction may be a good guide for what should be produced, though let us keep in mind that not all consumer satisfactions are valuable. The profit motive here, though, need not be in conflict with consumers' interests, where consumers know what they want, where it is not damaging, and when consumers voting for the products by way of purchase works both to the companies' benefit and the consumers'.

Even here, significant dangers exist. Capitalism sees wantonness as an excellence. Capitalism is ever eager to grow consumer appetite for its 'goods'; what is genuinely good for a person has a lower priority than satisfying whatever the person wants. Smith expresses some relevant worries which, interestingly, the pro-free-market Adam Smith Institute and Institute of Economic Affairs tend to ignore. He notes how many people toil to secure fleeting satisfactions: 'How many people ruin themselves by laying out money on trinkets of frivolous utility?... All their pockets are stuffed with little conveniences. They contrive new pockets, unknown in the clothes of other people, in order to carry a greater number. They walk about loaded with a multitude of baubles... the whole utility is certainly not worth the fatigue of bearing the burden.'

The market and its governments worship economic growth as measured by GDP. That, as discussed in Chapter 10, has no regard for the value or disvalue of the products, other than in market terms, be they Smith's baubles and conveniences or the locks, keys and firearms needed by citizens of a distrustful society – or, indeed, the weapons of war which many nations are keen to accumulate. Concentrating on GDP places us at the mercy of accountancy practices because, pithily put, how we measure and what we measure affect what we do and what we value.

Reflect on the fairy tale of the Princess and the Pea, as some have suggested. Those fortunate enough to secure more and more comforts often begin to notice more and more niggles, more and more dissatisfactions. The market's solution is to encourage still more purchases. When fully aware of that, we may rightly argue that capitalism – and what it offers and what, if lucky, we get – alienates us from the natural world and from our own nature. Many are rich in baubles, but impoverished in spirit, whatever they may think.

Some of the above disquiets are not essentially grounded in who owns the resources, but how those resources are used – whether to create more luxuries or to benefit the poorest; whether to enhance lives in ways other than tingles or just to multiply the tingles. On the latter, recall Chapter 4's Plato on itching and scratching – for a life of repeated satisfactions. The 'nastiest of men' are driven by seeking the greatest returns for themselves. Contrast with social ownership where the community as a whole has inputs: at least greater likelihoods then exist of resources being used to benefit all society's members. Further, with some good fortune, if individualism's self-interest is absent, there is a better chance that not all values will be reduced to acquisition. That is not to suggest that public bodies are thereby free from scandal and corruption. Public service can be corrupted by the greed that stimulates markets; public bodies may be so starved of funds – or so disparaged by free-market politicians – that demoralization sets in.

DOUBLE STANDARDS

Neo-liberalism's freedom is grounded in the individual, personal or corporate. People are seen as individual (or family) atoms, possessive, lacking solidarity with others, their freedom requiring minimal State interference. Focus on freedom sometimes brings together the political left and right. The political right values the freedom to trade, to buy and sell; hence, they may support legalization of cannabis, regardless of what they think of its merits. The political left value people being free to live their lives as they want, if to their benefit; hence, they may support the legalization, believing cannabis's benefits outweigh harms.

Neo-liberals condemn the State for interfering in private lives and the corporate: how dare the State urge people to reduce intake of sugar! Corporations, of course, also aim to affect human behaviour – their consumers. True, the State introduces laws to discourage certain sales; but the corporate world knows how to encourage sales. One cannot get by now without a mobile phone, without the internet, without the latest eating 'experiences'. Under the disingenuous claim of just seeking to preserve people's freedom, there are numerous instances of the corporate world preventing, or at least delaying, State regulations to protect consumers.

Neo-liberalism's advocacy of liberty contains the deceit of one-sidedness. Liberty requires *well-informed* choices; the corporate world has little interest in that. Humans, being human, are easily misled: items often strike us as more valuable the greater the price tag; wine, if we are told it is from an expensive bottle, can taste better. A different simple case is: 'Sale: 70% reduction'. Of course, only in small print do we read the 'up to'.

Neo-liberalism prioritizes corporate freedom – to give priority to returns for shareholders – over public interest. Commerciality, confidentiality clauses and refusal to release product trial results all aim to prevent the public from gaining knowledge. Governments over the years have introduced legislation for compensation to be paid to passengers when trains and planes are significantly late in arriving; the result has often been that operators announce officially longer journey times. Governments may be slow to wake up, for one reason or another, over what is going on. There has, for example, been a gradual awareness of the dangers of bacteria becoming resistant to antibiotics; consequently, British farms have trumpeted the radical decline in antibiotics deployed in poultry production – but things are not as they seem. Considerable use, it transpires, is made of ion-ophores as antibiotics, possibly with similar dangers, yet they are classed as 'feed additives' and so are not counted in official figures.

The farming example once again illustrates how the outcome of 'free markets' may be beneficial neither to society and nor, in this case, to chickens. Were markets not driven by consumer demand for the cheapest food and by corporate demand for maximum profits, the chickens could be looked after in better conditions; as a result, they would have healthier lives, be less likely to contract the nasty diseases and so less likely to need the ionophores. Of course, there are complexities here, not least because millions of people, even in wealthy liberal democracies, are in poverty; so it is glib to blame them for chasing after the cheapest food. They lack any effective lib-erty to do otherwise; they lack the power – though probably not as much as do the chickens.

Liberty is undermined through power imbalances, notably through wealth inequalities; yet neo-liberals cast that to one side. People have the liberty to contract, but what liberty is that when, on the international stage, the poor countries have to accept the deals offered by the wealthy corporations – or when the poor within a country have to accept harsh terms offered by employers? Trade unions are typically perceived by neo-liberals as threats to the free trade in labour, though the unions are trying to do for their employ-ees what the corporations do for their shareholders. Vast inequali-ties in wealth and in power tend to lead to conflicts between 'those that hath' and 'those that hath not'. As Alex de Tocqueville, an early sociologist investigating social conditions, reported of Paris in 1848: 'I saw society cut into two: those who possessed nothing united in a common greed; those who possessed something, united in a common terror. There were no bonds, no sympathies between these two great sections...'

⁕

The primary role of government is, many maintain, to protect people's freedoms. What, then, should we make of the insistence by some that freedom still exists even when there is significant inequality of wealth and income? Despite being poor, the poor live in a free society – the neo-liberals proudly announce – and lack of money does not interfere with their freedom, though obviously it limits *exercise* of that freedom. At least, the State does not get in the way: there are no laws restricting people's liberty to buy designer handbags, yachts and BMW cars; within a country, people are at liberty to travel across states and counties –and, in many cases, they have the freedom to travel abroad.

That reasoning is faulty. Your freedom to go to the opera is radically restricted if you lack a ticket – and you lack a ticket because you lacked money to buy a ticket. Money gives you permission to secure many things; without the money, you lack that permission, hence you lack the freedom. Mind you, to the poor, the argument may appear arcane: it is as bad for the poor whether they lack the freedom or lack the means to exercise it.

The card then played to keep the myth of freedom going is 'aspiration'. If people's lack of the fine things in life is 'just' a matter of lack of wealth – as opposed to laws forbidding ownership – then one day, maybe, through hard work or a lottery win... Well, hope can keep people going; it can, though, eventually lead to despair.

HAPPY LAND – AND DANCING BEARS

We recall Happy Land. We may think what is as remarkable as the laws of that land is the fact that nobody there is at all surprised at those laws. They judge, feel, believe they are holding to things just as they should be. What is remarkable about our lands of neo-liberalism is that, despite the financial crises, despite the vast inequalities of wealth, the poverty on the streets – despite a few people highlighting those indisputable facts – many, many people, including even many of those having a bad time, are convinced that there is no alternative.

TINA – 'there is no alternative' – was a mantra of the 1980s, from Margaret Thatcher. Neo-liberals pointed to the disasters in the Soviet Union and elsewhere as showing that alternatives to neo-liberalism inevitably fail – as if those versions exhaust all possibilities. It seems as if most of us, including critics of neo-liberalism, cannot conceive of possibilities other than neo-liberalism and the failures modelled on the Soviet Union. Capitalist neo-liberalism is the best we have for running a society; that is the zeitgeist. Here come the bears.

In south-western Bulgaria there exists the Dancing Bears Park, a park managed by Four Paws, an animal-welfare organization. Four Paws has been freeing performing bears from circuses and villages. Those bears had been captured soon after birth and trained to dance and entertain. The training involved much suffering (for the bears, that is) – dancing on hot coals – but led to the bears becoming conditioned, domesticated, without, so to speak, minds of their own. They were led into living a sort of lowly human life, working all year round (no hibernation), fed with bread and alcohol. They lost the ability to hunt, to move freely, to decide for themselves. When Four Paws 'frees' them, they are confined, but now within the park; they gradually learn to behave a little more like bears, though they could never survive in the wild.

The lives of the freed bears have been compared to how people have learned to cope, with varying degrees of success, after communist regimes collapsed into capitalism, a ruthless gang-like capitalism. People freed from the communist yoke are akin to the released bears: they are unsure how to use their freedom. After the collapse of totalitarian East Germany – the German Democratic Republic (GDR) – some *Ostalgie*, nostalgia, arose for the old days

of ordinary life, albeit impoverished. Some hanker after that communist past; at least people then possessed a sense of community,
despite shortages and lack of capitalist glitz. The hankering, though,
does not explain why many of the young, who never lived under the
communist regimes, are also unhappy with the neo-liberals' capitalist replacement. There are other well-known cases where values
have arisen through bad times: people have often valued the comradeship that arose in days of war.

Let us use the bears to suggest that we, here in neo-liberal societies, are so enmeshed in the zeitgeist's praise for capitalism and
free markets that, however hard we try, most of us lapse into thinking that ultimately there can be no alternative. It is, in fact, akin to
indoctrination; our beliefs in free markets seem insensitive to the
evidence of free-market disasters. To reiterate, despite 2008's global
financial crash, the resultant devastations for numerous people in
many countries, nothing much has changed regarding how markets, global companies, rating agencies dominate – save for the fact
that, if anything, they dominate even more. We should remind ourselves, though, that the ethos of a society is not fixed; it can change,
radically change even – and it need not be for the worse. We should
also note that, unlike Happy Land, the neo-liberal ethos is not all-
embracing; were it so, then this book and similar books would not
be written, save as fantasies.

Small groups, over the centuries, have attempted changes,
breaking from the then economic ethos. In the United States, with
the 1837 financial crisis and factory closures, hundreds of thousands became homeless; 'the land stinks with suicide' wrote the
philosopher-poet Ralph Waldo Emerson. Small communities were
attempted, either because of religious faith in a 'New Jerusalem' or
belief that science could provide the means for achieving a perfect
society. As mentioned earlier, the communities included George
Ripley's Brook Farm and Robert Owen's New Harmony. Their belief

was that society could be based fundamentally on cooperation, not competition, that distortions of the family should be overcome in favour of the community, that all work could be dignified – and that women should not be subordinated to men.

The above attempts have been dismissed as failures – those communities vanished – but that is a misleading dismissal. In some respects, what those communities sought did partly arrive in the wider society, with welfare programmes, free education, public libraries and ideas of equal rights.

Fifty years ago, concerns for the environment and animal welfare were much mocked as belonging solely to hippies, sandals and beads – to the long-haired and those who thrived on lentils. Fifty years ago, men could be sent to gaol for engaging in homosexual activities – and talk of same-sex marriages would have been laughed out of court. Look at how different many Western societies – and their political leaderships – are today.

Picturing how to overcome neo-liberalism is a difficult affair, for its myths of freedom and TINA permeate society. Those in power and wealth, accustomed to their social status and authority often through generations, probably just accept that how things are is how things ought to be. Most people, at some basic level, also seem to believe that is so and are, apparently, happy with their lot as consumers; they are content to live in a country where many very poor people only just manage, if that, to scrape a living, being virtually outsiders to the societies in which they live. Many people simply accept the vast discrepancies in people's health and longevity. Neo-liberalism offers the panacea of hope and aspiration to those doing not too badly; perhaps one day they too could own the superior car, the yacht and pay for private schooling.

Should the above acceptances count as manifestations of authentic preferences? Should we accept what people say – or should we recognize that things are not going well, whatever they say, believe and feel? Let us at least not fall for the reply that all is well, because society's ethos results from how 'the people' have voted. As seen in the first two chapters, 'democratic' outcomes manifest neither what a majority of people want nor what may be in their overall interests. With the free market's encouragement of individualism and self-interested motivations, dare the point be made that people are not ideal participants in democratic processes grounded in electorates voting for (what is assessed by them as) the common good?

In Happy Land, virtually everyone accepts the ethos; how things are is how they must be. In Western democracies, the ethos is that neo-liberalism is the only way, even morally the right way. True, there have been many protests: 'Occupy Wall Street'; 'Occupy London'. Resistance, though, is minimal. After all, corporations will set up elsewhere, if paying more tax here; chief executives would prefer – is that really true? – life in Saudi Arabia, if paying less tax. Yes, there are pockets of resistance to free markets: in the United Kingdom, the NHS struggles to retain its socialist grounding. Here it is worth contrasting with the US private-healthcare system, which is far more costly than the NHS, has a reputation for unnecessary medical interventions and, until 'Obamacare' legislation, excluded millions of the poorest. Doctors in both countries, though, may frequently be wondering what has happened to their calling: their patients have to be seen as customers requiring a contracted service; detailed paperwork and interventions may be undertaken to 'cover' themselves against customers' complaints which would otherwise be stimulated by some zealous lawyers; and insurance companies typically instruct doctors never to say sorry in case legal liabilities are created. Instead of medical professionals working together with patients to improve the patients' health, they are being forced into the business paradigm of suppliers and consumers, having to act in their own self-interest. It does not have to be that way.

Indeed, it does not have to be that way; we are misled into thinking that it is 'natural' that people should be self-interested, should seek eminence – that it is natural to possess the 'dog eats dog' mentality. Day after day, we breathe the air of neo-liberalism, of polluted values; it is difficult to reach a fresher atmosphere for clearer thinking. Of course, some deeply invested in the free-market ethos may merely pretend to believe in its overall benefits, simply to justify the status quo and their own positions. Some may truly hold the belief; the wealthy can be as trapped in the ethos as others, blind to how distorted their lives may be – though at least they have the comforts of acquisitions, the comfort of physical comfort.

This chapter's question comes down to how best to coordinate people socially and what to trade off with what. The assumption is that there is, on the one hand, free-market individualism which carries the dangers of promoting self-interest, inequalities and disparagement of the poor; there is, on the other hand, collectivism with dangers of totalitarianism, forcing people into one mould. That binary choice is another myth.

Few would seriously contend that free markets would lead to the best arrangements in sewerage services and nuclear electricity supplies; few would argue that collectivism involves everyone being compelled to wear the same-size shoes. There are cases and cases, degrees and degrees, as there are when encountering another seemingly binary distinction between values grounded in the individual and those in the community. Egoistic attached stances (for personal fulfilment) and universal detached ones (for community benefits) can coexist, if properly navigated.

VIEW FROM A DISTANT PLANET

Suppose observers from a distant planet were told how Western liberal democracies maximized the well-being of all their citizens, how they respected the rights of everyone to life, liberty and dignity.

Those observers then look more closely for themselves and see poverty on the streets, gross inequalities in well-being, in living conditions and lifespans. They learn that the twenty-six richest billionaires in 2018 own as many assets as the 3.8 billion people who constitute the poorest half of the planet's population. They hear the wealthy speaking, with political free-market endorsement, of how they deserve their wealth and do not deserve to be taxed so much.

Would not the observers be astonished at the leaders' incompetence, deceit or self-deception? Would not the observers be amazed at how, apparently, the best way of securing a good life for all involves gambling on stock exchanges, with vast sums being made via teeny discrepancies in prices over a few milliseconds? Would the observers fall for the idea that directing resources to satisfy demands for designer handbags, baubles and trinkets and ever bigger cars served one and all better than using those resources to provide clean drinking water for those who are without?

Suppose the observers from the distant planet offered a radically different vision of society – one where acquisitional eminence was not supremely valued; one where there existed considerably greater equality of income and wealth; one where taxation levels or remuneration caps, or people's sense of community, achieved that greater degree of equality; one where people held to the belief that healthcare, education and housing should be determined on the basis of need, not on wealth. Would we – *ought we to* – stamp our feet in disgust at such a vision? Is it really impossible for us, one day, to be so well-disposed to the vision that we seek its implementation?

Suppose that most people reject the vision, insisting that the current state of society, the ethos of neo-liberalism, is how things must be – how things morally ought to be and how they could not be otherwise. How should 'the people's' rejection be judged? Ought not the observers from the distant planet challenge that rejection just as we should challenge the 'happy' citizens of Happy Land?

For those who do badly out of today's society, yet reject the vision, perhaps they are akin to happy slaves or, more likely, unhappy slaves who believe their slavery is but a temporary rung on the ladder to prosperity. The ladder, maybe unbeknownst by them, is illusory.

For those who do reasonably well out of society, perhaps their rejection is akin to slave owners rejecting the abolition of slavery; they are rejecting the vision out of self-interest, playing safe with what they have. More accurately, they reject the vision out of perceived self-interest, perceived playing safe – for they too are dominated by the ethos of acquisition, blind to other values and blind to how things are for others.

For those who do exceptionally well out of society – well, they reject the vision because they swallow, or pretend to swallow, the manifest falsehoods that they deserve millions of pounds a week for being a talented footballer, chief executive or owner of inherited estates with large rental incomes.

Here is Keynes again:

> When the accumulation of wealth is no longer of high social importance, there will be great changes in the code of morals... All kinds of social customs and economic practices, affecting the distribution of wealth and of economic rewards and penalties, which we now maintain at all costs, however distasteful and unjust they may be in themselves, because they are tremendously useful in promoting the accumulation of capital, we shall then be free, at last, to discard.

An ungrounded optimism is Keynes's 'when' for the accumulation of wealth shines brightly in neo-liberalism's love of free markets. Markets may be free, but they neither free the poor – the poor cannot afford to buy – nor do they free the rest, be they wealthy or 'just managing', for they are driven to buy yet more.

Free markets do not set the people free.

EPILOGUE

In denial

Once upon a time, in some out of the way corner of that universe of numberless twinkling solar systems, there was a star upon which clever beasts invented knowing. That was the most arrogant and mendacious minute of 'world history', but nevertheless, it was only a minute. After nature had drawn a few breaths, the star cooled and congealed, and the clever beasts had to die.

Friedrich Nietzsche

We have been in denial. Well, we have been in denial, if – *if* – we accept current understanding of our biology. Every thought, every twinkle of the eye, every cough, every stroke of the keyboard, every scanning of these words – all are results of neurological changes within. Miss Fortuna – good luck – would need to be radically on our side for whimsical-like electrical impulses and chemical signals to be so patterned that, when we engage with shapes on paper and sounds from mouths, we encounter things that *make sense*. Miss Fortuna would be all the more generous were those encounters to be not merely with sense, but also with truth.

Of course, those very philosophical reflections also suffer from such unreliable sources; they too may be nothing better than meaningless babble. We should lapse into silence. Even this reasoning is open to the same criticism. To get anywhere, we have to vote for Miss Fortuna's good offices – well, so it luckily or nonsensically seems. We go on, speaking and writing with meaning. We believe we can make sense that is not 'nothing but' electrical impulses and chemical signals. We have to live by that myth, if myth it be.

In the quotation above, Nietzsche has been seen as possibly casting doubt on all truth and knowledge, or at least on anything presented as objective truth and knowledge. We resist allowing such casting lines to drag us into seas of meaningless babble, but we may yet experience a drowning within the smaller seas of this book's fifteen chapters. Not merely have the chapters shown that, in practice, we wallow in deceit – or, more kindly, live by myths – but also that when we rise to theory, to ideals, to how things *ought* to be, we are at a loss. We are in denial.

It is relatively easy to open our eyes to the myths by which, in reality, we live. We know that typically politicians, corporate leaders, the media, the law, the powers-that-be, the great and the good, conspire to blind us and bind us to how things are. We ride seas, on waves of babble, immersing ourselves within. We usually conspire with the babble, falling in line, following the ease of acquiescence, of our own self-interests or simple self-deception. Here are some reminders of the myths.

We admire Western democracy, yet we all know its failings. Oddly, we may feel reassured by Winston Churchill's quip: 'Democracy is the worst form of government, except for all the others.' We well know that 'democratic' governments are not the result of informed electorates, of fair distributions of knowledge, of everyone having the same access to voting. We know well that the mantra 'the people have spoken' is nothing but persuasive rhetoric, to be praised when it suits, condemned when not.

Our democracies promote the value of freedom, of laws securing maximum liberty for people, yet we are not so blind not to realize that freedom is radically reduced by poverty. Furthermore, a little reflection leads us to see that much of what we want is driven by powerful vested interests, interests that have little interest in our interests, our well-being. Our so liberally-minded anti-discrimination laws are silent on the vast discriminations against those who lack money – who lack knowledge, who lack power.

Praise is given to equal opportunities, yet we are all aware that liberal democracies endorse freedoms that manifestly undermine those equal opportunities. The wealthy buy better education for their offspring; the private schools – paradoxically so-called 'public schools' in Britain – often receive government encouragement through tax concessions. We speak of what people deserve, yet play down the huge role of good (and bad) luck in what they do (and do not) achieve.

There are howls of official protest at anything smacking of racism or ethnicity-ism, yet most nations explicitly provide preferential entry to those who show some suitable descent linked to their nationals. The most obvious example is the 1948 creation of Israel explicitly for Jewish people – causing Palestinians to flee their homes – followed by Israel's 1950 Law of Return, allowing 'return' to all and only those of a Jewish heritage. Paradoxically, the Law of Return welcomes those who have never lived in Israel yet may 'return', and excludes those Palestinians who did live in Israel for whom a return would indeed be a return.

Throughout liberal democracies, there is the rhetoric of basic human rights, of respect for all people, of life being sacred; yet governments and well-off voters typically favour more luxuries for themselves than necessities for others. True, few government ministers, senators or congressmen would have the courage blatantly to announce that, instead of funding essential social care for the elderly poor, they choose expenditure on grand banquets, tax concessions for the wealthy, and projects for the already privileged

– but that is the reality. Mahatma Gandhi, who led India into independence from Great Britain, was asked what he thought of Western civilization; his reply was: 'It would be a very good idea.'

Many more myths – puzzles and deceptions – could have been cited in this sociopolitical arena – from the sources of crime and the justification of imprisonment to our international responsibilities for future generations to the increases in sufferings and deaths in Britain from air pollution and inadequate welfare provision. Chapters could have discussed the relationship between terrorism and war or the immorality of threatening the use of nuclear weapons – that is, threatening the deliberate destruction and horrendous sufferings of millions – let alone the reality of the vast waste of resources in maintaining such weapons.

We could have reflected upon the mistreatment of animals destined for the abattoir, the loss of different species or destruction of rainforests. We might have questioned more the so-called respect for life; in a wealthy country, babies, usually of the right sort of parents, are deemed so precious that vast resources are deployed to keep them alive, although they lack any sense of themselves as subjects with a future. Contrast with children who do have such a sense, yet are left to scavenge – and die – in squalor.

The latter observation touches on population control: why assume that increasing numbers of human beings are good? Rational debate can be smothered through fear of accusations of racism; the accusations arise because fertility rates are high in countries such as Somalia, Afghanistan and South Sudan, but low in most European and some South East Asian countries. That leads to questions of population distribution between countries as well as to the effects on other species. In Britain, considerable resources are devoted towards overcoming the infertility of those wanting to have 'their' children; the consequence is fewer people ready to adopt abandoned children, 'other's' children. Once again, we tend to value 'our own' over others; attached values trump the detached.

George Orwell famously wrote, from the viewpoint of the swine, 'All animals are equal, but some are more equal than others.' He had the Soviet Stalinist authorities in mind, but the swinish quip vividly draws attention to the double-speak of numerous authorities, be they liberal democratic, totalitarian or theocratic. Allow me to reiterate: poverty restricts access to justice, education, health and awareness of life's possibilities – poverty destroys dignity – yet our 'civilized' liberal democracies rest on poverty both within and without.

The above examples of myths that we live by may well lead us to fall in with Kant's observation, 'Out of the crooked timber of humanity, no straight thing was ever made.'

Our societies self-advertise as beacons of democracy, liberty, equal rights, humanity and justice. Here is a little more Nietzsche from the same work as this Epilogue's opening quotation, *On Truth and Lies in an Extra-Moral Sense* (1873): 'Man has an invincible inclination to allow himself to be deceived and is, as it were, enchanted with happiness when the rhapsodist tells him epic fables as if they were true, or when the actor in the theatre acts more royally than any real king.'

We have that inclination not solely regarding the applications of praiseworthy concepts such as liberty and equality, but over those very ideals themselves. The ideals enchant us, yet we are at sea over what they mean. We mouth the words; yet we mouth senselessly.

Readily do we speak of fairness, but we have little idea of what constitutes fair remunerations, fair distributions of wealth, fair levels of taxation. We proclaim equality of opportunities and treating people equally, but we uphold national borders and are baffled over what, within a nation state, would count as equal opportunities for all. As touched upon, there are deep metaphysical puzzles here about what counts as *my* identity, *my* responsibility, *my free choices*, let alone the identity of a nation. There are deep puzzles over what even counts as 'the same'. Should killing and letting die be treated, morally so, as the same? How should we tell?

Our personal attachments receive priority over ones of detachment. Our family, our friends, our nation, take priority over their families, their friends, their nations. We declare respect for all human life, yet allow some lives going very, very well to trample on lives of others, of lives going very badly indeed. We admire the cultural institutions, the museums, the created wonders of the world; we should be appalled at the sufferings that brought them about, yet paradoxically we are so pleased that they were brought about. As Nietzsche wrote, in *Thus Spake Zarathustra* (1883–91): 'Have you ever said Yes to a single joy? O my friends, then you said Yes too to all woe. All things are entangled, ensnared, enamoured.'

To repeat the ancient saw, noted in the Prologue: all things conspire.

While law-makers and judges, philosophers and politicians, may speak of weighing up such factors as the above – striking a 'balance' between competing interests, competing values – the factors and values would seem to be incommensurable. How should one 'balance' the liberty to own land with the consequent restrictions on the liberty of others to roam those lands? How can we measure the value of free speech against the value of not offending others? The 'weighing' and 'balancing' are smokescreens for... *muddling through*.

The monster, we may regretfully acknowledge, is the human condition; it gives rise to the myths that we live by, myths that we pass by, usually with eyes firmly closed. Its form is the self-deception in which we engage, hiding reality by soaring descriptions of how fine our liberal democracies are; its form is the absurdity of our reach for ideals of which we ultimately can make no sense. It is the contradiction summed by Samuel Beckett as 'I can't go on; I go on'.

The book's chapters may hence lead some to shrug shoulders: 'Well, if we cannot even make sense of the ideals, why bother?' The reply is that although we lack a grip on the destination, we have some idea of the right direction – and the monster, the human condition, compels at least some of us to go on, arguing for that direction.

Some may conclude that the only rational response is to start again, from scratch. That is impossible. We should adopt the metaphor of Austrian philosopher and member of the twentieth-century Vienna Circle, Otto Neurath, of our being aboard a ship. We are in the middle of the ocean on a ship that is leaking. Rationally, we do not throw ourselves into the raging waters, foolishly thinking we can rebuild the ship from scratch. Rather, we make use of what we have to keep afloat; we do repairs here, with less important bits of shipping from over there – and then work back to over there from here. We make do with what we have; and what we have, regarding this book's topics, is a sense of humanity, of solidarity – well, at least to some degree, if we work at them.

The poor – the dispossessed, the hungry – in many ways lack the agency to make significant choices, an ability typically understood as essential for a fully human life. Now, we could challenge that understanding by doubting whether any of us are truly autonomous, truly agents. After all, that we are is another myth we live by, that we quietly pass by. Few, if any, though, seriously want to live lives as buffeted about by society, just as leaves on trees are blown by the breeze. Even if we sincerely believe ourselves completely causally determined, enmeshed in networks of causes and effects deriving from a primeval slime – even if it is true that we are – we still have to decide whether to put on the red dress or the blue. We have to live by the myth that we are free to make choices; and we know, we know so well, that available choices could and ought to be better for millions.

⑈

Let us head towards a close, beginning with Simone Weil, a French intellectual of the early twentieth century. Albert Camus described her as 'the only great spirit of our times'. Here is Weil, teaching in 1933: 'Human beings are so made that the ones who do the crushing feel nothing; it is the person crushed who feels what is happening. Unless one has placed oneself on the side of the oppressed, to feel with them, one cannot understand.'

Our problem is how to coax people into following Weil and re-placing them on the side of the oppressed. 'Can you not see?' we appeal – to those who stay put, in their privileged lives, feeling nothing at the world's distress. Trying to alter behaviour – to develop the moral discomfort of not being at home when at home – we employ rhetoric against self-interest, against greed, against 'dog eats dog'. Even atheists – and I write as an atheist – nod in recognition at Jesus's words reported in the Gospel According to Mark: 'For what shall it profit a man, if he shall gaine the whole world yet lose his owne soule?'

⑈

In the Prologue, Marx told of Perseus's magic cap worn to cover eyes and ears, to make-believe that there were no monsters. No words will make us discard the cap for good – or ill – for how well-disposed to our monstrous lives could we ever be that we discard all the dressings of myth? I lose myself in music, in the mysterious upliftings of choral works, operas and chamber music – and in wine too – yet I then find myself; I find myself with the guilt at this privilege, the privilege of guilt indeed, and also the despair at the surrounding realities of suffering. I write words such as these. That is, of course, a reflection on personal psychology, even a psychological pathology.

The words of this book – words grounded in those whimsical-like electrical impulses and chemical signals, transmissions between cells, courtesy of Miss Fortuna – may be so patterned that when we read them we feel not so at home.

The perils of poverty, its homelessness, its alienation, are for all to see; there are, though, perils of privilege, the perils of the privileged's complacency and their conceit of feeling at home when not truly at home – when not at home with humanity. The reflections throughout this work point to a variety of interconnected perils, of the myths of proclaimed ideals and the myths of their realizations; the reflections perhaps will help us to resist yanking the magic cap down so tightly. They may even help us to have feelings for the words from Oliver Goldsmith – and not just feelings, but also motivations to urge change:

> Ill fares the land, to hastening ills a prey,
> Where wealth accumulates, and men decay.

The words of this book may well have shed some darkness on the mantras of our liberal democracies; paradoxically that darkness may, just possibly may, shed some light.

Notes and References

These notes are uncluttered with publishers and page numbers; all will be revealed by an internet search for the title or text. Typically, the articles and reviews are freely available online. To avoid incongruities of references to, say, the seventeenth-century writings of Spinoza, yet with publication dates such as 2018, first publication dates are given. Let me express my indebtedness to all the authors and translators of the texts referenced here.

PROLOGUE: ON HIDING WHAT WE KNOW

Philosophers' works that I recommend for this book's topics – and into which I have dipped and owe much – include those by G. A. Cohen, Raymond Geuss, Jonathan Lear, Bernard Williams and Jonathan Wolff. *The Stanford Encyclopaedia of Philosophy*, online, has valuable entries, including extensive bibliographies. Please also read Noam Chomsky for some telling evidence and reflections on the operations of liberal democracies.

The 1225 Magna Carta's Clause 29, which derives from the 1215 version, is still proclaimed. It includes: 'We will sell to no man, we will not deny or defer to any man either justice or right.' How many people may painfully laugh at such commitments, being deprived of legal aid to get before the law or in detention or in the process of deportation? I speak of Britain, especially the consequences of keen church-going Theresa May's Home Office stances from 2010.

Franz Kafka's *The Trial* (published posthumously, 1925) tells of the law. The law's gatekeeper bars entry to the supplicant even when bribed – for, says the gatekeeper: 'I am taking this only so that you do not think you have left anything undone.' The pike comes from Isaiah Berlin's 1958 'Two Concepts of Liberty'. 'More equal than others' is from George Orwell's *Animal Farm* (1945).

1: WHAT'S SO GOOD ABOUT DEMOCRACY?

For Plato, please see Malcolm Schofield, *Plato: Political Philosophy* (2006). For the Hume/Rousseau relationship – generous good-humoured Hume trying to handle paranoid Rousseau and Sultan – try David Edmonds and John Eidinow, *Rousseau's Dog: Two Great Thinkers at War in the Age of Enlightenment* (2007).

For governments and the people, there is Richard Tuck, *The Sleeping Sovereign* (2006). Ultimate sovereign power in a democracy, it is controversially argued, is with the people through plebiscites; the people's popular votes authorize governments which may then act in ways distant from the democratic.

Regarding collective choice, Kenneth Arrow's theorem – his General Possibility Theorem – shows that, on reasonable assumptions, preference voting can lead to contradictions. Please see Amartya Sen, *Rationality and Freedom* (2002), and, for the 'olive oil, sea air, and heroines' observation, his *Collective Choice and Social Welfare* (2018).

Here is a paradox resulting from ordered preferences, using the Condorcet Cycle, from my *This Sentence Is False, An Introduction to Philosophical Paradoxes* (2009). The order of a society's preferences should be determined by the order of individuals' preferences; but suppose:

Max prefers improved medical facilities to tax reduction and prefers tax reduction to increased defences.

Tina prefers tax reduction to increased defences and increased defences to improved medical facilities.

Dan prefers increased defences to improved medical facilities and improved medical facilities to tax reduction.

Counting preferences, funding medical facilities defeats tax reduction 2:1. Tax reduction defeats funding defences 2:1. So, funding medical facilities should surely defeat funding defences; yet, count up the preferences and we see that funding for defence defeats funding medical facilities, 2:1. We strike inconsistency.

2: HOW DEMOCRACY LIES

Here is a political distortion: 'catgate'. In 2011, Theresa May, then British Home Secretary, eager to be rid of the Human Rights Act, claimed that under the Act a Bolivian man avoided deportation because he lived with his cat. Public outrage was stirred. The truth was other than Mrs May claimed. As the Judicial Office noted, 'The Home Office conceded that they had mistakenly failed to apply their own policy for dealing with unmarried partners... the cat had nothing to do with the decision.' See Nicholas Blake, 'Be careful what you wish for', *London Review of Books* (2018). Curiously, Mrs May and media allowed the distortion to remain captive within the public's mind.

Thanks to Clare Hepworth for drawing my attention to the Yeats. For electoral skulduggery, please see Zachary Roth, *The Great Suppression: Voting Rights, Corporate Cash and the Conservative Assault on Democracy* (2016). For a comprehensive review, try David Cole, 'How voting rights are being rigged', *New York Review of Books* (2016). Politicians' semi-detached relationship to truth is on display in Adam Macqueen, *The Lies of the Land* (2018). Electoral fraud is nothing new; for ancient Athens, please see Mary Beard, 'Power to the people?', *Times Literary Supplement* (2016).

Votes are often affected by prejudices. In the United States' population, willingness to vote for Catholic Jews, African American females, Mormons, homosexuals, is apparently over 55 per cent, but for atheists usually not more than 45 per cent. Do not trust non-believers, it seems, because they lack fear of supernatural surveillance and punishment.

Please see Steve Clarke, Russell Powell and Julian Savulescu (eds.), *Religion, Intolerance and Conflict: A Scientific and Conceptual Investigation* (2013).

England is acclaimed as the mother of parliaments. For a touch of reality, please see Ben Wright, *Order, Order! The Rise and Fall of Political Drinking* (2016). An admired social reformer, surviving the Irish Troubles, was Gerry Fitt, Northern Ireland MP. He would request a gin and tonic in the morning, adding, 'But no ice'; the clanging of ice cubes would be too much, given his inevitable hangover from nights before. That is a benign case of MPs' alcohol relationships. Some are far from benign; they cast doubt on certain MPs' integrity, voting behaviour and, indeed, respect for others.

I occasionally use 'race', a concept discredited by certain academics, though prevalent in 'anti-racism' legislation and everyday language. The discrediting assumes that the term is understood by most as identifying a genetic essence that sharply distinguishes groups, even though (I guess) most people lack any idea of essences. Kwame Anthony Appiah, highly critical of 'race', uses instead 'racial identity' to designate a group based on belief or pretence that its members possess an inherited racial essence. Please see K. A. Appiah and Amy Gutmann, *Color Conscious: The Political Morality of Race* (1996). My use of 'race' is the everyday sense whereby, say, the Chinese are typically accepted as having a different culture and set of characteristics from that of Swedes.

3: FREEDOM AND DISCRIMINATION: BURQAS, BIKINIS AND ANONYMOUS

The seminal emphasis on liberty, though lacking Chapter 4's nudging and 'true wants', is John Stuart Mill, *On Liberty* (1859). Raymond Geuss, *Public Goods, Private Goods* (2001), analyses different public/private distinctions. 'Anonymous' was inspired by Sophie Bolat and her work on privacy invasions (MA dissertation, Open University, 2012), as also were reflections throughout this book. Virginia Woolf, writing on Montaigne – *The Common Reader* (1925) – describes private life as 'infinitely the dearest of our possessions'.

For Venetian masks, please see James H. Johnson, *Venice Incognito: Masks in the Serene Republic* (2011). For current prohibitions on face coverings, please see articles by Eva Brems, Chair of Human Rights Law, University of Ghent.

4: SHOULD WE WANT WHAT WE WANT?

Harry G. Frankfurt highlighted 'wantons' in 'Freedom of the Will and the Concept of a Person', *The Journal of Philosophy* (1971). John Elster introduced 'adaptive preferences' with Aesop in *Sour Grapes* (1983). For women's preferences, please see Serene J. Khader, *Adaptive Preferences and Women's Empowerment* (2011).

Manipulations of politics and consumers are extensive; for one arena, try Pamela Haag, *The Gunning of America: Business and the Making of American Gun Culture* (2016). For numerous concerns: Kalle Grill and Jason Hanna (eds.), *The Routledge Handbook of the Philosophy of Paternalism* (2018).

5: LIVES AND LUCK: CAN MISS FORTUNA BE TAMED?

Plato's arguments with nuances (ignored in my chapters) are analysed in Malcolm Schofield, *Plato: Political Philosophy* (2006). An influential polemical challenge to Plato is Karl Popper, *The Open Society and Its Enemies* (1945). Some historical quests for fairness are in Miriam Eliav-Feldon, *Realistic Utopias: The Ideal Imaginary Societies of Renaissance, 1516–1630* (1982). That groups did worse than others was often blamed on cultures: witness 'the Negro Problem', raised by W. E. B. Du Bois in 1897, speaking of 'immorality, crime and laziness among the Negroes'.

People typically put their successes down to themselves, but their failures down to circumstances. Ways of luck are raised by Bernard Williams and Thomas Nagel in Daniel Statman (ed.), *Moral Luck* (1993). Please also see Neil Levy, *Hard Luck Undermines Free Will and Moral Responsibility* (2011).

6: THE LAND OF JUSTICE

For many topics here, there are Serena Olsaretti (ed.), *The Oxford Handbook of Distributive Justice* (2018), and thoughtful papers by Jonathan Wolff: for example, 'Fairness, Respect, and the Egalitarian Ethos' in *Philosophy and Public Affairs* (1998), a 'revisited' version online.

For individuals' responsibility and State compensations, please see Yascha Mounk, *The Age of Responsibility: Luck, Choice and the Welfare State* (2017). Even with shallow digging, we encounter many insidious ways that restrict options; see Diane Reay, *Miseducation: Inequality, education and the working classes* (2017). For the dispossessed's reality in England since Conservative governments' implementation of austerity policies, please watch the moving *I, Daniel Blake* (2016), a film directed by Ken Loach, written by Paul Laverty. It should be compulsory viewing for our leaders.

7: PLUCKING THE GOOSE: WHAT'S SO BAD ABOUT TAXATION?

An excellent collection is Martin O'Neill and Shepley Orr (eds.), *Taxation: Philosophical Perspectives* (2018). It includes Véronique Munoz-Dardé and M. G. F. Martin, 'Beggar your neighbour', challenging Nozick's preference for voluntary gifting. For organ donation related to FDS, please see John Harris, 'The Survival Lottery' (1975).

Tax systems in part may aim to reduce unfair economic inequalities, while upholding inequalities grounded in 'free' choices. The Gini Index is a dubious measure of economic inequality; please see Cappelen and Tungodden in the collection above. There are also questions of the relevance of the marginal utility of wealth.

With taxation policies, the democratic worry arises regarding what 'the people' will accept; political parties vie accordingly. Sometimes the ideal offered is taxation fairness (were that to be a clear concept) over whole lifetimes. Both approaches should yield to taxation as but one element of overall governmental policy, the policy aim being, one hopes, a flourishing society – though that too lacks determinate clarity.

8: 'THIS LAND IS OUR LAND'

For oddities of border control, please see Frances Stonor Saunders, 'Where on Earth are you?', *London Review of Books* (2016). Clair Wills, *Lovers and Strangers: An Immigrant History of Post-War Britain* (2017), sets one scene.

The Israel/Palestine conflict manifests the tragedy of two groups each proclaiming exclusive rights to the same territory. Israel's 1948 establishment as the Jewish State, with United Nations' support, led to Palestinians fleeing their homeland. In today's Gaza, there live well over a million Palestinians in 140 square miles, viewed as an open-air prison. The inhabitants suffer many human-rights violations, courtesy both of Israel and even their own leaderships; and Israel itself frequently suffers rocket attacks. An ideal solution ('Impossible?' we say) would be one-State; please see Karl Sabbagh, *A Modest Proposal... to solve the Palestine–Israel conflict* (2018). For discussion – and despair – on Israel, Judaism and Jewish life, please see my co-authored work with Rabbi Dan Cohn-Sherbok, *Jews: Nearly Everything You Wanted To Know But Were Too Afraid to Ask* (2018).

9: COMMUNITY IDENTITY: NATIONALISM AND COSMOPOLITANISM

For nation states and cosmopolitan ideals, there is Willem Schinkel, *Imagined Societies: A Critique of Immigrant Integration in Western Europe* (2017). K. A. Appiah discusses distinctions of colour, creed, country, class and so forth in *The Lies That Bind: Rethinking Identity* (2018). The curiosity of the United Kingdom is analysed in David Edgerton, *The Rise and Fall of the British Nation* (2018).

Research on Malthus is presented in Alison Bashford and Joyce E. Chaplin, *The New Worlds of Thomas Robert Malthus: Rereading the 'Principle of Population'* (2017).

Once we accept 'collective identity', we should engage 'collective responsibility'. The German people, after the Second World War, were typically held collectively responsible for the Nazi atrocities. Were that a fair assessment, then the Americans and British were collectively responsible for the saturation bombing of Dresden.

For C. P. Cavafy, please see E. M. Forster, 'The Poetry of C. P. Cavafy', where Forster discusses that 'Greek gentleman in a straw hat, standing absolutely motionless at a slight angle to the universe'.

10: WHAT'S SO GOOD ABOUT EQUAL REPRESENTATION?

The evidence of heightism is in Tanya S. Osensky's *Shortchanged: Height Discrimination and Strategies for Social Change* (2017); it relates to people above and below average height and of them on average (be it as mean or median). There are exceptions, often commented on for that very fact; Napoleon Bonaparte is oft cited (wrongly so, apparently) as a short man in a powerful position. The matter here is being discussed within the context of a nation and not introducing complexities of how some nationalities are shorter than others – and not dealing with extreme medical conditions related to dwarfism.

Instead of preventing discriminations against the short, we could seek to prevent height discrepancies; people, though, typically cannot help their height. 'Typically' for, in the US, some parents deploy recombinant growth hormones on their healthy but 'shorter than normal' children; smallness is being considered, unwisely, as an illness requiring treatment. Another unwise path is that of the teeny minority of the small who undergo dangerous operations to extend their legs (the length, not the number).

Turning to gender equality, for nineteenth-century movements – encountering the Owenites, Bristol socialism, and Helena Born and Miriam Daniell – please see Sheila Rowbotham, *Rebel Crossings: New Women, Free Lovers and Radicals in Britain and the United States* (2016). The silencing of black women in the US is surveyed by Patricia Williams, 'Intimate injustice', *Times Literary Supplement* (2018).

For some current, albeit dubious, reasoning, try the otherwise impressive Stella Creasy, British Labour MP, 'Calling the male Harriet Harmans: why equality in politics benefits men as well as women', *New Statesman* (2018). If – as Creasy implies – women are better at some leadership requirements than men, then appointments should be on that basis, not on a 50:50 gender balance, unless other factors come into play.

With gender and sexuality, there is much interest in biology 'on average'. The adult male brain is 150 grams heavier than the female's and, just within the neocortex, the male has 4 billion more neurons than the female; apparently, there are no significant differences in IQ tests. I rely on Christof Koch of the Allen Institute for Brain Science, Washington. Let us, though, be sceptical of the relevance of such tests and such quantitative neurological details. By the way, Gavin Evans, in *Mapreaders & Multitaskers: Men, Women, Nature, Nurture* (2017), denies any relevant neurological differences between men and women. For quantitative comparison – solely out of interest, I suppose – the neocortex of the long-finned pilot whale is estimated at 37 billion neurons, of bees just 1 million, yet bees have remarkable recognitional capacities.

11: HUMAN ~~DUTIES~~ – *OOPS* – HUMAN RIGHTS

Detailed considerations are within Adam Etinson (ed.), *Human Rights: Moral or Political?* (2018). For emphasis on obligations, please see Onora O'Neill, *Justice Across Boundaries* (2016). A vivid work related to genocides is Philippe Sands, *East West Street* (2016); there is also the excellent analysis by Jonathan Glover, *Humanity: A Moral History of the Twentieth Century*, 2nd ed. (2012). Please see Peter Pomerantsev, 'Murder in Mayfair', *London Review of Books* (2016), for the murder of Russians in London.

I am indebted to works by Raymond Geuss (which drew, I think, an analogy with witches) and to N. Ann Davis, Richard Keshen and Jeff McMahan (eds.), *Ethics and Humanity: Themes from the Philosophy of Jonathan Glover*, for many observations, especially James Griffin, 'What

Should We Do About Torture?' For aid programmes, try William MacAskill, *Doing Good Better: Effective Altruism and a Radical New Way to Make a Difference* (2016), and Peter Singer's thought-provoking works. For UK poverty and life expectancy, a quick start is Danny Dorling's 'Short Cuts', *London Review of Books* (2017). Period-poverty information is from Anna Dahlqvist, *It's Only Blood: Shattering the Taboo of Menstruation* (2018). My thanks to Emma Williams for alerting me to duties in the Universal Declaration.

12: FREE SPEECH: THE TOWER OF BABEL; THE SERPENT OF SILENCE

A splendid essay, source of some examples here, is David Bromwich, 'What are we allowed to say?', *London Review of Books* (2016). For social media, please see Dean Cocking and Jeroen van den Hoven, *Evil Online* (2018), and Roger Crisp's commentaries. Sensitivities of the wealthy are perhaps explained by exposures discussed in Bastian Obermayer and Frederik Obermaier, *The Panama Papers: Breaking the Story of How the Rich and Powerful Hide Their Money* (2017), and Paulo Z. Montalban, *Paradise Papers: Offshore Investment of the Rich and Powerful* (2017).

Paul Cartledge, *Democracy, A Life* (2016), looks at ancient Greece's free speech. For the 'marketplace of ideas', please see Alvin I. Goldman, *Knowledge in a Social World* (1999), and Bernard Williams, *Truth and Truthfulness* (2004). Are scientific analyses paradigms of rationality? For doubts, note the treatment of neuropathologist Waney Squier and her challenges to established views on baby shaking.

The Katie Hopkins piece is from Britain's *The Sun*, 17 April 2015. For misreporting, please see the LSE report, *Journalistic Representations of Jeremy Corbyn in the British Press*, available from LSE's Department of Media and Communications. For an example of life in Britain for some of the black community, try Benjamin Zephaniah, *The Life and Rhymes of Benjamin Zephaniah: The Autobiography* (2018).

There are many examples – pamphlets such as *Islam out of Britain* – where 'free speech' falls foul of anti-discrimination laws and risks reprisal

dangers. In 2005, the Danish paper *Jyllands-Postern* published caricatures of Muhammad; such cartoons have been linked to subsequent
terrorist acts, the torching of embassies and deaths. I thank Angela Joy
Harvey for various examples and despair over free-speech restrictions –
relating also to Chapters 3 and 14.

Some attempted silencing in 2019 has been of the Regius Professor
Nigel Biggar and his *Ethics and Empire* project mentioned earlier, where
some positive features of colonial rule are presented. Apparently some
colleagues support him privately, but dare not publicly. A different
restriction relates to Egon Schiele's contorted nudes exhibited at Britain's Royal Academy (2018–19). The exhibition's advertisements were
censored, with coverings sporting 'Sorry, 100 years old but still too dar-
ing for today'.

13: REGRETS, APOLOGIES AND PAST ABUSES

That we have personal regrets, even though blameless, came to the
philosophical fore through Bernard Williams, 'Moral luck', which, with
Tom Nagel's reply, is in Daniel Statman (ed.), *Moral Luck* (1993). For
comprehensive extension to impersonal regrets – and source of some
thoughts here – please see R. Jay Wallace, *The View from Here* (2017).
For the Holocaust links to Jewish Israel, please see my work with Dan
Cohn-Sherbok, cited in Chapter 8's notes.

Public art, statues, place names have often celebrated ideals – well, the
then ideals. A community's ideals come and go. In Florence, in front
of Palazzo della Signoria, in 1504, Donatello's *Judith* was replaced by
Michelangelo's *David*. *Judith* had been installed under Florence's 'evil
constellation', as it was later seen; *David* represented the new republic. Pre-installation, *David* was pelted with stones just because of the
republican symbolism. Please see John T. Paoletti, *Michelangelo's David:
Florentine History and Civic Identity* (2015).

Which items rightfully belong to whom? That question links (as seen
in Chapter 9) to preserving the identity of distinct groups – collectives,

nations, cultures. In the United States, there are discussions about returning museum items, funerary objects and so forth to recognized indigenous tribes, based on relevant kinship, geography, biology, language and folklore; please try James O. Young and Conrad G. Brunk (eds.), *The Ethics of Cultural Appropriation* (2012).

14: 'BECAUSE I'M A WOMAN': TRANS IDENTITIES

Regarding gender self-certification, there is the thoughtful work of Kathleen Stock and Sophie Allen – work that has led them to receive unwarranted abuse as transphobic. For specific controversy, try Alex Sharpe, 'Foxes in the Henhouse: Putting the Trans Women Prison Debate in Perspective'. Rebecca Reilly-Cooper analyses a related area with 'Gender is not a spectrum', an Aeon paper (2016); and thanks to Ardon Lyon for the Anglo-Saxon/Norman thought.

Rachael Padman's response to Germaine Greer is a letter, *London Review of Books*, 16 June 2016; such a reading is most odd, even by a physicist. We may wonder what to make of – and what self-certifiers may make of – observations such as Teiresias's on sexual pleasure, reported by Hesiod: 'Of ten parts, a man enjoys one only, but a woman's sense enjoys all ten in full.'

15: HAPPY LAND

For empirical data about neo-liberalism and its myths, please see works of Ha-Joon Chang. Disparagement of State intervention often appears blind to successes of State capitalism such as some in Norway. For land, please see Brett Christophers, *The New Enclosure: The Appropriation of Public Land in Neoliberal Britain* (2018). Substantial analyses of neo-liberalism and financial crashes are by Mariana Mazzucato, Joseph Stiglitz and Ann Pettifor.

There are ways in which corporations may seek to protect themselves from creditors at least to gain some time; in the United States, they can file for Chapter 11 under the US bankruptcy code. For practices apparently legal and corporately necessary, consider Sir Philip Green, one-time owner of the British retail chain BHS; during his ownership, he extracted hundreds of millions through interest, rents, dividends, leading to its 2016 collapse with its employees' pension fund, once healthy, left in deficit. See Mazzucato, *The Value of Everything* (2018).

For how municipal ownerships worked reasonably successfully, there is Tom Crewe, 'The Strange Death of Municipal England', *London Review of Books* (2016).

Turning to distant history, Adam Smith's famous work, *An Inquiry into the Nature and Causes of the Wealth of Nations* (1776), relies on the moral stance of his *The Theory of Moral Sentiments* (1759). David Hume's influence on Smith is explored in Dennis Rasmussen, *The Infidel and the Professor: David Hume, Adam Smith and the Friendship that Shaped Modern Thought* (2017).

Lacking Adam Smith's 'humanistic foundations' (often apparently overlooked by modern Smith followers), there is Joseph Townsend's *Dissertation on the Poor Law* (1786). Townsend tells of Juan Fernández's South Seas Island and how, with the introduction of goats and then dogs, populations increased and decreased, a balance being established, as the weakest were 'to pay the debt of nature'. Nature here was a kind of 'invisible hand'. For that hand as in some way divine, please see Harvey Cox, *The Market as God* (2016), and Dotan Lesham, *The Origins of Neoliberalism: Modeling the Economy from Jesus to Foucault* (2016).

Yanis Varoufakis, in *And the Weak Suffer What They Must? Europe, Austerity and the Threat to Global Stability* (2016), brings to light capitalism's practice on the international stage. He quotes Thucydides on the Athenian generals' treatment of the impotent Melians: 'the strong actually do what they can and the weak suffer what they must.' The Melians ask whether that is a sensible self-interested approach; after all, when the Athenians eventually fall, they would 'be visited by the most terrible vengeance, watched by the whole world'.

For poverty facts, please see the World Inequality Report 2018, coordinated by Lucas Chancel. Free markets working against society's benefit include, as reported in the Financial Times, 12 September 2018, activities of Nostrum Laboratories, cited in the main text. Casper Pharma acted similarly, with Martin Shkreli raising an AIDS cancer drug from $13.50 to $750. In Britain, Atnahs – perfectly legally, it seems – in 2016 raised the price of antidepressants from £5.71 to £154 a packet and insomnia treatment from £12.10 to £138. That, of course, costs the NHS millions. Interestingly, Vijay Patel, who set up the company, received the OBE honour in January 2019. Please see London's The Times, 7 January 2019.

For United States healthcare, there is Elisabeth Rosenthal, An American Sickness: How Healthcare Became Big Business and How You Can Take It Back (2017): the original non-profit Blue Cross and Blue Shield accepted more or less all proposers and spent around 5 per cent on marketing; since turning into 'for profits', 20 per cent is spent on marketing. Please also see Catharine Smith, 'Why the United States, One of the World's Richest Countries, Struggles With Diseases of Poverty' (online, 30 January 2018).

Examples in the text of money corrupting values – there are many more – derive from Michael Sandel, What Money Can't Buy: The Moral Limits of Markets (2013). See also Samuel Bowles, The Moral Economy (2017). For dancing bears, I am indebted to Witold Szablowski, Dancing Bears: True Stories of People Nostalgic for Life Under Tyranny (2018).

Economists who argued against Hand include Tawney, Polanyi, Thompson as well as Marx and Engels, as shown in Tim Rogan, The Moral Economists (2018). Transforming human nature occurs in some utopian visions; one is William Morris, News from Nowhere (1890). To overcome greed, pride and envy, some utopians exclude all private ownership save of oneself; others – F. A. Hayek and Ayn Rand – see utopias as shunning the State (more or less), as if all sin is State-based sin. Of course, matters are not so 'black-or-white'; were everyone to receive sufficient healthcare, education and leisure, then there would be no problem if some prefer to spend excess income on privately-owned satin sheets when in hospital while others make do with polyester, preferring instead trips to Disneyland.

EPILOGUE: IN DENIAL

I came across the end quotation, from Oliver Goldsmith's 'The Deserted Village' (1770), in Tony Judt's fine collection of essays, Ill Fares the Land (2010).

Many people, once with eyes opened, recognize the sufferings, injustices and immoralities here described. Some see automation, artificial intelligence and changes in food production as solutions, but while they may generate new ways of living, there is no good reason to think that there would be improved distributions of goods, with the well-to-do consuming less and workers working less, having more fulfilled lives. To secure those ends, we need a better or revised grasp of human nature.

Had nature constituted us differently, making us far more community-minded, sympathetic and ready to help others, the world could have been so much better. With that, people may agree, yet still baulk at seeking to achieve that 'so much better' by changing society. I wonder why. It may be fear of the risks; it may be people's mistaken thought that all is going well when things are going well *for them*.

This work is asking whether things can be going well for them – for you, for me – when they are going so manifestly unwell for so very, very many others. With that thought, another book could be written directly on the myths of our personal lives going well – myths concerning love, sexuality, family, 'life-plans', 'fidelity to oneself' and, indeed, happiness. For here, though – with the poignancy of the ending to the fore – let us once again emphasize the question:

> Can things really be going so well for you, for me, for us, when they are going so manifestly unwell, so horrendously unwell, for so many, many, many others?

Acknowledgements

Naming names would generate a list far too long. Numerous people – philosophers and non-philosophers – over many years have stimulated me intellectually, motivationally and 'muddlingly' (muddles can help); some of them have, more recently, suffered my many sighs about this particular work. By their sufferings, they are known. I give them many thanks, sincere thanks.

Regarding the practical, let me thank the library staff: in particular Laura Doran and Annette Rockall of the Athenaeum, for efficiently and encouragingly collecting and returning London Library books, all glanced at, often with sighs, some read, others unread. Also, my appreciation goes to Atlantic Books, especially in the form and substance of James Pulford, for challenges to, and labours on, my authorial substance and form. Sarah-Jane Forder is the fine copy-editor for this book and 'thereby' (I may get away with one more) working with Sarah-Jane has been a pleasure and pretty painless too. I have learnt a lot. Mike Harpley commissioned this work and a certain special agent, Jonathan Pegg, helped it on its way; to both go my thanks.

While I was completing this work, Michael Clark – (another) good friend, good philosopher, good humoured – died. More accurately, he took his own life. More accurately still, he tripped off to Zurich, to Dignitas, to receive the means for his 'accompanied' suicide.

Michael was a strong supporter of Humanists UK. He rightly considered it appalling that when people in the United Kingdom are wanting, needing and desperate to bring an end to life in a reasonable manner – when they are suffering without hope – they require the information, financial resources and physical ability to travel abroad, to a country with a respectful understanding of how some people have finally had enough. The current treatment of sufferers such as Michael is another example of how hollow can be the claim by various governments, religions and human-rights legislation to support the dignity of all human beings.

Michael and I would sometimes reflect on a comment by an early twentieth-century Cambridge philosopher, C. D. Broad. Broad, always interested in the possibility of an afterlife, would say, 'All we can do is wait and see. Or wait and – don't see.'

Michael, being a man of reason – as well as a philosopher – was convinced that, on death, it was the latter: we wait – and don't see.

Index